CONTENTS

ISBN 0 85147 671 6

First Edition   1975
Second Edition, fully revised   1977

©Autobooks Ltd 1977

843

Printed and bound in Brighton England for Autobooks Ltd by G Beard & Son Ltd

B

Passat, Dasher 1973-77 Autobook

by the Autobooks Team of Technical Writers

Volkswagen Passat N 1973-77
Volkswagen Passat L 1973-77
Volkswagen Passat LS 1973-77
Volkswagen Passat TS 1973-75
Volkswagen Passat GLS 1976-77
Volkswagen Dasher 1973-77

Autobooks

Autobooks Ltd. Golden Lane Brighton BN1 2QJ England

The AUTOBOOK series of Workshop Manuals is the largest in the world and covers the majority of British and Continental motor cars, as well as the majority of Japanese and Australian models.

Whilst every care has been taken to ensure correctness of information it is obviously not possible to guarantee complete freedom from errors or to accept liability arising from such errors or omissions.

ACKNOWLEDGEMENT

We wish to thank Volkswagen GB Limited for their co-operation and also for supplying data and illustrations. Considerable assistance has also been given by owners, who have discussed their cars in detail, and we would like to express our gratitude for this invaluable advice and help.

INTRODUCTION

This do-it-yourself Workshop Manual has been specially written for the owner who wishes to maintain his vehicle in first class condition and to carry out the bulk of his own servicing and repairs. Considerable savings on garage charges can be made, and one can drive in safety and confidence knowing the work has been done properly.

Comprehensive step-by-step instructions and illustrations are given on most dismantling, overhauling and assembling operations. Certain assemblies require the use of expensive special tools, the purchase of which would be unjustified. In these cases information is included but the reader is recommended to hand the unit to the agent for attention.

Throughout the Manual hints and tips are included which will be found invaluable, and there is an easy to follow fault diagnosis at the end of each chapter.

Whilst every care has been taken to ensure correctness of information it is obviously not possible to guarantee complete freedom from errors or omissions or to accept liability arising from such errors or omissions.

Instructions may refer to the righthand or lefthand sides of the vehicle or the components. These are the same as the righthand or lefthand of an observer standing behind the vehicle and looking forward.

CHAPTER 1

THE ENGINE

1:1 Description

Engines of three different sizes are used in the range of cars covered in this manual, their dimensions being as follows:

	Bore	Stroke	Capacity
1300	75 mm	73.4 mm	1297 cc
1500	76.5 mm	80 mm	1471 cc
1600	79.5 mm	80 mm	1588 cc

Apart from the differences which are associated with the engine capacity sizes, the engines are identical in design features and have the same equipment except where stated in the text of this or later chapters. Reference should also be made to **Technical Data** in the **Appendix**.

A cutaway view of the engine is shown in **FIG 1:1**. It is a four-cylinder in-line, four-stroke, water-cooled unit. An alternator and a water pump are engine driven by a conventional V-belt arrangement in which the belt is tensioned by adjusting the position of the alternator. An electrically operated and thermostatically controlled ducted fan draws cooling air through the radiator which is positioned off centre to the left.

The cylinder block is in cast-iron into which the cylinder bores are machined directly. Worn or scored bores may be remachined to take oversize pistons. The cylinder head is in aluminium alloy and carries a single overhead camshaft.

The cams operate directly onto interchangeable tappet discs which are available in a range of thicknesses. Fitment of discs of appropriate thickness into the recess in the main tappets enables the valve clearances to be accurately set. Two valve springs are fitted to each inlet and exhaust valve. The camshaft and an intermediate shaft are driven from the crankshaft by a toothed belt which runs 'dry' and is guarded by a sheet metal cover. Toothed pulleys which engage this belt are fitted to the crankshaft, the camshaft and the intermediate shaft. The belt is tensioned by an adjustable jockey wheel. The intermediate shaft and the camshaft run at half engine speed. The intermediate shaft drives the ignition distributor and the oil pump. A mechanical diaphragm type fuel pump is actuated by an eccentric on the intermediate shaft. A pressed steel oil sump encloses the bottom of the cylinder block. The capacity of the sump is approximately $6\frac{1}{2}$ pints (3.7 litres).

The forged steel crankshaft runs in five shell type bearings. Axial float is controlled at the centre bearing. The crankshaft is balanced by four web counterweights in the case of the 1297 cc engines and by eight in the case of the 1471 and 1588 cc engines. Worn journals and crankpins may be reground to take appropriate undersize diameter bearing shells. Light alloy, steel reinforced, pistons carry two compression rings and one oil control ring. Gudgeon

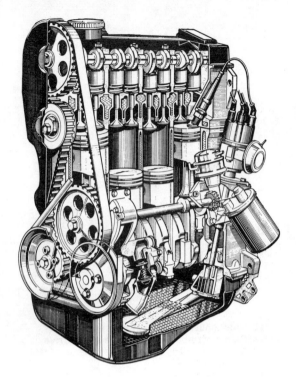

FIG 1:1   Cutaway view of engine

pins are retained by circlips. Connecting rods are in forged steel with detachable bearing caps. The bearings are shell-type. The camshaft, intermediate shaft and all main and big-end bearings are pressure lubricated. A renewable element fullflow oil filter is provided.

The flywheel carries the clutch assembly in the case of manual transmission models with the clutch plate operating straight onto the flywheel rear face. In the case of automatic transmission models, the driving plate carries the torque converter. In both cases the starter motor pinion engages a peripheral ring gear. The front wheel drive transmission bellhousing is attached directly to the rear of the cylinder block.

The single Solex carburetter draws air through an air cleaner unit in which the element is removed for cleaning but is not renewed on a routine basis. The carburetter type varies for different models. Ignition is by coil and distributor of Bosch manufacture.

The combined engine and transmission unit is carried on three bearings. As will be seen from **FIG 1:2**, the engine is substantially cantilevered forward of the two forward mountings which are supported by a subframe in which the front suspension arms are pivoted. To reduce overall height, the engine is tilted 20 degrees to the right.

No starting handle is provided but, with the number plate removed from below the front bumper, access is available to the hexagon head of the bolt which retains the toothed camshaft drive wheel to the crankshaft (see **Section 1:13**). A suitable box spanner to which an extension and a cross piece have been welded will be found invaluable for such operations as valve clearance checking, renewal of the camshaft drive belt etc., which require the engine to be turned by small amounts.

1:2 Maintenance

Engine oil level:

Check the oil level with the car on level ground and, if the engine has been running, wait for at least a minute after the engine has stopped. Remove the dipstick, wipe it dry. re-insert fully, withdraw and check the level. If necessary, add oil to bring the level up to slightly below the 'MAX' mark. Use the same grade and brand of oil as that already in use. It is undesirable to mix grades or brands. If the grade or brand is to be changed, do so when the engine oil is being changed. Approximately 2 pints (slightly over 1 litre) is required to raise the level from 'MIN' to 'MAX'.

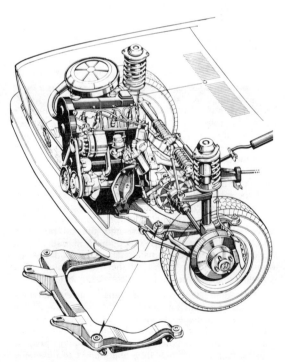

FIG 1:2   The engine, transmission, front suspension and steering

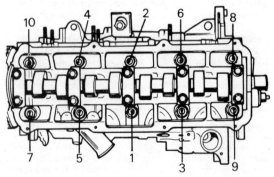

FIG 1:3   Cylinder head bolt tightening sequence

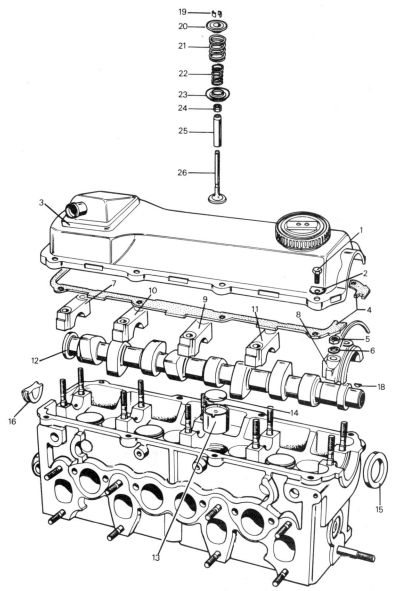

FIG 1:4 Cylinder head and valve gear components

Key to Fig 1:4 1 Bolt   2 Washer   3 Camshaft cover   4 Gasket   5 Nut   6 Washer   7 Rear bearing cap   8 Front bearing cap (No. 1)   9 Bearing cap   10 Bearing cap   11 Bearing cap   12 Camshaft   13 Tappet (cam follower) 14 Clearance adjusting disc   15 Oil seal   16 Plug   17 Gasket   18 Woodruff key   19 Cotters   20 Upper spring seat 21 Outer valve spring   22 Inner valve spring   23 Lower spring seat   24 Valve stem seal   25 Valve guide   26 Valve

Changing engine oil:

Change the oil every 5000 miles (8000 km). Drain off the old oil when the engine is hot. After draining completely, refit the drain plug (torque tighten to 22 lb ft (3 kg m)) and refill with new oil up to the 'MAX' level.

Use a multi-viscosity oil of reputable brand to the following specification.

Summer	20–W–20
Winter	10–W–20
All the year round	10–W–40

Water pump/alternator drive belt:

Every 5000 miles (8000 km), check and adjust the tension of the belt as described in **Chapter 4, Section 4:5.** Renew the belt every 60,000 miles (100,000 km) or earlier if it shows signs of wear.

Oil filter:

At ever other oil change, that is every 10,000 miles (16,000 km), renew the oil filter element as described in **Section 1:3.**

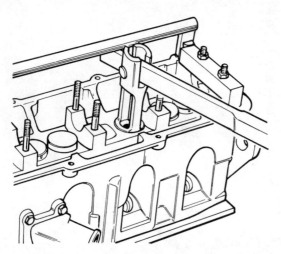

FIG 1:5   Removing valve spring retaining cotters

Valve clearances:

Every 20,000 miles (33,000 km), check and adjust the valve clearances as described in **Section 1:5.**

Camshaft drive belt:

Every 60,000 miles (100,000 km), remove and discard the toothed drive belt and fit a new belt as described in **Section 1:13.**

1:3 Oil pump and filter

As shown in **FIG 1:1**, the gear-type pump is driven from the lower end of the distributor drive shaft. The pump draws oil from the forward end of the sump through a gauze screen fitted to the suction duct which is integral with the pump cover. Pressure oil is delivered to the engine through the externally mounted fullflow disposable canister-type filter. If maintenance is neglected and the filter element becomes clogged, back pressure will build up and unfiltered oil will bypass the element. A non-adjustable relief valve is incorporated and excess pressure oil is returned to the sump. Oil pressure will normally be limited to 28 lb/sq in (2 kg/sq cm) at 2000 engine rev/min at an oil temperature of 80°C (176°F). Depending upon the vehicle model, either an oil pressure gauge or an oil pressure warning light is fitted. The oil pressure warning light switch contacts are closed when there is no oil pressure and, with the ignition switched on, the warning light will be illuminated. When the engine is started and oil pressure builds up, the contacts are opened and the warning light goes out. This should occur at 4 to 8 lb/sq in (.3 to .6 kg/sq cm).

Renewing the filter element:

Renew the element every 10,000 miles (16,000 km). Use a band type grip to unscrew the canister. Clean and lubricate the joint face with engine oil. Fit the new canister according to the instructions given on it. Tighten by hand only. After running the engine, check for oil leaks and top up the oil level as described in **Section 1:2.**

Removing the filter housing:

The filter housing is attached to the cylinder block by three socket headed bolts and a joint washer is provided. Remove the three bolts and dismount the housing. On refitment, tighten the bolts to a torque of 14 lb ft (2 kg m).

Removing and fitting the pump:

Remove the sump as described in **Section 1:15.** Remove two socket headed retaining bolts and withdraw the pump downwards.

Fitment is the reverse of this sequence. Position the drive lug to engage with the distributor drive shaft and torque tighten the retaining bolts to 14 lb ft (2 kg m).

Dismantling and assembling the pump:

Remove the pump as described earlier. Withdraw two bolts, remove the cover and withdraw the gears.

Wash off all parts in petrol and, in particular, ensure that the gauze screen is cleaned. The axial clearance between the gear and cover faces should not exceed .006 inch (.15 mm). The backlash clearance between the meshed gears should be within .002 to .008 inch (.05 to .20 mm).

Reassembly is the reverse of the dismantling sequence. Wet all parts with engine oil and tighten the two assembly bolts to a torque of 7 lb ft (1 kg m).

1:4 Removing and refitting the cylinder head

The cylinder head can be removed and refitted without removing the engine from the vehicle.

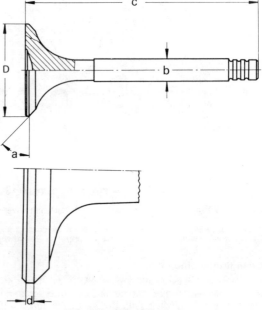

FIG 1:6   Valve dimensions

Key to Fig 1:6   Inlet valves: **D** 1.338 inch (34.0 mm) diameter   **b** .314 inch (7.97 mm) diameter   **c** 3.886 inch (98.7 mm)   **d** .02 inch (.5 mm)   **a** 45 deg.   Exhaust valves: **D** 1.220 inch (31.0 mm)   **b** .313 inch (7.95 mm) diameter   **c** 3.878 inch (98.50 mm)   **d** Zero   **a** 45 deg. Injection engines Inlet valves: **D** 1.496 inch (38.0 mm)

Removal:

1 Disconnect the battery earth connection. Drain the cooling system as described in **Chapter 4, Section 4:2.**

2 Remove the cylinder head to water pump hose and the cylinder head to heater hose. Remove the feed and return hoses from the carburetter.

3 Refer to **Chapter 2.** Remove the air cleaner. Disconnect the throttle control, the fuel feed pipe and the distributor vacuum pipe.

4 Detach the exhaust pipe from the engine manifold. Disconnect the wiring from the oil pressure warning light switch (or from the oil pressure transmitter) and detach the HT leads from the sparking plugs.

5 Remove the alternator/water pump drive belt as described in **Chapter 4, Section 4:5.** Refer to **Section 1:13.** Remove the camshaft drive belt cover. Detension and remove the camshaft drive belt. Remove the camshaft cover after disconnecting the breather pipe.

6 With the engine cool, refer to **FIG 1:3** and, following the numerical sequence, loosen off and withdraw the cylinder head holding down bolts.

7 Lift off the cylinder head and place it onto a clean smooth surface which will not damage the joint face. Remove and discard the cylinder head gasket.

Servicing the cylinder head:

Servicing the cylinder head and valve gear is covered in **Section 1:5.**

Decarbonizing the piston crowns:

With the cylinder head removed, carbon deposits can be scraped from the crowns of the pistons. Use lint free rag in all passage orifices to prevent ingress of foreign matter. Avoid the use of sharp tools which could damage the crown surfaces. Bring the piston which is to be worked on to the top of its stroke, work 'dry' (do not use paraffin) and carefully remove dislodged carbon.

Fitment:

Use a new cylinder head gasket and ensure that the joint faces of the gasket, head and cylinder block are clean. Do not use jointing compound on either the cylinder block, head or gasket faces. Fit the gasket correctly with the side marked 'OBEN' upwards.

Fitment and reassembly is the reverse of the removal sequence. Starting with No. 1 bolt and following the numerical sequence shown in **FIG 1:3**, gradually tighten the holding down bolts and finally torque tighten them to 54 lb ft (7.5 kg m). The camshaft timing procedure is included in **Section 1:13.** Check and adjust if necessary, the valve clearances as described in **Section 1:5.**

600 miles (1000 km) after refitting the cylinder head, retighten the holding down bolts in the order shown in **FIG 1:3** and using the following procedure: loosen each bolt in turn approximately 30 degrees and then retighten it to the specified torque of 8.5 kgm (61 lb ft) if the engine is warm or 7.5 kgm (53 lb ft) if it is cold.

Valve clearances must also be checked at this time as described in **Section 1:5** noting that if the engine is

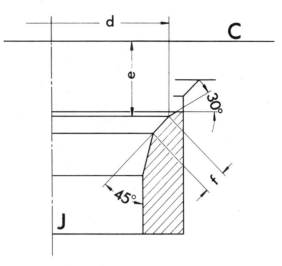

FIG 1:7 Valve seat insert dimensions. C is cylinder head face

Key to Fig 1:7 Inlet valve seats: **d** 1.306 inch (33.20 mm) **e** .354 inch (9.00 mm) **f** .069 inch (2.00 mm) Exhaust valve seats: **d** 1.212 inch (30.80 mm) **e** .378 inch (9.60 mm) **f** .094 inch (2.40 mm)

cold, a further check must be made when it is hot for the final adjustment. Always fit the adjusting discs with the lettering downwards.

1:5 Servicing the cylinder head

Cylinder head, camshaft and valve components are shown in **FIG 1:4.** Removal and fitment of the cylinder head is covered in **Section 1:4.**

Manifolds:

If a cylinder head is to be fully serviced or overhauled, remove the carburetter, both manifolds and the coolant elbows.

Combustion chambers:

Before removing the valves, decarbonize the combustion chambers and valve heads. Decarbonizing at this stage protects the valve seats. Use a scraper and wire brush and avoid the use of sharply pointed tools. Be careful not to damage the joint face.

Camshaft:

Before removing the camshaft, check the axial float. This should not exceed .006 inch (.15 mm) and is controlled by the forward bearing cap (No. 1). Remove the toothed drive wheel. Identify the caps to their positions and remove them in the following order: 5, 1, 3, 2, 4. Lift out the camshaft. Discard the oil seal 15 and check that the end plug 10 is not damaged. Camshaft runout at the centre bearing should not exceed .0004 inch (.01 mm).

On assembly, fit a new oil seal and torque tighten the bearing cap retaining nuts to 14 lb ft (2 kg m). Follow the reverse of the removal sequence. Torque tighten the drive wheel retaining bolt to 58 lb ft (8 kg m).

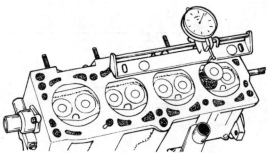

FIG 1:8   Measuring valve stem 'rock'

Valves:

With the camshaft removed, remove the adjusting discs 14 and the cam followers 13. Identify them to their positions. Using tool VW 541 as shown in **FIG 1:5** or an equivalent valve spring compressing tool, remove the cotters 19 and seats and springs 20, 21, 22 and 23. Remove the valve stem seals 24 only if they or the valve guides are worn.

Valve dimensions are given in **FIG 1:6**. Inlet valves may be remachined to correct worn seats. **Exhaust valves must not be machined** however and, if lapping to the head seat insert does not rectify worn or burned valve seats, new valves must be obtained.

Lap valves to their seats using a suction-type tool and, on completion, ensure that all traces of lapping paste are removed from the valves and the seats.

Valve springs:

Check valve springs against the following load/length figures. Renew if they do not meet the minimum load specified.

Spring	Length	Load
Outer	.916 inch	96 to 106 lb
	(22.3 mm)	(43.5 to 48 kg)
Inner	.719 inch	46 to 51 lb
	(18.3 mm)	(21 to 23 kg)

Valve seats:

No procedure is prescribed for renewing valve seats and, if lapping or machining will not restore their condition, a new cylinder head must be obtained. Valve seat dimensions are given in **FIG 1:7**.

Valve guides:

Valve guides which are excessively worn may be removed and new guides pressed in. **FIG 1:8** shows tool VW 689/1 and a dial indicator being used to measure valve 'rock'. A new valve is inserted into the guide so that the end of its stem is flush with the end of the guide and the 'rock' is then measured. Guides should be rejected if the 'rock' exceeds .039 inch (1.0 mm) in the case of an inlet guide or .051 inch (1.3 mm) in the case of exhaust valve guides.

Press out worn guides from the combustion chamber side with mandrel 10-206. Coat new guides with oil and press in from the camshaft side with the head cold until the shoulder on the guide just makes contact with the head and, finally, ream with tool 10-215. Re-work seats.

Cylinder head:

Distortion of the lower face (head to block face) must not exceed .004 inch (.1 mm) measured with feeler gauges under a straight edge. Camshaft bearing bore diameters should be within 1.0236 to 1.0244 inch (26 to 26.02 mm) and cam follower bores within 1.378 to 1.379 (35 to 35.02 mm).

Reassembly:

Reassembly is the reverse of the dismantling sequence.

Valve clearances:

Check and, if necessary, adjust the valve clearances after the cylinder head has been refitted to the cylinder block as described in **Section 1:4**.

Turn the camshaft until both valves of the relevant cylinder are closed. Using feeler gauges, measure the clearance between the back of the cam and the adjusting disc. Note the difference between this and the desired cold clearance of .006 to .010 inch (.15 to .25 mm) for an inlet valve or .014 to .018 inch (.35 to .45 mm) for an exhaust valve. If the clearance requires adjustment, remove the adjusting disc as described later. Adjustment is made by fitting a disc which is thinner or thicker than the disc which was fitted by the difference noted. Disc thicknesses are marked on their undersides and are available in .002 inch (.05 mm) steps from .118 inch (3 mm) to .167 inch (4.25 mm) in thickness. If clearances are being checked on a hot engine, work to the desired hot clearance of .008 to .012 inch (.20 to .30 mm) for inlet valves and .016 to .020 inch (.40 to .50 mm) for exhaust valves.

Removing an adjusting disc:

With both valves of the relevant cylinder closed, use either tool 10-209 or VW 546 to depress both cam

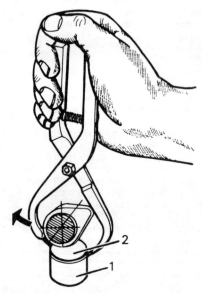

FIG 1:9   Removing an adjusting disc

Key to Fig 1:9   1 Cam follower (tappet)   2 Clearance adjusting disc

followers. Using special pincers 10-208 as shown in **FIG 1 : 9**, lift and swing out an adjusting disc. With the cam follower depressed, a disc may be pushed into position by hand.

Discs which are not worn or damaged may be used in any positions for which their specific thickness suits them. It is advisable always to measure the thickness of a used disc with a micrometer.

1 : 6 Removing the engine

In describing the engine removal and dismantling operations, some items of the emission control systems are omitted in view of the variety of applications. These must be removed or disconnected as appropriate, but do not interfere with an air conditioning system without professional assistance, see **Chapter 13, Section 13 : 12**.

In the following engine removal sequence the transmission is left installed in the vehicle. Have a suitable cradle ready to receive the engine. Refer to **FIG 1 : 10**.

1 Dismount the bonnet as described in **Chapter 13, Section 13 : 2**. Disconnect the battery earth connection 1. Remove the air cleaner 2 as described in **Chapter 2, Section 2 : 3**.

2 Disconnect the throttle control 3 at the carburetter. Refer to **Chapter 5, Section 5 : 4** and disengage the clutch cable adjuster from its bracket 4.

3 Remove the feed pipe 5 from the fuel pump and blank off the open end. Loosen the screws of the relay/fuse box and bend the harness clip open. Disconnect the heater control cable 7. Remove the engine front mounting and support 8 and 9 (these are arrowed 6 and 7 in **Chapter 2, FIG 2 : 4**).

4 Disconnect the following wiring: ignition coil 10, oil pressure switch (or pressure transmitter) 11, bypass air cut-off 14, alternator connections 15, cooling fan motor connections, cooling fan thermoswitch connections. Remove the starter motor as described in **Chapter 12, Section 12 : 4**.

5 Drain the cooling system and remove the radiator as described in **Chapter 4, Sections 4 : 2 and 4 : 3**.

6 Uncouple the exhaust pipe at the engine manifold. Remove the nuts which retain the engine mountings to the subframe. **Remove** the lower and **loosen** the upper engine/transmission bolts. On automatic transmission models, remove the torque converter bolts.

7 Refer to **FIG 1 : 11** and instal tool VW 785/1 to support the transmission. Using suitable lifting gear, raise the engine until the transmission housing just touches the steering gear. Adjust tool VW 785/1 so that, in this position, the transmission housing rests on the adjustable tool plate.

8 Remove the engine/transmission upper bolts which were loosened only at operation 6. Remove the intermediate plate, separate the engine mountings and lift and guide the engine out of the vehicle. Great care is required to avoid damage to the drive shafts, clutch and body contours.

Fuel injection and air conditioned models:

For cars fitted with continuous fuel injection and air conditioning, the following sequence is recommended. Do NOT disconnect the refrigerant pipes or hoses.

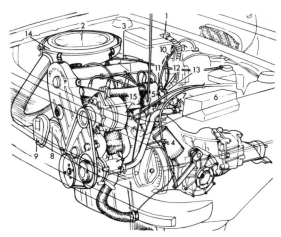

FIG 1 : 10   Engine removal, preliminary operations

Key to Fig 1 : 10   1 Battery earth connection   2 Air cleaner   3 Throttle control   4 Clutch control   5 Fuel feed pipe   6 Relay/fuse box   7 Heater control   8 Engine mounting   9 Engine mounting support   10 Ignition coil   11 Oil pressure transmitter   12 Distributor   13 Coolant temperature transmitter   14 Bypass air cut-off valve   15 Alternator

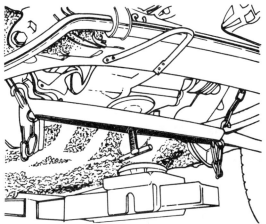

FIG 1 : 11   Supporting the transmission with tool VW 785/1

Remove the air filter and move the intake air distributor to one side. Remove the EGR valve, the horn and unbolt the compressor and move it out of the way. Unbolt the condenser and tie it on one side.

Remove the intake air duct, tie the condenser on one side then remove the radiator together with the electric fan.

1 : 7 Dismantling the engine

If the operator is not a skilled automobile engineer, it is suggested that he will find much useful information in Hints on Maintenance and Overhaul which is included in the **Appendix** and that he should refer to it before proceding with the dismantling of the engine.

1 Remove the engine as described in **Section 1 : 6**. Remove the water pump as described in **Chapter 4, Section 4 : 5**. Remove the alternator as described in

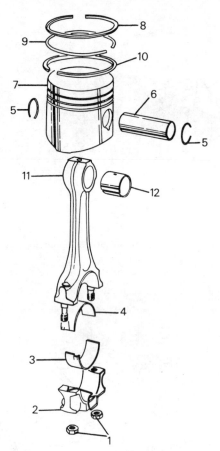

FIG 1:12 Piston and connecting rod components

Key to Fig 1:12   1 Nuts   2 Cap   3 Bearing shell
4 Bearing shell   5 Circlip   6 Gudgeon pin   7 Piston
8 Top compression ring   9 Lower compression ring   10 Oil
control ring   11 Connecting rod   12 Connecting rod small-
end bush

After cleaning and washing off components in petrol,
use compressed air to dry them and, to prevent rust, brush
clean engine oil over all steel parts. If rag is used for
cleaning operations, use only lint-free material. Blank off
all orifices to preclude the entry of dirt.

1:8 Pistons and connecting rods

Pistons and connecting rods can only be removed
upwards when the crankshaft is in position. It is necessary,
therefore, whether an engine is installed or removed from
the vehicle to remove the sump and the cylinder head
before the pistons and connecting rods can be withdrawn.

Removal:

1 Remove the cylinder head and the sump as described in
   Sections 1:4 and **1:15** respectively. Bring the
   crankshaft throw of the relevant cylinder to the bottom
   of its stroke.
2 Refer to **FIG 1:12**. Identify the bearing cap to its rod.
   Remove the retaining nuts 1 and dismount the cap 2.
3 Push the rod and piston assembly up the cylinder bore
   and withdraw it from the top. Collect the bearing shells
   3 and 4.
4 Remove the circlips 5. If the gudgeon pin 6 is tight in
   the piston bore, warm the assembly to approximately
   90°C (194°F) and, with due attention to the
   temperature, push the gudgeon pin out of engagement
   and separate the piston from the connecting rod.
5 Remove the piston rings and wash off the parts in
   petrol. Brush clean engine oil over steel parts to
   preclude rusting.

Fitment:

This is the reverse of the removal sequence. Warm the
piston to 90°C (194°F) to enable the gudgeon pin to be
fitted. Ensure that the circlips 5 are correctly seated in their
grooves. Wet the piston and rings with clean engine oil.
Position the ring gaps at 120 degrees to each other and use
an appropriate piston ring clamp to enter the piston into

Chapter 12, Section 12:5. Remove the distributor as
described in **Chapter 3, Section 3:4.**
2 Refer to **Chapter 2** and remove the carburetter and the
   fuel pump. Refer to **Section 1:3** and remove the oil
   filter housing. Remove the coolant and oil pressure
   transmitters.
3 Remove the clutch assembly as described in **Chapter
   5, Section 5:3** or, in the case of automatic
   transmission models, dismount the torque converter.
4 Refer to **Section 1:11** and remove the flywheel or, in
   the case of automatic transmission models, remove the
   driving plate; to **Section 1:4** and remove the cylinder
   head; to **Section 1:15** and remove the sump and to
   Section 1:3 and remove the oil pump.
5 Refer to **Section 1:8** and remove the pistons and
   connecting rods. Refer to **Section 1:12** and remove
   the crankshaft. Refer to **Section 1:13** and remove the
   intermediate shaft.

Dismantling procedures for the cylinder head, oil pump,
pistons and connecting rods etc are covered in their
relevant Sections.

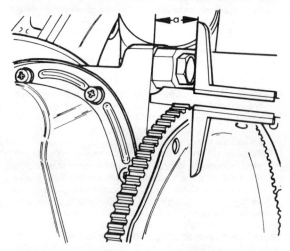

FIG 1:13   Driving plate to cylinder block dimension

Key to Fig 1:13   a 1.232 ± .031 inch (31.3 ± .8 mm)

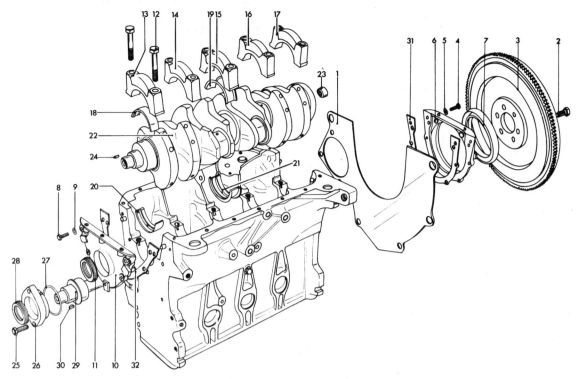

FIG 1:14 Components of the cylinder block and crankshaft

Key to Fig 1:14   1 Intermediate plate   2 Bolt   3 Flywheel   4 Bolt   5 Spring washer   6 Rear oil seal flange   7 Oil seal   8 Bolt   9 Spring washer   10 Front oil seal flange   11 Oil seal   12 Bolt   13 Front main bearing cap   14 Main bearing cap   15 Centre main bearing cap   16 Main bearing cap   17 Rear main bearing cap   18 Lower bearing shell   19 Lower centre bearing shell (flanged)   20 Upper bearing shell (grooved)   21 Upper centre bearing shell (flanged)   22 Crankshaft   23 Needle roller bearing (pilot)   24 Woodruff key   25 Bolt   26 Intermediate shaft oil seal flange   27 Oil seal ring   28 Oil seal   29 Intermediate shaft   30 Woodruff key   31 Gasket   32 Gasket

the top of the cylinder bore. Lubricate and fit the bearing shells. Fit the cap and torque tighten the retaining nuts to 33 lb ft (4.5 kg m).

1:9 Pistons and rings

Pistons:

Where, as in the case of the 1471 cc engine, two compression ratio versions of the engine are available, two types of piston are manufactured. Those with dished crowns give a compression ratio of 8.5:1 and are fitted to Dasher models. Those with flat crowns give a compression ratio of 9.7:1 and are fitted to Passat models. All 1297 cc Passat models have pistons with dished crowns to give a compression ratio of 8.5:1.

Piston crowns carry an arrow (fit with arrow pointing to front of engine), its diameter in mm and its weight class code. All pistons in one engine should be in the same weight class (weight difference should not exceed 17 grams). The piston diameter should be measured about $\frac{5}{8}$ inch (16 mm) up from the bottom of the skirt and at right angles to the axis of the gudgeon pin. The desired (new or after overhaul) piston to cylinder bore clearance is .0012

inch (.03 mm) and the recommended wear limit is .0028 inch (.07 mm).

In addition to the basic (new vehicle) size, pistons are available in three oversizes. Each size and oversize is coded into three grades. The overhaul of the cylinder block (see **Section 1:16**) must be completed before pistons can be selected to match its bores.

Details of piston diameters, both standard and oversize, will be found in **Technical Data** in the **Appendix**.

Rings:

The two top grooves carry compression rings. The bottom groove carries the oil control (scraper) ring. The lower compression and the oil control rings must be fitted the correct way up with TOP towards the piston crown.

Groove widths and ring thicknesses are standard for all engines and, with a ring in its groove, the ring to groove clearance should be .0008 to .002 inch (.02 to .05 mm) with a wear limit of .006 inch (.15 mm). Ring gaps, measured by feeler gauge with the ring pushed down squarely into the cylinder bore by approximately .6 inch (15 mm), should be .012 to .018

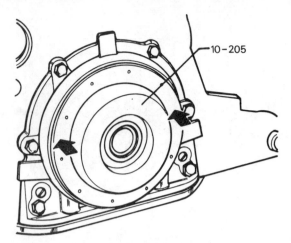

FIG 1:15 Rear oil seal fitment

inch (.30 to .45 mm) for compression rings and .010 to .016 inch (.25 to .40 mm) for oil control rings. The wear limit recommended in all cases is .040 inch (1.0 mm).

1:10 Connecting rods

The desired big-end clearance with its crankpin is .0012 to .0032 inch (.03 to .08 mm) diametrically. The wear limit recommended is .0047 inch (.12 mm). Diametrical clearance may be conveniently measured using Plastigage as described in **Section 1:12**. Tighten the connecting rod cap to a torque of 33 lb ft (4.5 kg m) and do not turn the rod on the crankpin while making the Plastigage check. It is recommended that axial clearance between a connecting rod and the crankshaft web should not be greater than .010 inch (.25 mm).

In addition to bearings which suit new crankpin diameters, three sizes of bearings are available to suit crankpins which have been reground undersize. It follows that, before big-end bearing shells can be selected, the overhaul of the crankshaft (see **Section 1:12**) must have been completed.

Gudgeon pins run with a clearance in the connecting rod small-end bushes.

No attempt should be made to salvage a bent, twisted or damaged connecting rod.

If any connecting rod is found to be unserviceable, it must be renewed and on these engines that means renewing the other three also as connecting rods are supplied only in sets of four.

1:11 Flywheel

The flywheel or, in the case of models fitted with automatic transmission, the torque converter driving plate, can be removed with the engine installed in the vehicle after removal of the transmission as described in **Chapter 6** or **Chapter 7**. Removal of the clutch as described in **Chapter 5, Section 5:3** in the case of manual transmission models or removal of the torque converter as described in **Chapter 7** is also necessary.

The flywheel is spigotted to the rear end of the crankshaft and is secured to it by six bolts. On manual transmission models the flywheel carries the clutch assembly (see **Chapter 5**) and the clutch plate operates directly on the rear face of the flywheel.

Removal and fitment:

Withdraw the retaining bolts and, using leverage if necessary, dismount the flywheel.

When refitting the flywheel, ensure that the crankshaft and flywheel spigots are clean and free from burrs. Position the flywheel, coat the threads of the six retaining bolts with Loctite and torque tighten them to 54 lb ft (7.5 kg m). Refer to **FIG 1:13** and, on automatic transmission models, measure the dimension **a** between the rear face of the cylinder block and the rear face of the torque converter driving plate. If necessary, shims must be fitted between the crankshaft and the driving plate to bring **a** within the 1.232 ± .031 inch (31.3 ± .8 mm) specified.

Flywheel rear face:

If the face on which the clutch plate operates is excessively scored it may be salvaged by machining. If the surface is damaged severely, however, a new flywheel will be required. Dishing of the face (inwards towards the centre) is acceptable up to a maximum of .003 inch (.08 mm).

1:12 Crankshaft and main bearings

The crankshaft and cylinder block components are shown in **FIG 1:14**. With the engine dismantling procedure given in **Section 1:7** completed to the relevant stage, the crankshaft removal sequence is as follows.

Removal:

1 Refer to **Section 1:13** and remove the alternator/water pump pulley and camshaft driving wheel from the crankshaft. The intermediate plate 1 was withdrawn during the engine removal sequence and the flywheel 3 will have been removed as described in **Section 1:11**.

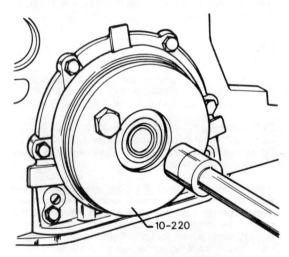

FIG 1:16 Rear oil seal fitment

2 Remove the six bolts and washers 4 and 5 and dismount the rear oil seal flange and joint washer 6 and 31. Extract and discard the rear oil seal 7.

3 Remove the five bolts and washers 8 and 9 and dismount the front oil seal and joint washer 10 and 32. Extract and discard the front oil seal 11.

4 Remove the bearing cap retaining bolts 12, identify the caps 13, 14, 15, 16 and 17 to their positions and remove them. Lift out the crankshaft.

5 Collect all bearing shells noting that those for the centre bearing (19 and 21) are axial float control bearings and that bearing shells which have no lubrication grooves fit into the bearing caps and not into the cylinder block.

6 If the transmission shaft pilot bearing 23 is unserviceable, it may be extracted using puller 10-202. Removal of the intermediate shaft and its associated parts (25 to 30) is covered in **Section 1 : 13**.

7 Remove all traces of old jointing washers. Clean off all components by washing in petrol and brush clean engine oil over all steel components to preclude rusting.

Inspection :

With the crankshaft supported in V-blocks at the front and rear journals, the runout measured at journals 2, 3 or 4 should not exceed .0024 inch (.06 mm).

If there has been a journal bearing or a big-end bearing failure, the crankshaft oilways must be checked to ensure that there is no obstruction and any transfer of bearing metal must be carefully removed before the crankpins and journals are examined for damage. Neither crankpin nor main journal ovality should exceed .0012 inch (.03 mm).

Crankpin to connecting rod big-end clearances (see **Section 1 : 10**) and main bearing clearances are best measured by using Plastigage as described later in this section. The main bearing cap retaining bolts should be tightened to 47 lb ft (6.5 kg m) and the crankshaft must not be turned while making the Plastigage checks. The desired main bearing clearance is .0012 to .0032 inch (.03 to .08 mm) with a wear limit of .0067 inch (.17 mm).

If crankpin or main journal clearances are excessive, the crankshaft must be reground to suit undersize diameter bearing shells. There are three stages of undersize crankpins and also three stages of undersize main journals for which bearing shells are available. Which stage to regrind to will depend upon the extent of the wear or damage. Only after completing the salvage operations can the big-end or main journal bearings which are appropriate to the new diameters be selected. Crankpin and main journal diameters for new and for the three stages of regrind are tabulated in **Technical Data** in the **Appendix**.

Crankshaft end float is controlled by the flanged centre bearing shells. End float is measured by feeler gauge. The desired clearance is .003 to .007 (.07 to .17 mm) with a recommended wear limit of .010 (.25 mm).

Fitment :

The fitment sequence is the reverse of that described for removal of the crankshaft. Use mandrel VW 207c to fit a new pilot bearing 23 if it was removed. Fit the new rear oil seal by pushing it over fitting sleeve 10-205 as

shown in **FIG 1 : 15** and, as shown in **FIG 1 : 16**, use tool 10-220 to press it home until flush. Use tool 10-203 as shown in **FIG 1 : 17** to fit the new front seal.

Assemble the bearings wetted with engine oil and torque tighten the bearing cap retaining bolts to 47 lb ft (6.5 kg m). Confirm that the axial float is within limits.

Plastigage :

The installed clearance of crankshaft main bearings and connecting rod big-end bearings is best measured by using this proprietary plastic 'thread' as follows.

1 Select the diameter of Plastigage which covers the clearance to be measured. Place a length of the thread on the relevant journal along its full width and slightly off centre.

2 Fit the bearing shell and cap and tighten the retaining bolts or nuts to the torque specified for them. The Plastigage will be squeezed down to the clearance dimension of the bearing and its width will increase. **Do not turn the crankshaft or connecting rod while the Plastigage is in position.**

3 Remove the bearing cap and shell and, using the Plastigage scale which is provided with the thread, read off the clearance. The maximum width of the Plastigage will indicate the minimum bearing clearance and the minimum width, the maximum clearance.

1 : 13 Camshaft and intermediate shaft drive

The camshaft and intermediate shaft are driven by toothed belt from a wheel on the forward end of the crankshaft. They both run at half crankshaft speed. The belt runs 'dry' and is guarded by a sheet metal cover. An adjustable tensioner pulley is provided. The components are shown in **FIG 1 : 18**.

The drive belt has a recommended life of 60,000 miles (100,000 km) and should be renewed at intervals of this milage irrespective of its apparent condition.

Drive belt removal :

Remove the alternator/water pump drive belt 1 as described in **Chapter 4, Section 4 : 5**. Remove the cover

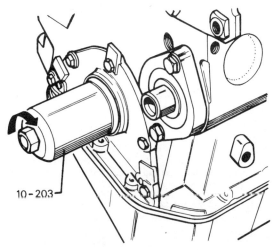

FIG 1 : 17 Front oil seal fitment

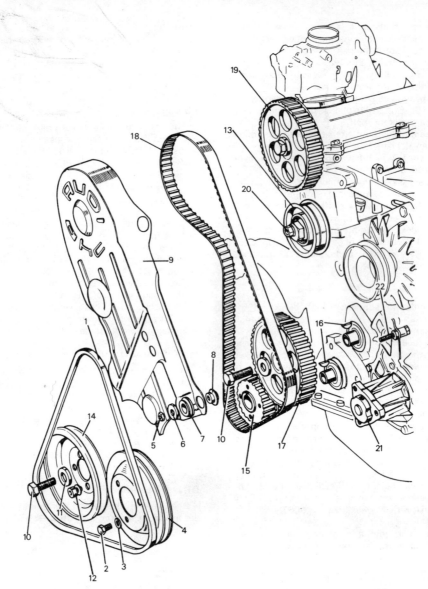

FIG 1:18   Components of the camshaft and the alternator/water pump drives

Key to Fig 1:18   1 V-belt   2 Bolt   3 Spring washer   4 Pulley   5 Nut   6 Washer   7 Rubber bush   8 Bush
9 Cover   10 Bolt   11 Washer   12 Socket headed bolt   13 Tensioner   14 Pulley   15 Toothed wheel (crankshaft)
16 Woodruff keys   17 Toothed wheel (intermediate shaft)   18 Camshaft drive belt   19 Toothed wheel (camshaft)
20 Tensioner locking nut   21 Water pump drive flange   22 Bolt

9. Detension the belt by loosening the retaining nut 20 and turning the tensioner pulley 13 on its eccentric. Push the belt axially forwards off the camshaft drive wheel 19 and disengage it from the wheels 17 and 15.

Drive belt fitment and camshaft timing:

1 With No. 1 cylinder on TDC of its compression stroke, turn the intermediate shaft wheel 17 until, as shown in **FIG 1:19**, the markings on the wheels are in line (see arrow).

2 Turn the camshaft wheel 19 until, as shown in **FIG 1:20**, the arrowed mark is aligned with the top of the camshaft cover flange.

3 Fit the drive belt and, by turning the pulley 13 on its eccentric, tension the belt. Lock the tension by tightening nut 20 to a torque of 32 lb ft (4.5 kg m). Tension is correct when, using only thumb and index finger between the camshaft wheel and the intermediate wheel, the belt can just be twisted through 90 degrees.

4 Turn the crankshaft through two complete revolutions and confirm that the marks align correctly. Refit the parts which were removed and tension the alternator/water pump drive belt as described in **Chapter 4, Section 4:5.**

Drive wheel removal and fitment:

Removal and fitment of the camshaft wheel is covered in **Section 1:5.** Removal of the crankshaft drive wheel is effected after removing the drive belt as described earlier by removing the four bolts 12 in **FIG 1:18** and dismounting the V-belt pulley 14 and the single bolt 10 (or, if pulley 14 and wheel 15 are not to be separated, by removing only bolt 10). The intermediate shaft wheel may be removed after withdrawing bolt 21. On refitment, torque tighten bolts 10 and 21 to 58 lb ft (8 kg m) and bolts 12 to 14 lb ft (2 kg m).

Intermediate shaft and oil seal:

To remove the intermediate shaft, dismount the distributor as described in **Chapter 3, Section 3:4** and the fuel pump as described in **Chapter 2, Section 2:5.** Remove the camshaft drive belt and the intermediate shaft wheel as described earlier. Refer to **FIG 1:14.** Remove the two bolts 25 which retain the oil seal flange and withdraw the flange and seal. Remove the seal ring 27. Withdraw the intermediate shaft 29. Fitment is the reverse of this sequence. If the oil seal is unserviceable, press it out and, using mandrel VW 519, press in a new seal.

1:14 Distributor drive

The distributor is driven by a skew gear which is integral with the intermediate shaft (see **FIG 1:1**). This gear mates with the matching gear on the distributor shaft which is shown in **Chapter 3, FIG 3:1.** This 1:1 ratio drive with the intermediate shaft running at half crankshaft speed provides the 1:2 ratio for the distributor.

The engine oil pump is driven from the lower end of the distributor shaft.

1:15 Oil sump

To provide clearance for the removal of the sump with the engine installed in the vehicle, the engine has to be temporarily supported from above and its mountings released. **FIG 1:21** shows the engine support 10-222 straddling the engine compartment with its supporting hook engaging the lifting lug at the rear of the cylinder head.

When automatic transmission is fitted, the vacuum hose for the primary throttle pressure must be removed and in some cases it may be necessary to lower the sub-frame.

Drain off the engine oil before removing the twenty socket headed bolts which retain the sump to the cylinder block. An extension of 7 to 8 inches in length (175 to 205 mm) for the socket wrench will be required as shown in **FIG 1:22.**

When refitting, ensure that both faces are clean and free from old gasket and jointing compound. Use a new gasket and tighten the twenty bolts to a torque of 7 lb ft (1 kg m). The sump drain plug should be tightened to a torque of 22 lb ft (3 kg m).

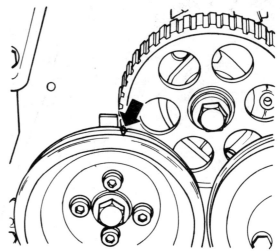

FIG 1:19   Crankshaft and intermediate wheel timing marks

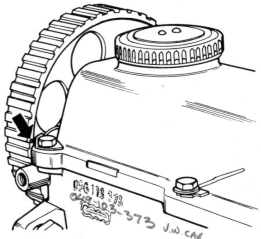

FIG 1:20   Camshaft timing mark

1:16 Cylinder block

Before the cylinder block bores can be honed or rebored, the engine must be completely dismantled. A cylinder block which is cracked should be rejected and a new block obtained. The flatness of the top face should be within .004 inch (.1 mm) measured with feeler gauges and a straight edge.

Use a comparator gauge to measure the cylinder bores. Take measurements at about $\frac{3}{8}$ inch (10 mm) from the top and from the bottom of each bore and also near the mid-stroke position. For each engine capacity, three rebore stages are specified and oversize pistons are available to suit them. There are three gradings for each stage. Decide, from the measurements taken, which rebore stage will correct the bores and have the work carried out. It will then be possible (see **Section 1:9**) to determine which pistons must be obtained to match the bores.

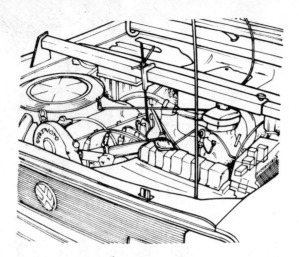

FIG 1:21 Engine supporting beam

1:17 Assembling the engine

Assembly instructions are given in the text of each relevant Section. These are largely the dismantling procedures in reverse but, as they may not always be so, the point should be checked against the information given in the text. It is then simply a matter of tackling the work in the correct sequence, of applying normal automobile engineering practice, fitting only VW replacement parts, using new gasket and joint washers and ensuring that joints are well made.

If the engine has been completely dismantled, the assembly sequence will be the reverse of that described in **Section 1:7**. If the engine has been only partially dismantled, reverse the sequence which was followed when carrying out the partial dismantling.

Refer to sectional and chapter texts and to **Technical Data** for torque tightening figures, clearances and end play information. At each stage of assembly check, where relevant, the free rotation of the assembly or component. Ensure that nuts and bolts are correctly tightened and, where applicable, properly locked.

Assemble working parts wetted with engine oil and use oil resistant sealing compound where relevant. It is important to ensure that joints are well made as it may not easily be possible to rectify an oil leak which is not discovered until assembly and installation of the engine has been completed. For this reason also, scrutinize carefully the condition of oil seals and, if their condition is not perfect, fit new.

1:18 Installing the engine

Installing the engine into the vehicle is basically the reverse of the removal sequence described in **Section 1:6**. When the installation has been completed and all systems made serviceable, run the engine up to normal temperature and adjust the carburetter as described in **Chapter 2**. Check over and correct leaks from pipe and hose connections.

600 miles (1000 km) after reassembling and installing the engine, retighten the cylinder head holding down bolts as described in **Section 1:4**.

1:19 Engine mountings

With the engine supported by lifting tackle or by tool 10-222 as shown in **FIG 1:21**, the two engine mountings 22 in **Chapter 8**, **FIG 8:2** can be removed and new mountings fitted. Similarly the engine front support (arrowed 6 and 7 in **Chapter 2**, **FIG 2:4**) can, if necessary, be dealt with. Torque tighten the mounting retaining nuts to 29 lb ft (4 kg m).

Similarly, with the engine supported and the suspension arm pivot bolts removed (see **Chapter 8, Section 8:4**, operation 4 only), the subframe can be removed after releasing the two engine mountings and withdrawing the four retaining bolts 23 in **FIG 8:2**. This allows unserviceable bonded rubber bushes 20 in **Chapter 8**, **FIG 8:2** to be renewed. Torque tighten the subframe retaining bolts to 50 lb ft (7 kg m) on refitment.

1:20 Emission control system

This Section is only relevant to Dasher models imported into the USA. Since, however, emission control regulations in California are not the same as those for other States in the USA, emission control equipment is not identical on all models and engines have accordingly been given series letters to indicate whether the equipment fitted conforms to Californian regulations or to those of the other States. Emission control equipment may relate to the engine, to the fuel system or to the ignition system and reference should also be made to **Chapter 2, Section 2:10** and to **Chapter 3, Section 3:8**.

Engine series letters:

XZ	Manual transmission models for California.
XY	Automatic transmission models for California.
XW	Manual transmission models for other States.
XV	Automatic transmission models for other States.

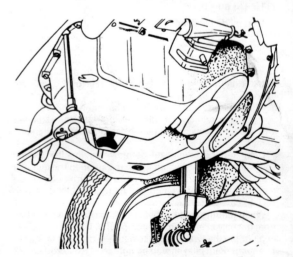

FIG 1:22 Removing sump retaining bolts

Exhaust gas recirulation (EGR):

In this system (see **FIG 1 : 23**) a metered quantity of exhaust gas is diverted from No. 4 cylinder exhaust port 6, through the filter 8 and EGR valve 9 into the inlet manifold 4. This has the effect of lowering the combustion temperatures and so reducing the emission of oxides of nitrogen in the exhaust. The diameter of the orifice in the exhaust manifold is .157 inch (4 mm) on manual transmission models and .276 inch (7 mm) on automatic models.

The system is designed to operate only in the mid-throttle range and when the temperature valve is above $46° \pm 3°C$. See **FIG 1 : 24** which shows how vacuum is applied to the EGR valve. There is always a vacuum being applied to the two-way valve 2 and this is opened to the EGR valve passage by means of the throttle valve micro switch at throttle openings of between 30 and 67 deg. (manual) or 23 and 63 deg. (automatic). This combined method of operation ensures full engine efficiency when cold, at idle speeds or when full power is required.

Checking the EGR valve:

Refer to **FIG 1 : 25**. With the engine hot and running at idle speed, disconnect the vacuum hose from the EGR valve as indicated by the arrow.

Disconnect the hose from the anti-back fire valve and attach it to the vacant union on the EGR valve. The idle speed should now show a decrease. If it does not, either the EGR valve or filter is blocked or the return line from the valve.

Refer to **FIG 1 : 26**. Run the engine at idle speed and operate the micro switch (arrowed) on the throttle valve.

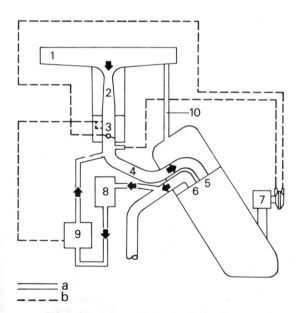

FIG 1 : 23   Exhaust gas recirculation system

Key to Fig 1 : 23   1 Air cleaner   2 Air intake   3 Carburetter   4 Inlet manifold   5 Inlet valve   6 Exhaust valve   7 Distributor   8 Filter   9 Gas recirculation valve   10 Breather pipe   a Air and exhaust gas pipes   b Vacuum pipes

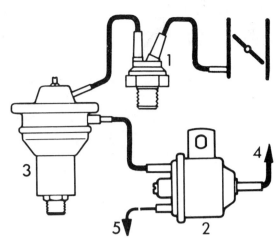

FIG 1 : 24   Diagram showing the actuation of the EGR valve

Key to Fig 1 : 24   1 Temperature valve   2 Two-way valve   3 EGR valve   4 To vacuum servo unit   5 To micro switch

The engine should now lose speed or even stall. If it does not, either the EGR valve is faulty, the micro switch is faulty, the filter or return line is blocked or the two-way valve is not operating.

If any of these components is proved to be faulty, a new part must be fitted as no repairs are possible, although the EGR valve may be cleaned. The specified interval for cleaning the EGR valve is 15,000 miles and is indicated by the EGR warning light in the speedometer on later cars. After checking and cleaning the system, the elapsed mileage recorder on the speedometer drive must be reset to zero by pressing the white button marked EGR.

Catalytic converter:

This is a device fitted in the exhaust pipe by means of which the CO in the exhaust is still further reduced. A mileage recorder will illuminate the CAT warning light in the speedometer at 30,000 miles to indicate that the converter is due for renewal. This is the same recorder as Is used tor the EGR system warnings and must be reset, after renewal, by pressing in the CAT button.

The warning lamp will also be illuminated if the converter overheats—a temperature sensor is included for this purpose. Over-heating can be caused by an engine fault such as incorrect mixture or timing, incorrect operation of one of the emission systems or prolonged high speed driving or towing a heavy trailer. The lamp will usually go out if speed is reduced.

To check the converter, remove the bolts holding it in position and unscrew the temperature sensor. Hold it up to a strong light and look through both ends to see if the ceramic insert is blocked. If it is, renew the converter and reset the elapsed mileage recordor.

Fuel tank filler pipe:

Since those cars equipped with catalytic converters must use a non-leaded fuel and American fuel station pumps are fitted with smaller diameter nozzles for non-leaded fuels, the filler pipe has a small bore insert and spring loaded flap to prevent the use of normal leaded fuel pump nozzles.

Exhaust afterburning:

On **XY and XZ series engines**, by injecting air into the incandescent exhaust gases immediately after they leave the engine cylinders, further combustion of unburned hydrocarbons is encouraged and the final exhaust gases when they leave the exhaust pipe contain less carbon monoxide (but more of the less noxious carbon dioxide) than would be the case with untreated gases.

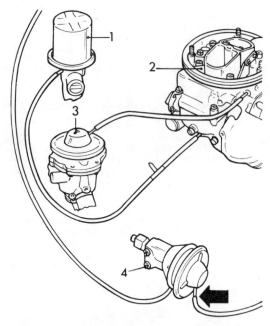

FIG 1 : 25   Checking the EGR valve temperature valve circuit

Key to Fig 1 : 25   1 Anti-backfire valve   2 Carburetter
3 Diverter valve   4 EGR valve

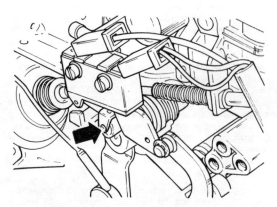

FIG 1 : 26   Checking the EGR valve micro switch circuit

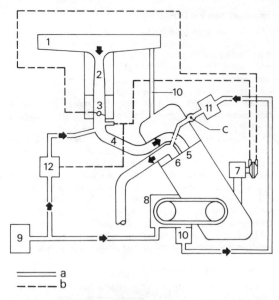

FIG 1 : 27   Emission control exhaust afterburning

Key to Fig 1 : 27   1 Air cleaner   2 Air intake   3 Carburetter   4 Inlet manifold   5 Inlet valve   6 Exhaust valve
7 Distributor   8 Belt driven air pump   9 Filter   10 Breather pipe   11 Backfire valve   12 Deceleration valve   C Air gallery

The system is shown diagramatically in **FIG 1 : 27**. The air pump 8 is belt driven from the forward end of the crankshaft and draws in ambient air through a filter 9. Pressure air is delivered via air gallery **C** to a nozzle in each exhaust port adjacent to each exhaust valve. To preclude reverse flow of exhaust gases (this could occur if the pump became defective, if its belt drive should fail or if the pump relief valve should become inoperative) a non-return valve 11 is fitted immediately before the air gallery. When the throttle is closed suddenly, an unburned (excessively rich) petrol/air mixture may be exhausted from the cylinders and this, when diluted by air from the nozzles, will become a combustible mixture in the exhaust pipe and silencers. On subsequent opening of the throttle, it will be ignited by the hot exhaust gases and a backfire will occur. To minimize this risk, the inlet manifold 4 is provided with a connection to filtered ambient air via valve 12 which at high inlet manifold depression (on deceleration with throttle closed and a fast running engine) admits air to the manifold. The resulting weakening of the petrol/air mixture burns more readily in the cylinders and is expelled as normal (non-combustible) exhaust gas.

Air pump belt drive:

Every 10,000 miles (17,000 km), check the belt tension and adjust if necessary. The tensioning procedure is similar to that described in **Chapter 4, Section 4:5** for the alternator/water pump drive belt.

Air filter:

Renew the element of filter 9 every 20,000 miles (33,000 km).

Deceleration valve:

If backfires occur, either the deceleration valve 12 is not opening on decelerations because it is defective or because there is a leak in its 'vacuum' line. The valve may be checked by removing the filter to valve hose at the valve and, with the engine idling, alternately detaching and attaching its 'vacuum' line at the valve. Each time the line is attached, it should be possible to feel air being drawn into the valve at its inlet. A defective valve must be renewed.

Air pump:

A defective air pump cannot be repaired and must be replaced by a new unit.

General:

Every 10,000 miles (17,000 km), check over all emission control equipment pipes, hoses and connections. Since emission control standards are strict where the requirements are mandatory, any actual or suspected malfunctioning which the owner cannot readily correct himself should be referred to an Agent who is equipped to diagnose and rectify faults and able to supply any replacement parts which may be required.

1:21 Fault diagnosis

(a) Engine will not start

1 Defective ignition coil
2 Faulty distributor capacitor
3 Dirty, pitted or incorrectly set distributor points
4 Ignition leads loose or insulation faulty
5 Water on HT leads
6 Battery discharged, corrosion of terminals
7 Faulty or jammed starter motor
8 Sparking plug leads wrongly connected
9 Vapour lock in fuel line
10 Defective fuel pump
11 Defective carburetter choke
12 Blocked fuel filter
13 Blocked carburetter jet(s)
14 Valves leaking or sticking
15 Camshaft or ignition timing incorrect

(b) Engine stalls

1 Check 1, 2, 3, 4, 5, 10, 12, 13 and 14 in (a)
2 Sparking plugs defective or gaps incorrect
3 Excessively retarded ignition
4 Mixture too weak
5 Water in fuel system
6 Fuel tank air vent blocked
7 Incorrect valve clearances

(c) Engine idles badly

1 Check 2 and 7 in (b)
2 Air leak at inlet manifold joint
3 Carburetter adjustment incorrect
4 Mixture too rich
5 Worn piston rings
6 Worn valve stems or guides or stem seals
7 Weak valve springs
8 Air leak at carburetter joint
9 Deceleration valve defective (emission control models)

(d) Engine misfires

1 Check 1, 2, 3, 4, 5, 8, 10, 12, 13, 14 and 15 in (a)
2 Weak or broken springs

(e) Engine overheats (see Chapter 4)

(f) Compression low

1 Check 14 in (a), 5 and 6 in (c) and 2 in (d)
2 Worn piston ring grooves
3 Scored or worn cylinder bores

(g) Engine lacks power

1 Check 3, 10, 13, 14 and 15 in (a), 2, 3, 4 and 7 in (b), 5 and 6 in (c), 2 in (d) and check (f)
2 Leaking joint gasket
3 Dirty sparking plugs
4 Incorrect valve clearances

(h) Burnt valves or seats

1 Check 14 in (a)
2 Excessive carbon deposits round valve seats

(j) Sticking valves

1 Check 2 in (d)
2 Bent valve stem
3 Scored valve stem or guide
4 Incorrect valve clearance

(k) Excessive cylinder wear

1 Check 11 in (a)
2 Lack of oil
3 Dirty oil
4 Piston rings gummed up or broken
5 Connecting rod bent

(l) Excessive oil consumption

1 Check 5 and 6 in (c)
2 Ring gaps over limit
3 Oil return holes in piston(s) choked
4 Oil level too high
5 External oil leaks

(m) Main or big-end bearing failure

1 Check 2, 3 and 5 in (k)
2 Restricted oilways
3 Worn main journal or crankpin
4 Loose bearing cap(s)
5 Extremely low oil pressure

(n) Engine vibration

1 Loose alternator
2 Engine mountings loose or defective
3 Misfiring due to mixture, ignition or mechanical fault
4 Air cleaner loose
5 Air pump loose (emission control models)

NOTES

CHAPTER 2

THE FUEL SYSTEM

2:1 Description

Fuel is drawn from a 10 gallons (11 gallons on estate cars) capacity tank at the rear of the vehicle by a mechanical diaphragm-type pump which is mounted on the lefthand side of the cylinder block. The pump is operated by an eccentric on the intermediate shaft which runs at half crankshaft speed. A fuel filter is fitted inside the pump, and a strainer may also be included at the fuel tank outlet pipe. Later cars have an in-line filter located at the front of the engine.

The fuel tank is provided with a float and arm type of contents transmitter which operates electrically in conjunction with a fuel gauge mounted in the instrument panel. Contents readings are given only when the ignition is switched on.

A single Solex downdraught carburetter is fitted and, depending upon the engine capacity, compression ratio and other features, this may be a single venturi or a twin venturi type. All carburetters incorporate a fully automatic choke for starting from cold. The choke is controlled thermostatically by the temperature of the engine coolant which is circulated through the choke housing. All carburetters incorporate an accelerator pump. The throttle control is by Bowden-type flexible cable.

A dry-type paper element is fitted to the canister air cleaner/silencer mounted immediately above the carburetter. Cleaners fitted to single venturi carburetters differ from those fitted to twin venturi carburetters. The main difference is that those fitted to twin venturi carburetters incorporate a heated air entry connection and are provided with a means of automatic control of air intake temperature. All cleaner canisters incorporate a connection to which the cylinder head cover breather pipe is coupled.

Models which are imported into countries in which emission control is mandatory are provided with appropriate equipment. This may be covered in one of the Sections but is summarised in **Section 2:10**. Reference may also be made to **Chapter 1, Section 1:20** and **Chapter 3, Section 3:8**.

Fuel octane ratings:

It is recommended that fuel of the following ratings is used.

Engines with compression ratios of 8.2
  and 8.5:1   ..   .. 91 octane
Engines with compression ratio of 9.7:1 .. 98 octane

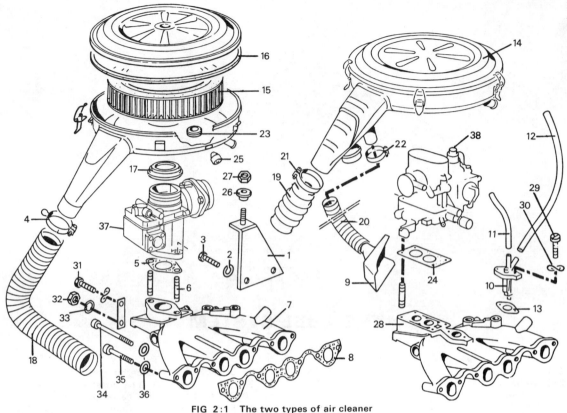

FIG 2:1 The two types of air cleaner

Key to Fig 2:1   1 Mounting bracket   2 Washer   3 Bolt   4 Hose clip   5 Gasket   6 Stud   7 Manifold   8 Gasket
9 Warm air collector   10 Valve   11 Hose (to vacuum unit)   12 Hose (to carburetter)   13 Gasket   14 Air cleaner
assembly   15 Element   16 Canister cover   17 Joint   18 Flexible duct   19 Flexible duct (cold air)   20 Flexible duct
(warm air)   21 Hose clip   22 Hose clip   23 Mounting inset   24 Gasket   25 Plug   26 Grommet   27 Nut   28 Manifold   29 Bolt   30 Washer   31 Bolt   32 Nut   33 Washer   34 Bolt   35 Bolt   36 Washer   37 PDSIT carburetter   38 TDID or
DIDTA carburetter

2:2 Maintenance

Fuel pipes and connections:

At regular intervals of, say, 5000 miles (8000 km), check
the fuel pipes and ensure that there are no leaks at the
pump or carburetter connections. Similarly check the
coolant feed and return pipes to the automatic choke
housing.

Air cleaner:

Every 10,000 miles (16,000 km) or more frequently in
dusty terrain, remove and clean the element as described in
Section 2:3. Every 20,000 miles (33,000 km), discard the
element and fit a new replacement.

Fuel filter:

Every 10,000 miles (16,000 km), clean the filter as
described in Section 2:4.

Idling speed:

Every 5000 miles (8000 km) or whenever necessary,
check and adjust the idling speed as described in Section

2:7, Section 2:8 or Section 2:9. Before carrying out
any adjustment that may be required, ensure that the
ignition distributor points gap is correctly set, that the
ignition timing is correct and that the sparking plugs are
serviceable and that their gaps are also correctly set. These
ignition maintenance procedures are covered in Chapter
3, Sections 3:4, 3:6 and 3:7.

The engine must be at normal operating temperature
when checking and adjusting the idling speed. The correct
idling speed is as follows.

| All Passat models | 950±50 rev/min |
| All Dasher models | 925±75 rev/min |

Emission control equipment:

Maintenance recommendations are included in
Section 2:10. Since emission control limits are critical,
maintenance must never be neglected and a competent
Agent should be employed to deal with all procedures for
which special facilities are needed or which an owner
cannot readily deal with himself.

2:3 Air cleaner

The components of the alternative types of air
cleaner/silencer are shown in FIG 2:1.

Cleaning or renewing the element:

Unclip and remove the cover from the canister assembly. Lift out the element. Dislodge the dust from the element by agitating it thoroughly and blowing off with compressed air if available. Taking care that no dust enters the carburetter, clean the interior of the canister. Clean the inside of the canister cover.

Fit the new or cleaned element. Refit the cover and ensure that the retaining clips are securely engaged.

Removing and fitting the air cleaner canister:

Loosen the hose clips and pull off the cold air hose and the breather hose. In the case of Dasher and appropriate Passat models, uncouple the preheated air hose. In the case of Dasher and relevant Passat models which are provided with automatic control of the temperature of the preheated intake air, identify and disconnect all pipes from the canister. Remove the element as described earlier. Remove the retaining nut and dismount the canister from the mounting bracket.

Fitment is the reverse of this sequence. Ensure that all pipes and hoses are correctly reconnected and that their retaining clips are securely tightened.

Intake air preheating (non-automatic control):

On models which do not have automatic control of the preheated air temperature, observe the following compromise guide lines which will ensure that the carburetter is supplied with intake air at the approximately correct temperature for differing climatic conditions and seasonal variations.

When the ambient temperature is **above** 15°C (60°F):
1 Secure the air cleaner intake hose to the wheel housing by pushing the ball head of the hose clip securing screw into the rubber grommet.
2 Open the fresh air slide in the radiator grille.

When the ambient air temperature is **below** 15°C (60°F):
1 Push the air cleaner intake hose onto the adaptor on the exhaust manifold.
2 Close the fresh air slide in the radiator grille.

Intake air preheating (automatic temperature control):

When the ambient air temperature is **above** 15°C (60°F), open the fresh air slide in the radiator grille. When the ambient air temperature is **below** 15°C (60°F), close the fresh air slide in the radiator grille. Testing is covered in **Section 2:10**.

2:4 Fuel filter

Up to 1975 the fuel filtration was performed by the gauze element, 5 in **FIG 2:2**, in the fuel pump, later cars have an in-line filter which must be renewed every 18,000 miles (30,000 km). This is simply a matter of disconnecting the two hoses from the old unit and connecting them to the new filter, noting the arrow pointing in the direction of fuel flow. Earlier filters are cleaned as follows:

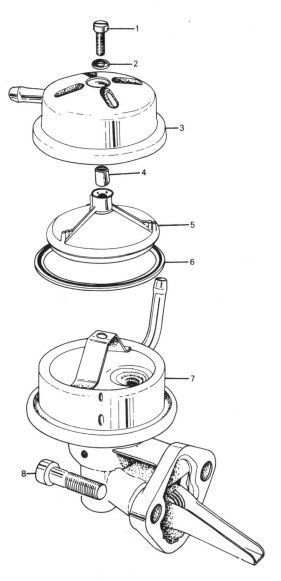

FIG 2:2 Components of the fuel pump

Key to Fig 2:2 1 Screw 2 Washer 3 Cover 4 Bush
5 Filter 6 Joint seal 7 Pump 8 Bolt

Cleaning the filter:

As a safety precaution, uncouple the battery earth connection before removing the pump cover. Remove screw 1, dismount the cover 3 and collect the washer 2 and bush 4. Lift off the filter 5 and the joint seal 6. Use compressed air to clean the filter. Confirm that the joint seal is serviceable or obtain a replacement.

Reassembly is the reverse of this sequence. Align the indentation in the rim of the cover with that in the pump body. Run the engine and check for fuel leaks.

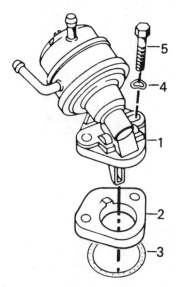

FIG 2:3 Pump mounting parts

Key to Fig 2:3 1 Pump mounting flange 2 Insulation piece 3 Gasket 4 Washer 5 Bolt

2:5 Fuel pump

The mechanically actuated diaphragm-type pump is mounted on the lefthand side of the cylinder block immediately forward of the ignition distributor. It is operated from an eccentric on the intermediate shaft. An insulation distance piece is interposed between the pump flange and the cylinder block to prevent excessive heat transfer to the pump. The pump cannot be overhauled and, should it become defective, must be removed and replaced by a new unit.

Removal:

1 As a safety precaution, uncouple the battery earth connection. Disconnect the feed and return hoses from the pump. Blank off the feed pipe to preclude possible leakage or siphoning.

2 Refer to **FIG 2:3**. Withdraw the two retaining bolts 5 and collect the washers 4. Lift off the pump.

3 Dismount the insulation distance piece 2. Remove and discard the joint washer 3.

Fitment:

Fitment of the fuel pump is the reverse of the removal sequence. Use a new joint washer 3. Ensure that both faces of the insulation distance piece 2 are clean. Torque

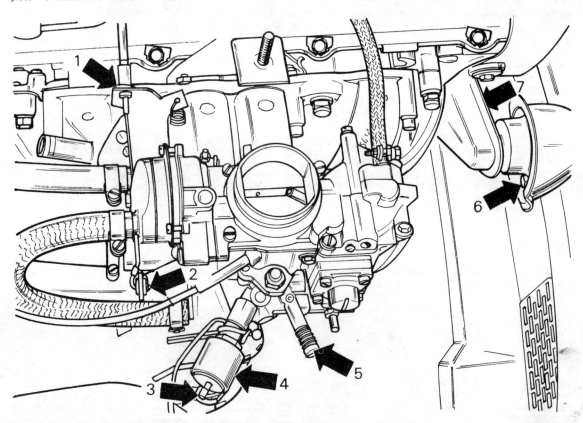

FIG 2:4 The PDSIT carburetter with cleaner dismounted

Key to Fig 2:4 1 Throttle cable adjuster 2 Throttle cable/lever connection 3 Bypass valve wiring connection 4 Bypass valve 5 Bypass screw 6 and 7 Front support

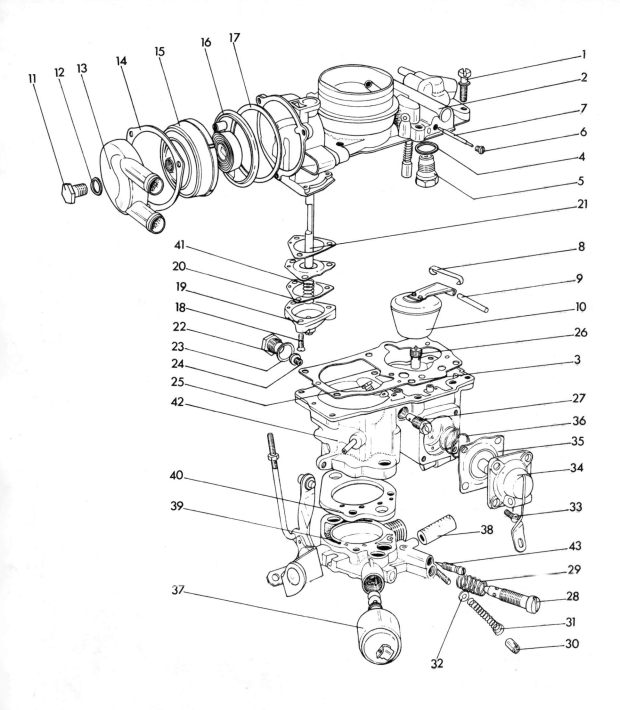

FIG 2:5 Components of the Solex 35 PDSIT carburetter

Key to Fig 2:5   1 Screw   2 Upper housing   3 Gasket   4 Washer   5 Needle valve   6 Screw   7 Pin   8 Retainer
9 Float pivot pin   10 Float   11 Bolt   12 Gasket   13 Hose connection flange   14 Ring   15 Choke   16 Adjuster ring
17 Gasket   18 Screw   19 Cover   20 Gasket   21 Diaphragm and pull rod   22 Plug   23 Sealing ring   24 Main jet   25 Air
correction jet   26 Power jet   27 Pilot jet   28 Bypass screw   29 Spring   30 Adjusting nut   31 Spring   32 Washer
33 Screw   34 Pump cover   35 Pump diaphragm   36 Spring   37 Bypass cut-off valve   38 Hose   39 Throttle valve
assembly with linkage   40 Intermediate flange   41 Spring   42 Lower housing   43 Volume control screw

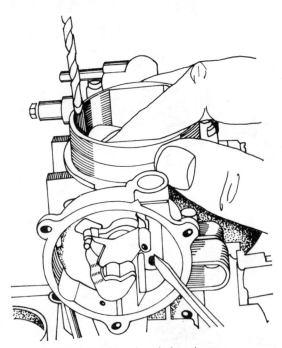

FIG 2:6 Adjusting choke valve gap

tighten the retaining bolts 5 to 14 lb ft (2 kg m). Reconnect the feed and delivery hoses. Check, after running, that the pipe connections are secure and that there is no oil leak at the pump to cylinder block joint.

Fuel pressure:

Incorrect fuel pump delivery pressure can account for faults ranging from weak mixture and poor performance to carburetter flooding and high fuel consumption. Pump delivery pressure is measured with the pump installed. A suitable T-piece and an accurate pressure gauge are required.

Fit the T-piece into the fuel delivery line immediately before the carburetter. Connect the pressure gauge to the third limb of the T-piece. Run the engine at about 2000 rev/min and, with the gauge at carburetter level, note the pressure recorded. This should be between 2.8 and 3.5 lb/sq in (.2 to .25 kg/sq cm). If the pressure is not within these limits a new pump should be fitted.

Stop the engine and observe the pressure. It should initially remain substantially constant and only fall away progressively. If the pressure drops off quickly, a faulty carburetter needle valve should be suspected.

2:6 Controls

Choke:

A fully automatic choke is incorporated in each type of carburetter. It is thermostatically controlled by the temperature of the engine coolant which is circulated through the choke housing. There is no manual choke control, but on later cars an auxiliary electrical heater is fitted in addition to the water heating system. A temperature switch in the coolant circuit switches the electric heater on and off in the range between 10° and 15°C.

A modified version has also a slow acting heater which is supplied at only 9 volts and cuts out at 25° to 30°C.

Accelerator:

The carburetter throttle control is by Bowden-type flexible cable to an extension lever above the accelerator foot pivot. The outer cable is retained at the bulkhead and at an adjuster which is arrowed 1 in FIG 2:4.

To disconnect the cable, withdraw the clip 2 at the throttle lever and uncouple the cable. Loosen the adjuster 1 and withdraw the cable from the bracket.

Adjustment, when necessary or on refitment is made at 1.

Automatic transmission:

The adjustment of the throttle cables on these models is described in Chapter 7.

2:7 Solex 35 PDSIT carburetter

The components of this single venturi carburetter are shown in FIG 2:5. Jet sizes and other data are tabulated in Technical Data in the Appendix.

Carburetter removal and fitment:

Although carburetters are not identical for all models covered by this manual, the procedure sequence for the removal and fitment of the carburetter is the same for the three types covered in this Chapter. The following series of operations is consequently also applicable to the Solex 32/35 TDID and to the Solex 32/35 DIDTA carburetters and is therefore not repeated in Section 2:8 or 2:9.

Removal:

1 Disconnect the battery earth cable. Partially drain the cooling system as described in Chapter 4, Section 4:2.
2 Remove the air cleaner as described in Section 2:3. Disconnect the throttle control as described in Section 2:6.

FIG 2:7 Measuring accelerator pump quantity

3 Uncouple the coolant feed and return pipes from the automatic choke housing. Uncouple the fuel feed pipe from the carburetter.

4 Identify and disconnect all vacuum pipes from the carburetter. Disconnect the wiring from the bypass cut-off valve.

5 Remove the nuts and washers which retain the carburetter to the intake manifold. Lift off the carburetter and the joint gasket.

Fitment:

Fitment is the reverse of the removal sequence but, before fitting the carburetter, ensure that adjustments which have to be made with the carburetter dismounted have been carried out. Ensure that the joint faces are clean. Ensure that all pipe connection clips are securely tightened. Run the engine up to normal temperature. Check for leaks and adjust the idling speed as described later.

Adjusting choke valve gap:

Remove the carburetter as described earlier. Refer to **FIG 2:5** and remove bolt 11 and washer 12. Remove the hose connection flange 13, ring 14 (retained by three screws which are not shown), choke 15, adjuster ring 16 and gasket 17.

Refer to **FIG 2:6**. Press the vacuum diaphragm rod as far as it will go. Open the throttle valve about half way. Close the choke valve until the lever rests on the upper stop of the rod. In this position the choke valve gap should be .181±.006 inch (4.60±.15 mm) and is best measured, as shown in the illustration, with the shank of a drill. Adjust, if necessary, at the screw in the centre of the cover 19.

Assembly is the reverse of the dismantling sequence but refer to **FIGS 2:9** and **2:10** and note the alignment of the notches.

Adjusting throttle valve gap:

Remove the carburetter as described earlier. Close the choke valve. The throttle valve gap should be .0256±.002 inch (.65±.05 mm) and is best measured with the shank of a drill. Adjust, if necessary, by turning the two nuts on the connecting rod.

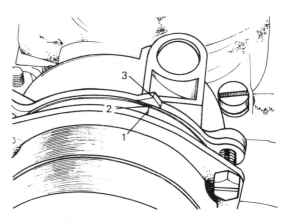

FIG 2:9 Automatic choke alignment

Key to Fig 2:9   1 Notch   2 Notch   3 Lug

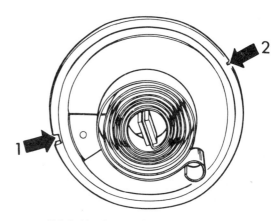

FIG 2:10 Automatic choke adjustment

Key to Fig 2:10   1 Adjusting notch   2 Control notch

Float chamber fuel level:

With the vehicle standing on level ground, run the engine for about a minute. Uncouple the battery earth connection. Remove the air cleaner as described in **Section 2:3**. Disconnect the fuel feed pipe so that no more fuel can enter the float chamber. Refer to **FIG 2:5**, remove six screws and washers 1 and lift off the carburetter upper housing assembly 2.

Using a depth gauge, measure the distance from the surface of the fuel to the carburetter joint face. Take the measurement a little way from the wall of the chamber to avoid the meniscus. The level should be .550±.040 inch (14±1 mm) below the joint face. If the level is not within this limit, remove the float needle valve 5 and washer 4. If the level is too high fit a thicker washer 4 and vice versa. The new washer should be that much thicker (or thinner) than the amount by which the fuel level was too high (or too low).

Reassemble and check the adjusted level by repeating the procedure after again running the engine.

FIG 2:8 Accelerator pump stroke adjustment

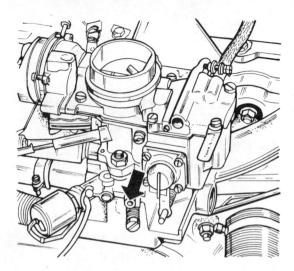

FIG 2:11   Mixture adjustment (volume control) screw is arrowed

Accelerator pump injection quantity:

Each time the throttle is opened rapidly, the accelerator pump injects a quantity of fuel into the venturi. The quantity is adjustable by altering the stroke of the pump. If the quantity is excessive, fuel consumption will be increased or, if insufficient, rapid acceleration performance will be poor. By leading the injected fuel to a calibrated container as shown in **FIG 2:7**, the quantity can be measured.

Run the engine to fill the float chamber. Disconnect the battery earth cable. Remove the air cleaner as described in **Section 2:3**. Open the choke valve and use a retainer to keep it in the open position. Fit a small bore S-shaped tube (the official tool set is VW 119) to the accelerator pump outlet and operate the throttle until fuel emerges from the tube. Hold the calibrated container under the pipe and open the throttle rapidly five times. Note the amount of fuel collected and divide by five. The quantity should be .90±.15 cc in the case of 1296 cc engines and 1.15±.15 cc in the case of 1470 cc engines. Adjustment is made at the pump operating rod by rotating the adjuster. Refer to **FIG 2:8**. Moving the adjuster in the **a** direction will reduce the fuel quantity and vice versa.

Idling speed:

Do not attempt to finally set the idling speed to 950±50 rev/min **unless the engine is at normal operating temperature** with the oil temperature at approximately 60°C (140°F). Adjust the idling speed only at the bypass screw (arrowed 5 in **FIG 2:4**). It may be necessary, in parallel, to adjust the mixture setting screw which is arrowed in **FIG 2:11**. If access to CO testing equipment is available, refer to **Section 2:10** and work to the limits quoted for Passat models.

Bypass air cut-off valve:

Some earlier engines may have a tendency to run on after the ignition has been switched off. The remedy is to remove the valve 4 in **FIG 2:4** after removing the wiring 3 and to fit a later type valve (part no. 056 129 412) which can be identified by the asterisk stamped on one of the hexagon flats.

Jets:

Use only petrol and compressed air to clean jets. Do not attempt to clean them by probing the orifices as this will ruin their calibration.

Jet and air bleed sizes are tabulated in **Technical Data** in the **Appendix**.

Dismantling and reassembly:

Where only partial dismantling of the carburetter is required to enable a specific operation to be performed or adjustment to be made, the relevant dismantling procedure is included under the adjustment or operation heading. It is not likely that an owner will find it necessary to extensively dismantle a carburetter but, if necessity does arise, the sequence order in which the components are numbered in **FIG 2:5** should be followed. It is recommended that the extent of the dismantling should be limited to that required by the purpose for which the dismantling was initially dictated. Do not attempt extensive dismantling without first removing the carburetter as described earlier.

On reassembly, ensure that the relevant settings and adjustments are made.

2:8 Solex 32/35 TDID carburetter

The components of this twin venturi carburetter are shown in **FIG 2:12**. Jet sizes and other data are tabulated in **Technical Data** in the **Appendix**.

Carburetter removal and fitment:

Although carburetters are not identical for all models covered by this manual, the procedure sequence for the removal and fitment of the carburetter is the same for the three types covered by this Chapter and the sequence of operations given in **Sections 2:7** is also applicable to the Solex 32/35 TDID carburetter.

Adjusting throttle valve gaps:

The adjustments of the throttle valve gaps is carried out in two separate operations, one for each throttle valve. After completing these adjustments, check and adjust the idling speed as described later.

1st stage gap adjustment:

Remove the carburetter as described earlier. Close the choke valve. Refer to **FIG 2:13**. The 1st stage throttle valve is that nearest to the bypass cut-off valve and its gap should be .026±.002 inch (.65±.05 mm). It is best measured with the shank of a drill. Reset the 1st stage throttle gap, if necessary, by adjusting the connecting rod arrowed in the illustration.

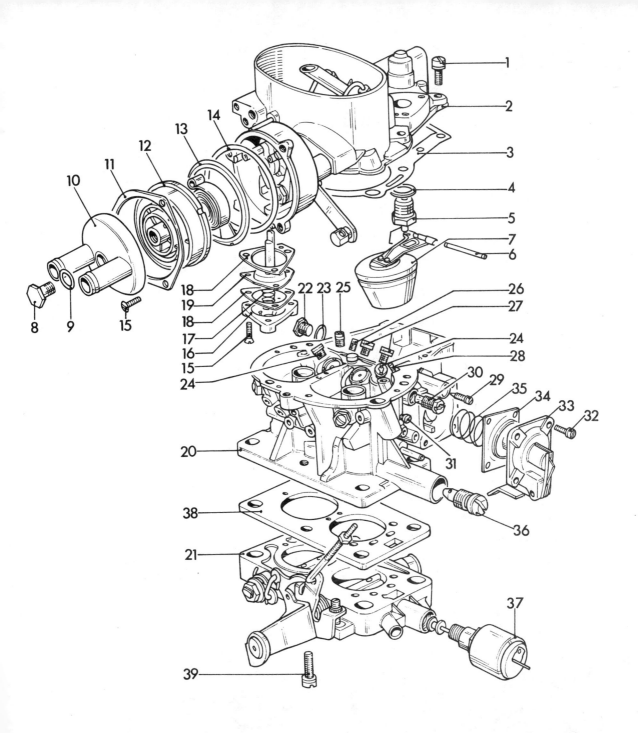

FIG 2:12   Components of the Solex 32/35 TDID carburetter

Key to Fig 2:12   1 Screw   2 Upper housing   3 Gasket   4 Washer   5 Needle valve   6 Float pivot pin   7 Float   8 Bolt   9 Sealing ring   10 Hose connection flange   11 Ring   12 Choke   13 Adjuster ring   14 Gasket   15 Screw   16 Cover   17 Spring   18 Gasket   19 Diaphragm   20 Lower housing   21 Throttle valve assembly with linkage   22 Plug   23 Sealing ring   24 Air correction jet   25 Pilot air jet   26 Auxiliary pilot jet   27 Main jet   28 Auxiliary air jet   29 Volume control screw   30 Pilot jet   31 Plug   32 Screw   33 Pump cover   34 Diaphragm   35 Spring   36 Bypass screw   37 Bypass cut-off valve   38 Intermediate flange   39 Screw

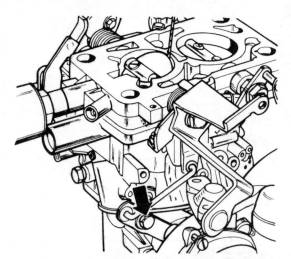

FIG 2:13   1st stage throttle valve gap adjustment

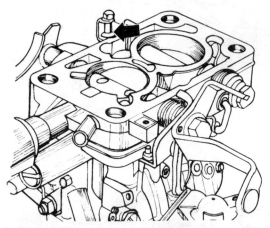

FIG 2:14   2nd stage throttle valve gap adjustment

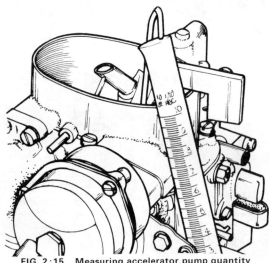

FIG 2:15   Measuring accelerator pump quantity

2nd stage gap adjustment:

It should not be necessary to adjust the 2nd stage gap on a routine basis but the procedure is as follows.

Unlock the adjusting screw which is arrowed in **FIG 2:14** and unscrew it until the 2nd stage throttle is fully closed. Screw in the adjusting screw by one half turn and relock.

Accelerator pump injection quantity:

The procedure is as described under this heading in **Section 2:7** but refer to **FIG 2:15**. The fuel quantity should be .9±.15 cc per stroke. Adjustment is at the bellcrank lever which is arrowed in **FIG 2:16**.

Idling speed:

Do not attempt to finally set the idling speed to 950±50 rev/min **unless the engine is at normal operating temperature** with an oil temperature at approximately 60°C (140°F). Adjust the idling speed only by the bypass screw which is arrowed **A** in **FIG 2:17**. It may be necessary, in parallel, to adjust the mixture setting screw which is also indicated in this illustration and is arrowed **B**. If access to CO testing equipment is available, refer to **Section 2:10** and, for CO limits, to **Technical Data** in the **Appendix**.

Bypass cut-off valve:

The tendency in earlier engines to run on after the ignition is switched off can be corrected by fitting a later type cut-off valve which can be identified by it having an asterisk stamped on one of its hexagon faces. The part No. of this later type valve is 056 129 412.

Jets:

Refer to the recommendations given under this heading in **Section 2:7**.

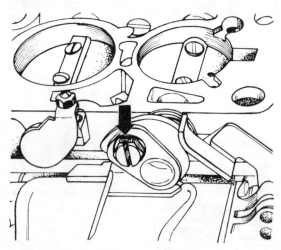

FIG 2:16   Accelerator pump stroke adjustment

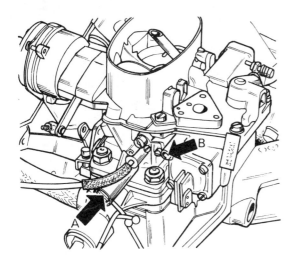

FIG 2:17   Idling speed and mixture adjustment points

Key to Fig 2:17   A Bypass screw   **B** Volume (mixture) screw

Dismantling and reassembly:

Follow the recommendations given under this heading in **Section 2:7** but refer to **FIG 2:12** and not to **FIG 2:5**. Note that **FIG 2:10** is relevant in conjunction with **FIG 2:18**.

2:9 Solex 32/35 DIDTA carburetter

This twin venturi carburetter is fitted to Dasher engines. Its components are as shown in **FIG 2:12** for the Solex 32/35 TDID carburetter but, additionally and not shown in **FIG 2:12**, it is provided with a throttle dashpot which is shown in **FIG 2:19**. Jet sizes and other data are tabulated in **Technical Data** in the **Appendix**.

Removal and fitment:

Although carburetters are not identical for all models covered by this manual, the procedure sequence for the removal' and fitment of the carburetter is the same for the three types covered by this Chapter and the sequence of operations given in **Section 2:7** is also applicable to the Solex 32/35 DIDTA carburetter.

Adjusting throttle valve gaps:

The procedure is as described under this heading in **Section 2:8** for both the 1st and 2nd stage throttle valves.

Accelerator pump quantity:

The procedure for the measurement of the accelerator pump injection quantity is as described under this heading in **Section 2:8**. The desired injection quantity is also the same.

Dashpot adjustment:

Refer to **FIG 2:19**. With the throttle valve closed, press the plunger of the dashpot fully in. The clearance **a** should be .04 inch (1 mm). If adjustment is required, loosen the

locknuts, turn the body of the dashpot in the appropriate direction until the clearance at **a** is as specified. Retighten the locknuts and recheck the clearance.

Now open the throttle fully and use spacing washers as shown in **FIG 2:20** to fill the gap **b** between the locking ring and the bush in the bracket.

Idling speed:

Do not attempt to finally set the idling speed to 925±75 rev/min **unless the engine is at normal operating temperature** with the oil temperature at approximately 60°C (140°F). Adjust the idling speed only at the bypass screw which is arrowed **A** in **FIG 2:17**. In parallel with the adjustment of the bypass screw, the mixture will have to be monitored using CO testing equipment and the CO content of the exhaust kept within emission control limits.

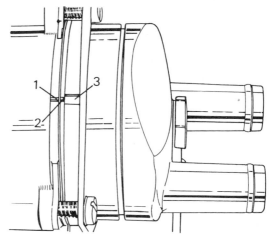

FIG 2:18   Automatic choke alignment

Key to Fig 2:18   1 Notch   **2** Notch in ring   **3** Notch in choke

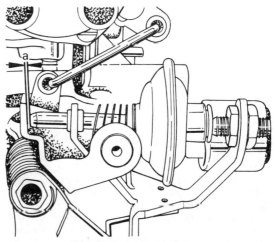

FIG 2:19   Throttle dashpot

Key to Fig 2:19   Set clearance **a** to .04 inch (1 mm)

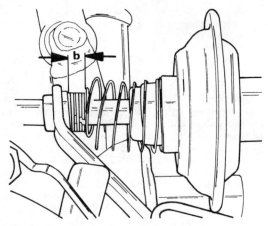

FIG 2:20 Adjusting the dashpot. Fill the gap with spacers while holding the throttle fully open

The procedure differs between models which meet Californian control requirements and those of other States. Both procedures are covered in **Section 2:10**.

The mixture adjustment screw is arrowed **B** in **FIG 2:17**.

Bypass cut-off valve:

Note the information given in **Section 2:8** under this heading and, if relevant, fit a later type valve.

Jets:

Refer to the recommendations given under this heading in **Section 2:7**.

Dismantling and reassembly:

Follow the recommendations given in **Section 2:7** under this heading but refer to **FIG 2:12** and not to **FIG 2:5**. Note that **FIG 2:10** is relevant in conjunction with **FIG 2:18**.

2:10 Zenith 2B2 and 2B3 carburetters

These double barrelled carburetters are fitted to later models of both Passat and Dasher models and although they have many points of similarity with the Solex carburetters described earlier, they are in fact quite different.

The throttle in the first barrel is mechanically operated from the accelerator pedal and a vacuum system is used to open the secondary throttle as operating conditions demand. A separate float chamber and float is provided for each barrel so that each has its own fuel supply.

Most of the jets are grouped together in the body as shown in **FIG 2:21** while the main jets are mounted in the float chamber cover. Specifications for these will be found in **Technical Data**.

Unnecessary adjustment or dismantling is not encouraged in order to ensure compliance with emission requirements, but those operations which may be carried out without professional assistance will be described where they differ from the other carburetters.

Adjusting the idle speed and mixture (emission control):

The correct idle speed with manual or automatic transmission is between 900 and 1000 rev/min and is to be set using the idle speed (by-pass) screw arrowed in **FIG 2:22**. The throttle stop screw is set at the factory and must not be moved.

If, for any reason, the throttle stop screw's position has been modified, it must be reset to its basic position as follows:

Remove the plastic cap on the head of the screw and turn the screw out until there is a clearance between its tip and the fast-idle cam/lever. Now screw in slowly until the screw just touches the cam lever and then for exactly a quarter of a turn more.

Refit the limiter cap.

The CO content must next be adjusted and it is most important to have the engine at full working temperature and the choke fully open.

The idle mixture adjusting screw is shown in **FIG 2:23** and at the specified idle speed the CO content should be 1% by volume when measured at the tailpipe. On USA versions fitted with a catalytic converter, a receptacle for the gas analyser probe is provided at the forward end of the converter and a volume percentage of 1.5 to 2.5 is specified at this position.

If adjustment of the mixture causes an alteration in the engine speed, this must be reset as described above.

Idle adjustment (non-emission control):

For cars operating in areas where strict control of exhaust emissions is not enforced, the following simplified procedure may be adopted.

Use the idle speed screw (**FIG 2:22**) to obtain a fairly fast-idle. It may be noted that this screw does not affect the mixture strength or the throttle position, it simply allows a fixed ratio of fuel and air to bypass the throttle plate.

Now use the mixture control screw (**FIG 2:23**) to the point where the engine is running at its fastest idle speed consistent with smoothness. This setting gives the correct idle mixture strength.

Turn in the idle speed screw to slow the engine down to the recommended speed, 900 to 1000 rev/min, if necessary, and finally 'trim' the mixture screw by turning it in a quarter of a turn. A new plastic cap should preferably be used to seal the mixture screw in this position.

Setting the dashpot:

When a dashpot is fitted, the clearance should be set as described in **Section 2:9**, but the gap at 'a' must be .12 inch (3 mm).

Throttle valve gap:

This is checked with the carburetter removed as described earlier and shown in **FIG 2:13**, but in this instance the gap is changed. On Passat models with manual transmission it is between .60 and .70 mm, with automatic transmission it is .70 to .80 mm, while on Dasher models it is between .45 and .50 mm.

Any adjustment necessary is made by means of the stop screw on the lever attached to the throttle spindle.

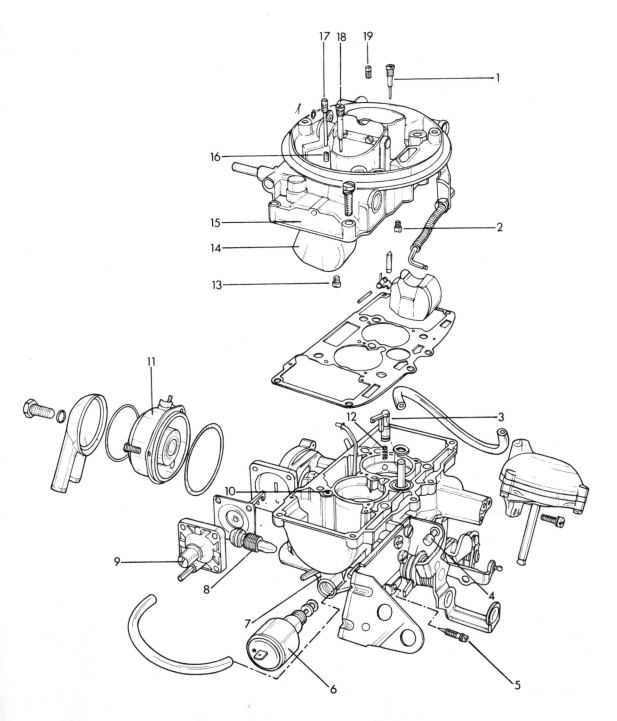

FIG 2:21 Exploded view of a typical 2B2 carburetter

Key to Fig 2:21   1 Secondary idle fuel and air jet   2 Secondary main jet   3 Pump injector   4 Throttle basic adjustment screw   5 Idle mixture screw   6 Fuel cut-off valve   7 Throttle valve gap adjustment   8 Idle speed screw   9 Choke adjustment   10 Enrichment valve   11 Automatic choke   12 Progression jet   13 Primary main jet   14 Float   15 Upper body   16 Primary bypass jet   17 Air correction jet   18 Primary idle fuel and air jet   19 Progression air jet

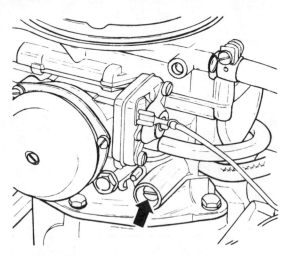

FIG 2:22 The idle speed adjusting screw on 2B2 and 2B3 carburetters

Choke valve gap:

This also is measured with a calibrated rod as described in **Section 2:7**. Close the choke valve fully, remove the cover from the automatic choke mechanism and push the operating link clockwise against its stop. The gap must now be as follows:

Passat, manual transmission	..	3.0 to 3.3 mm
automatic transmission	..	4.35 to 4.65 mm
Dasher	..	3.8 to 4.2 mm

Any adjustment required is made by means of the screw in the centre of the cover of the vacuum unit.

Float level:

As mentioned earlier, there are two fully independent float mechanisms and it should not be necessary to interfere with the settings set in production. If, however, adjustment should be required, proceed as follows:

Detach the carburetter top cover assembly in which the floats are mounted, hold it upside down and measure the distance between the bottom of the float (now on top) and the cover joint face. On the primary barrel float this should be 28 ± .5 mm (1.102 ± .02 inch), on the secondary float it should be 30 ± .5 mm (1.118 ± .02 inch). If any adjustment should be necessary, carefully bend the choke mounting brackets as appropriate.

2:11 Emission control system

Activated carbon filter:

A vented fuel tank filler cap will allow air to enter the tank as fuel is consumed but will not allow fuel vapour to leak to atmosphere. The noxious vapour is vented via a vapour pipeline to the activated carbon filter which is located on the lefthand forward side of the engine compartment. The filter is connected by hose to the air cleaner. Accumulated vapour in the filter is drawn into the air cleaner and consumed by the engine. Disposal of the vapour in this way reduces atmospheric pollution.

Every 10,000 miles (17,000 km), check that the hoses are serviceable and securely connected at the tank, filter

and air cleaner canister. Every 50,000 miles (85,000 km), remove and discard the activated carbon filter and fit a new replacement.

Intake control valve:

The temperature of the air intake preheated air is controlled by a valve and a vacuum unit. The valve may be of either of the two types shown in **FIG 2:24**. The lower (standard) type of valve is fitted to the intake manifold and, as dictated by the mixture temperature, controls the vacuum unit located in the air cleaner. The vacuum unit operates the hot/cold air flap. This type of valve is fitted to vehicles which are required to meet Californian emission control regulations.

The upper (double) valve is fitted to vehicles required to meet the emission control regulations of other States and is located in the lower part of the air cleaner.

In both cases pipe 1 is connected with the vacuum unit and pipe 2 is connected with the carburetter (the vacuum source).

Testing of the intake preheated air system is carried out when the engine is cold. The procedure is the same whichever type of valve is fitted.

Run the engine at idling speed. Pull the hose off the vacuum unit. If the system is operating correctly, the flap should cut off the flow of warm air. If the flap does not move, the valve or the flap actuating vacuum unit is defective or there is a leak in the vacuum system. Eliminate the possibility of a leak by careful examination of the pipes and pipe joints, If the trouble persists, run a pipe direct from the carburetter to the vacuum unit, run the engine and check whether the flap operates. If it does, the valve is defective. If it does not, the vacuum unit is defective.· Neither valves nor vacuum unit can be repaired and, if defective, should be replaced by a new unit.

Mixture adjustment (control of CO emission):

CO testing equipment is required for the following procedures.

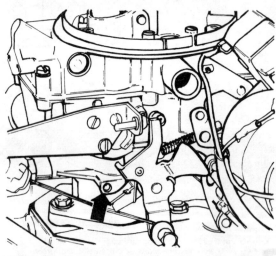

FIG 2:23 The idle mixture adjusting screw on 2B2 and 2B3 carburetters

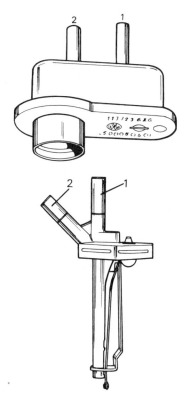

FIG 2:24 The two types of preheated air temperature control valves

Key to Fig 2:24 1 Connect to vacuum unit 2 Connect to carburetter (vacuum source)

Dasher models:

The adjustment procedure differs between Dasher models which are equipped to meet Californian requirements and are provided with exhaust afterburning (see **Chapter 1, Section 1:20**) and those which, without afterburning, are in line with the requirements of other States.

With afterburning – California:

Run the engine up to normal operating temperature. The oil temperature should be approximately 60°C (140°F). Disconnect the air delivery hose from the air pump and blank it off. Check and adjust the idling speed to 925±75 rev/min. Make the adjustment only at the bypass screw which is arrowed **A** in **FIG 2:17**. Set the exhaust CO content to 1 to 2 vol. % by means of the mixture (volume control) screw **B**. Recheck the idling speed and adjust if necessary. Recheck the CO content. When both the idling speed and the CO content are within the limits specified, reconnect the air feed to the nozzle gallery. The exhaust CO content should then drop to below 1 vol. %.

Without afterburning – other States:

Run the engine up to normal operating temperature. The oil temperature should be approximately 60°C (140°F).

Check and adjust the idling speed to 925±75 rev/min. Make this adjustment only at the bypass screw which is arrowed **A** in **FIG 2:17**. By means of the mixture (volume control) screw **B**, set the exhaust CO content to within .4 to 1.0 vol. %. Recheck and, if necessary, readjust the idling speed. Recheck the CO content. Repeat these adjustments until both the idling speed and the CO content are within the specified limits.

Passat models:

The 'without afterburning' procedure described earlier can be applied to Passat models. The CO content should be kept within a 1.3 to 1.7 vol. % range but, if there are no local emission control regulations which preclude a higher %, may be increased to as much as 3.5 vol. % to counter flat spots. This may be found to be needed in cold weather particularly.

Dashpot:

There can be a tendency for engines fitted with emission control equipment to stall when the throttle is closed suddenly. To overcome this, a dashpot is fitted to the carburetter of Dasher (but not to Passat) engines. The dashpot overrides the throttle control over the range of lower throttle openings and allows only gradually closing in the final stages. Adjustment of the dashpot setting is described in **Section 2:9**.

General:

Refer to the general recommendation given at the end of **Chapter 1, Section 1:20**.

2:12 Fault diagnosis (carburetters)

(a) Insufficient fuel delivered

1 Tank air vent restricted
2 Fuel feed pipe blocked
3 Air leak in feed to pump
4 Fuel filter requires cleaning
5 Fuel pump defective
6 Fuel vapourizing in pipeline due to heat
7 Defective fuel gauge (tank empty)

(b) Excessive fuel consumption

1 Carburetter requires adjustment
2 Fuel leakage
3 Dirty air cleaner element
4 Excessively high engine temperature
5 Carburetter air bleed(s) blocked
6 Defective automatic choke
7 Choke valve incorrectly adjusted
8 Idling speed too high
9 High fuel pump pressure
10 High float chamber fuel level
11 Brakes binding
12 Tyres under-inflated
13 Vehicle overloaded

(c) Idling speed too high

1 Incorrect adjustment
2 Throttle control sticking
3 Incorrect mixture adjustment
4 Worn throttle valve(s)

5 Worn throttle spindle(s)
6 Air leak at manifold joint

(d) Carburetter flooding

1 Check 9 and 10 in (b)
2 Dirt in needle valve
3 Worn needle valve
4 Punctured float

(e) No fuel delivery

1 Check all items in (a)
2 Fractured fuel feed line
3 Punctured fuel tank (tank empty)
4 Needle valve stuck in closed position

(f) Engine will not idle

1 Wiring discontinuity to bypass valve
2 Bypass valve defective

(g) Engine runs on

1 Check 2 in (f)
2 Early type bypass valve in use

2:13 The fuel injection system

Description:

The layout of the main components of the continuous injection system is shown in **FIG 2:25**, the fuel pressure control circuit being separated in **FIG 2:26**. The method of operation is as follows:

The electric fuel pump, fitted on the floor of the luggage compartment adjacent to the fuel tank, draws the fuel from the tank and delivers it to the fuel distributor through the accumulator and filter, the pressure relief valve maintaining a constant pressure of 4.6 bar, surplus fuel being returned to the tank. The fuel passes through the metering ports in the distributor and pressure regulating valves to the injection valves, located adjacent to the inlet valve in each cylinder.

The metering of the fuel supply is controlled according to the rate of flow of air to the engine through a venturi with a sensor plate in front of the throttle butterfly plate mounted on a counter-weighted lever. The air drawn into the engine lifts the sensor plate until a state of balance is achieved between the air flow, the control plunger and the balance weight. Since the plunger regulates the four fuel port apertures, the fuel delivered is corrected for any rate of air flow and position of the sensor plate. Fuel enrichment for cold starting is ensured by the injection of extra fuel into the manifold under the control of a thermo/time switch in the engine's cooling system.

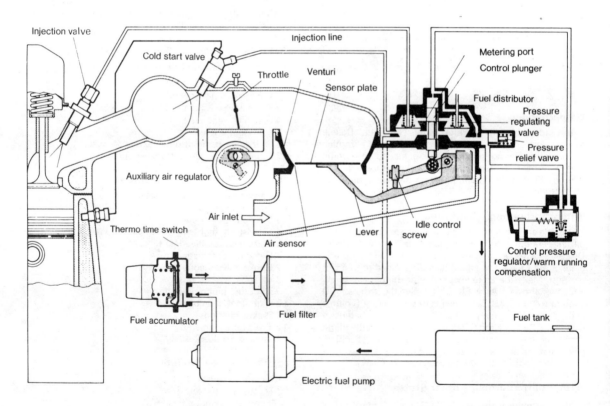

FIG 2:25   Diagram showing the main components of the Bosch Continuous Fuel Injection System

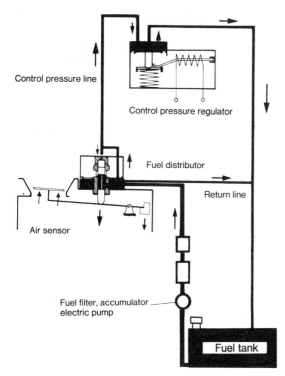

Control pressure line

Control pressure regulator

Fuel distributor

Return line

Air sensor

Fuel filter, accumulator electric pump

Fuel tank

FIG 2:26   Fuel pressure control circuit

The electric fuel pump is switched on when the starter is operated and runs only while the engine is running, movement of the sensor plate opening the contact on the air sensor switch. The bi-metal springs of the auxiliary air regulator and the control pressure regulator and warm running compensator are also heated when the fuel pump is switched on. The cold start valve is actuated by the thermo/time switch according to engine coolant temperature.

The fuel pressure accumulator is fitted in the fuel delivery line immediately after the pump and its purpose is to delay the initial pressure surge when the pump starts. This is necessary to prevent the control plunger from being pushed up before sufficient control pressure has built up. The accumulator also acts as a reservoir to maintain enough pressure in the system for a short time after the engine has been switched off in order to prevent vapour lock.

Testing and adjusting:

When carrying out checks on an engine that is not running but has the ignition switched on, always disconnect the plug at the air sensor switch and the positive wire to the alternator in the wiring harness.

Too much care cannot be taken to ensure the absolute cleanliness of all parts of the injection system.

All other engine services must be in order and correctly adjusted before making any adjustments or checks on the injection system.

Idle speed and mixture adjustment:

Ensure that the engine is at normal operating temperature, apply an electrical load by switching the headlamps on to main beam and turn on the air conditioner, if fitted.

Start up the engine and use the idle speed control screw, shown arrowed in **FIG 2:27**, to obtain an engine speed of 850 to 1000 rev/min and at the same time adjust the CO content to the specified percentage by means of a suitable tool, P377, inserted through the hole in the mixture control unit. This may be seen in **FIG 2:28** and is normally protected by a plug with a finger pull as shown.

The specified CO percentages are as follows:

California, all models	..	..	..	0.5 max.
Other States, manual	..	..	..	1.5 max.
	automatic	..	..	1.0 max.

All these readings being taken at the tailpipe.

When adjusting the CO, turning the adjusting wrench clockwise increases the CO content (rich mixture), turning it anticlockwise decreases the CO (weak

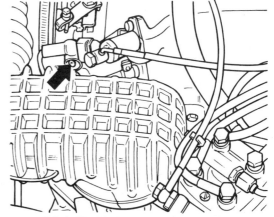

FIG 2:27   The idle speed control screw

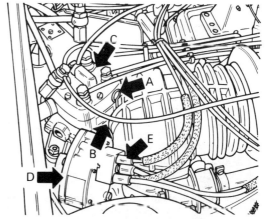

FIG 2:28   Showing the location of the CO adjustment point

Key to Fig 2:28   A Plug for mixture (CO) adjustment hole   B Location of mixture (CO) adjuster   C Mixture control unit   D Vacuum booster   E Vacuum connections

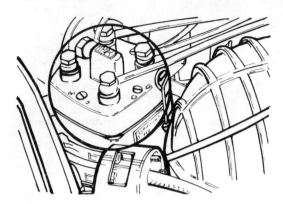

FIG 2:29 The mixture control unit

mixture). Do not press down on the adjusting tool as this will alter the position of the control plunger and may stall the engine. Use the tool very carefully and do not accelerate the engine while the tool is in position, but remove the tool after each adjustment and accelerate briefly before reading the CO meter.

If the CO cannot be adjusted to the specified value, the mixture control unit is defective and must be renewed. It is assumed that there is no fault in the ignition system and that the timing is correctly set to 3 deg. ATDC at idling speed.

Mixture control unit:

This is shown in **FIG 2:29** and is removed and refitted as follows:

Disconnect the air duct from the air sensor and the throttle valve housing. Clean all the connections carefully before disconnecting them and remove the control unit.

Use a new gasket under the upper part of the air sensor when refitting the mixture control unit and use a new seal at the air duct.

Fuel filter:

This component is mounted on the bulkhead in the engine compartment immediately below the air intake grille, it should be renewed at intervals of approximately 15,000 miles (25,000 km).

Clean the two screwed unions and disconnect them, release the filter mounting clips and lift the filter out.

The new filter is fitted in the reverse order, ensuring that the arrow on the filter case is pointing in the direction of fuel flow.

Fuel pump and pressure accumulator:

These two components are both mounted underneath the floor of the luggage compartment on the right of the fuel tank. If removal is necessary, first disconnect the battery and the leads to the pump, clean and disconnect the fuel pipe connections and remove the retaining nuts.

Before checking the delivery rate of the pump, check that the fuel filter is completely unobstructed, fitting a new one if in doubt.

Disconnect the fuel delivery line at the fuel distributor and hold it in a calibrated container of suitable size. Turn

on the ignition for exactly 30 seconds during which time the amount of fuel delivered must be at least 750 cc.

If the delivery rate is too low, disconnect the two leads from the pump and connect a voltmeter across them. This should show at least 11.5 volts. If the voltage is less than this, check the state of the battery.

Check the current draw at the pump by reconnecting the earth lead (large connector) and connect an ammeter in the positive lead. The current shown must not exceed 8.5 amps, if it does renew the pump. If the power supply is correct and the delivery rate too low, renew the pump after checking that the supply pipes and hoses are not obstructed.

The operating fuel pressure should be between 4.6 and 5.2 bar, this being controlled by the relief valve in the fuel distributor unit. The pressure in the system, 20 minutes after stopping the engine should be at least .69 bar, this being controlled by the pressure accumulator. If it is lower than this, make sure that the complete system is free from leaks before condemning the accumulator.

Fuel distributor:

This is shown in **FIG 2:28** and is removed by taking out the three retaining screws after cleaning and disconnecting the fuel line connections. Great care must be taken to ensure that the control plunger does not fall out of the unit when removing the distributor. If it is removed for any reason, wash it in clean petrol before refitting, noting that it is matched to the distributor and cannot be renewed separately.

Use a new seal when fitting the distributor and tighten the securing screws to a torque of 2.5 to 2.7 lb ft (.32 to .38 kgm) and seal the joint with paint. Use new seals at the fuel pipe connections and finally check the idle speed and mixture as described earlier.

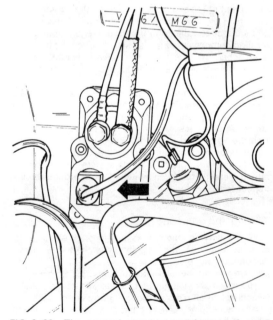

FIG 2:30 The control pressure regulator and warm running compensator

Control pressure regulator:

This unit, combined with the warm running compensator, is mounted on the inlet manifold as shown in **FIG 2:30**. A faulty unit is likely to give rise to the following symptoms: bad starting (particularly with a hot engine), faulty idling, hesitation or backfiring and high fuel consumption.

The equipment required for adequately testing the regulator is not likely to be available to the home operator and it is suggested that a service station be asked to check if its performance is suspect.

To remove, disconnect the wiring, clean and remove the fuel lines and remove the two securing screws. Always use new seals when refitting.

Auxiliary air regulator:

Poor starting or idling can be due to a defective air regulator and it can be checked as follows on a **cold** engine.

Disconnect the connectors at the control pressure regulator, mixture control unit, auxiliary air regulator and the positive wire to the alternator. Disconnect both hoses at the auxiliary air regulator and look through the unit to see that the gate valve is open. See **FIG 2:31**.

Reconnect the connector to the regulator unit and switch on the ignition. After about five minutes the gate valve must be seen to be fully closed. If it is not, check the power supply and if this is in order, renew the regulator, removal being effected by taking out the two retaining screws.

Thermo/time switch:

This component is screwed into the coolant adaptor on the engine block. Its purpose is to control the period during which the cold start valve is open to provide fuel enrichment by cutting off the current when the engine coolant reaches a pre-determined temperature, this is stamped on the switch body. If the switch does not operate at the correct temperature it must be renewed as no adjustment is possible.

Drain out sufficient coolant from the cooling system so that no loss will occur, disconnect the plug connector and unscrew the switch.

Cold start valve:

A sectional view of the cold start valve is given in **FIG 2:32**. It is bolted to the inlet manifold behind the throttle housing and, as will be seen, is an electromagnetic fuel injector. The valve is opened for starting a cold engine when the ignition is switched on and closed when the coolant reaches a predetermined temperature, these operations being effected by the thermo/time switch.

A simple but effective test for the valve is to unscrew it from the manifold and hold it, with the electric plug disconnected but the ignition on to operate the fuel pump, in a suitable container. The valve should show no sign of dripping fuel for at least one minute.

If the electric plug is now reconnected and the engine is cold, the valve should open and spray fuel in an even conical pattern. A faulty valve must be renewed and always use new seals and gaskets when fitting a valve after removal.

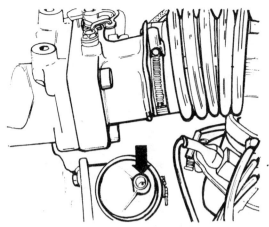

FIG 2:31   The auxiliary air regulator

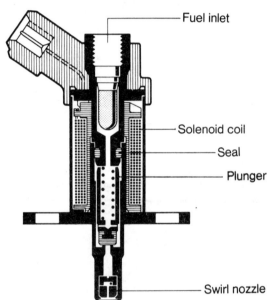

FIG 2:32   Section through the cold start valve

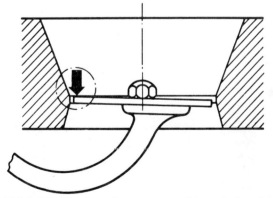

FIG 2:33   Showing the correct position of the air sensor

Injection valves:

These are located in the cylinder head by 'O' rings and may be pulled out for inspection, cleaning or replacement, disconnecting the fuel line at the valve. When refitting, soak new 'O' rings in clean fuel and press the valves firmly against their seats.

The correct opening pressure for an injection valve is between 2.45 and 3.55 bar and the maximum variation allowed in one set of valves is .59 bar.

Plastic fuel lines:

The correct way to remove a plastic fuel line from its adaptor is to apply heat with a soldering iron around the adaptor area and pull the pipe off. Never use an open flame and never cut the pipes as this might damage the adaptor and cause an uncurable fuel leak.

Never heat a new plastic pipe when fitting, a special tool, P385, is available to slide it over the adaptor.

If an injection line should require to be replaced, **always** use new lines which are supplied complete with connectors.

Air sensor assembly:

It is recommended that any malfunction in this part of the fuel injection system be checked by a qualified service station, with the necessary facilities.

The correct position of the sensor plate when there is no pressure in the system is shown in **FIG 2:33**. The upper edge of the plate must be flush with the beginning of the venturi and if it is too high it must be corrected. A slightly lower position, however, is permissible up to a maximum of .02 inch (.5 mm).

2:14 Fault diagnosis (fuel injection system)

(a) Engine does not start

1 Check (b)
2 Cold start valve defective
3 Thermo switch defective
4 Air sensor sticking

5 Auxiliary air regulator defective
6 Control pressure regulator defective
7 Fuel distributor defective

(b) Insufficient fuel delivered

1 Tank air vent obstructed
2 Fuel feed pipe blocked
3 Air leak in feed to pump
4 Fuel filter blocked
5 Defective fuel pump

(c) Difficult hot starting

1 Check 3 and 6 in (a)
2 Leaks in system

(d) Erratic idling

1 Check (a)
2 Injection valve(s) defective
3 Air leaks after sensor plate
4 Fuel leaks
5 Control plunger sticking
6 Incorrect warm control pressure

(e) Backfiring

1 Check 2, 6 and 7 in (a); 3 and 6 in (d)
2 Excessive variation in injector opening pressures

(f) High fuel consumption

1 Check 2, 5, 6, 7, 8 and 9 in (b) in **Section 2:12**; 2 and 6 in (a)
2 Incorrect control regulator pressure

(g) Engine runs on

1 Check 4 and 6 in (a); 2 in (d)

(h) Poor performance

1 Check 4, 5, 6 and 7 in (a); 2 and 5 in (d)
2 Filter requires renewal
3 Defective fuel pump

CHAPTER 3

THE IGNITION SYSTEM

3:1 Description

The components of a partially dismantled Bosch distributor are shown in **FIG 3:1**. The distributor is driven by the 1:1 ratio skew gearing on the distributor shaft and on the engine intermediate shaft which runs at half crankshaft speed. The engine oil pump is driven from the lower end of the distributor shaft. The distributor incorporates variable timing which is controlled centrifugally and also by a vacuum operated advance/retard unit. As engine speed increases, the centrifugal action of rotating weights pivoting against the tension of small springs, advances the contact breaker cam in relation to the distributor drive shaft and progressively advances the ignition timing. The vacuum control unit is connected with the intake depression by small-bore piping. At high degrees of depression it advances the ignition but, under load, at reduced degrees of depression the unit progressively retards the ignition timing.

A resistor is inserted in the battery lead to the coil which reduces the voltage applied to the coil while the engine is running. This is bypassed when the starter is operated so that full battery voltage is applied at this time in order to assist in starting a cold engine, particularly under adverse weather conditions.

The firing order is 1, 3, 4, 2 for all models covered by this manual. The distributor advance/retard characteristics (both centrifugal and vacuum) are not the same for all Passat and Dasher models. Note, in particular also, that, due to differing USA Federal and State emission control requirements, distributors (and other features) are not identical for Dasher models for California as against other States.

3:2 Maintenance

Distributor breaker points:

Every 5000 miles (8000 km), check and adjust, if necessary, the distributor points gap as described later. If the points are badly burnt, worn or if excessive transfer of metal has taken place, a new set of points should be fitted as described in **Section 3:4**.

Points gap setting:

Remove the distributor cap, rotor and dust seal and turn the engine until the points are fully open. Refer to **FIG 3:2** and, using a screwdriver as shown in the illustration and feeler gauges, set the points gap to .016 inch (.4 mm).

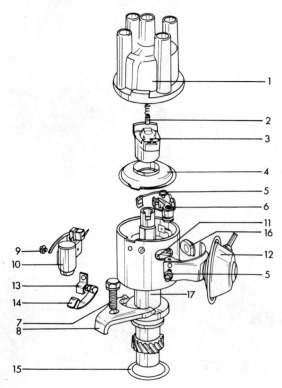

FIG 3:1 Components of the distributor

Key to Fig 3:1   1 Cap   2 Carbon brush and spring
3 Rotor arm   4 Dust seal   5 Screw   6 Set of contact
breaker points   7 Bolt   8 Clamp bracket   9 Screw
10 Capacitor   11 Spring washer   12 Vacuum unit   13 Clip
14 Spring   15 Joint washer   16 Plug   17 Body

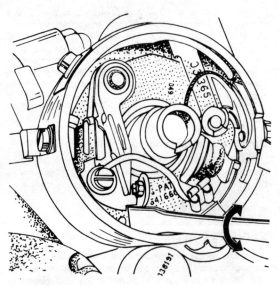

FIG 3:2 Adjusting the point gap

Distributor lubrication:

Every 5000 miles (8000 km), remove the distributor cap, rotor arm and dust seal. Refer to FIG 3:3 and apply a drop of oil to the points pivot 1 and a touch of multi-purpose grease to the cam and cam follower 2. Refit the seal, rotor and cap.

Ignition timing:

Every 5000 miles (8000 km), have the ignition timing checked stroboscopically and adjusted if necessary. The procedure is described in **Section 3:6** and timing data is given in that Section and also in **Technical Data** in the **Appendix.**

Sparking plugs:

Every 5000 miles (8000 km), remove the sparking plugs, clean them and reset the gaps as described in **Section 3:7.**

Every 10,000 miles (16,000 km), discard the plugs and fit a new set. Recommended types of sparking plugs for each model are listed in **Technical Data** in the **Appendix.**

3:3 Ignition faults

If the engine runs unevenly, set it to idle at about 1000 rev/min and disconnect and reconnect each high tension cable from its sparking plug in turn. Doing this to a plug which is firing properly will accentuate the uneven running but it will make no difference if the plug is not firing. Locate the faulty plug and, taking care not to touch any metal part of the lead while the engine is running, remove the insulated connector from the end of the cable. With the engine running, hold this lead so that the conductor is about $\frac{1}{8}$ inch (3 mm) away from the cylinder head. A strong, regular spark will confirm that the fault lies with the sparking plug which should be cleaned or renewed. If, on the other hand, there is no spark, suspect the cable or its connection at the distributor cap.

If the spark is weak and irregular, check the condition of the HT cable and, if it is perished or cracked, renew it. If no improvement results, check the distributor cap. It must be clean and dry. Check that good contact is being made between the centre carbon contact brush and the rotor arm and that there is no 'tracking' which will show as a thin black line between the electrodes or to a metal part in contact with the cap. 'Tracking' cannot be rectified except by fitting a new cap.

If the contact breaker points are serviceable and the gap is correctly set but there is no spark, refer to the relevant wiring diagram in the Appendix, use a 0 to 20 range voltmeter with its negative connected to a good earth and, with the ignition switched on, check that there is voltage throughout the LT circuit. Trace and correct the faulty cable, loose connection, defective resistor or unserviceable ignition switch.

If the circuit is in order but the trouble persists, the coil or capacitor must be suspect. These are best checked by substitution.

3:4 Distributor

A Bosch JFU 4 distributor is fitted to all models covered by this manual. Note, however, that the distributor series

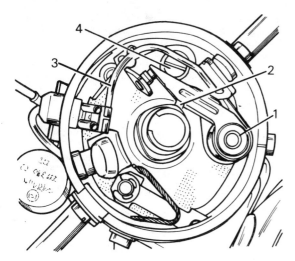

FIG 3:3 Distributor points and lubrication

Key to Fig 3:3 1 Pivot 2 Cam follower 3 Capacitor wire 4 Retaining screw

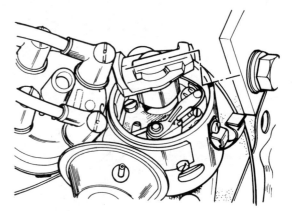

FIG 3:4 Aligning rotor and body marks

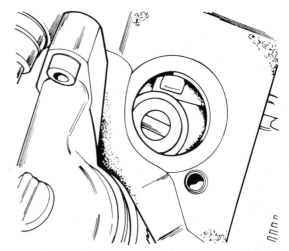

FIG 3:5 Oil pump drive lug alignment

number (this distinguishes the differing centrifugal and vacuum advance/retard characteristics) is not the same for all engine types.

Removal:

Unclip the distributor cap, withdraw the pipe from the vacuum unit and disconnect the LT wire. Rotate the crankshaft until the mark on the rotor arm is in line with the No. 1 cylinder segment position as shown in **FIG 3:4** and marked on the distributor body. Refer to **FIG 3:1**. Remove bolt 7 which retains the clamp bracket 8 and lift off the clamp bracket. Withdraw the distributor by pulling upwards and collect the joint washer 15. Note that the oil pump driving lug will be parallel with the axis of the intermediate shaft as shown in **FIG 3:5**.

Fitment:

Turn the oil pump drive shaft until its lug is parallel with the axis of the intermediate shaft as shown in **FIG 3:5**. Turn the crankshaft to the static timing point which is specified in **Section 3:6**. With the vacuum unit on the distributor pointing away from the cylinder block and the rotor and distributor body marks aligned, fit the distributor. Ensure that the joint washer is not omitted. Fit the clamp bracket and its retaining bolt. Tighten the bolt. Do not refit the pipe to the vacuum unit at this stage. Adjust the ignition timing as described in **Section 3:6**.

Overhaul:

Except for the following operations, no procedure is prescribed for the overhaul of a distributor by an owner and, if the defect cannot be rectified by the fitment of new points or a replacement capacitor, a new replacement unit should be fitted or the unserviceable unit should be passed to a specialist for repair and bench testing.

Fitting new points:

Remove the distributor cap, pull off the rotor and withdraw the dust seal. Refer to **FIG 3:3**. Disconnect the capacitor wire 3 and remove the beaker point assembly after removing the retaining screw 4. Fitment of the new set of points is the reverse of this sequence and must be followed by adjusting the points gap as described in **Section 3:2**.

Fitting a new capacitor:

Remove the capacitor attachment screw (9 in **FIG 3:1**) and withdraw the capacitor. Fit the new part and tighten the retaining screw.

3:5 Coil

The coil is a Bosch KW12V. Other than keeping its leads and surface clean and dry, no maintenance is required. A suspect coil is best checked by substituting one which is known to be serviceable. Alternatively a rough test may be

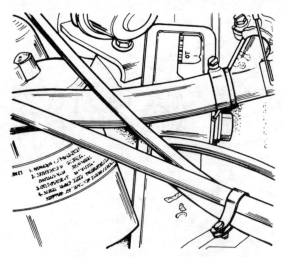

FIG 3:6   The TDC (OT) mark

FIG 3:7   The 30 deg. advance mark

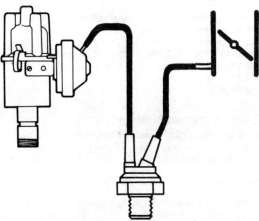

FIG 3:8   Showing the vacuum advance cut-off valve and its connections

carried out by withdrawing the HT feed cable to the distributor from the distributor cap centre position and holding it with insulated pliers so that its conductor is about .4 inch (10 mm) from the cylinder head. With the ignition switched on, turn the engine by means of the starter motor. A strong spark should result.

3:6 Timing the ignition

Confirm that the distributor breaker points are in good condition and that the gap is correctly set as described in **Section 3:2**.

Timing marks are inscribed on the circumference of the flywheel and can be seen through the small window in the transmission bellhousing as shown in **FIG 3:7**.

Static timing point:

When fitting a distributor as described in **Section 3:4**, turn the crankshaft to the No. 1 and No. 4 TDC position (the **OT** mark) with No. 1 cylinder valves both closed.

Stroboscopic timing checks, Passat models:

With the pipe to the vacuum unit disconnected (the vacuum advance/retard will be inoperative) and an electric tachometer wired into the ignition circuit, connect a stroboscopic lamp into the No. 1 cylinder HT feed so that it will be triggered when this cylinder fires. Run the engine and, with the stroboscopic lamp illuminating the flywheel through the bellhousing window, increase the engine speed and observe the 'stationary' timing reading. At 3000 rev/min this should be 30 degrees advance (30 degrees BTDC) as shown in **FIG 3:7**. If adjustment is needed, loosen the distributor clamp bracket bolt (7 in **FIG 3:1**) and turn the distributor body until the required reading is achieved. Turning the body clockwise will retard the timing and vice versa. On completion of the adjustment, tighten the clamp bolt to a torque of 14 lb ft (2 kg m) and refit the vacuum hose.

Stroboscopic timing checks, Dasher models:

Proceed as for the Passat models described earlier but **connect the vacuum hose(s)** to the distributor vacuum unit. Run the engine at 850 to 1000 rev/min. The reading obtained should be 3 deg. ATDC. If necessary, adjust as described for Passat models.

Later models Passat, 1975 onwards:

On these later cars a modified flywheel is fitted which carries an additional timing mark at 9 deg. BTDC which is used for certain engines. The timing procedure is similar to that described above, but an engine speed of 900 to 1000 rev/min is used. The specified timing for 1975 and 1976 models is tabulated below:

	Engine code	Vacuum hose(s)	Timing
1975	ZA, ZF, XX, FF, YJ, ZC (manual)	Off	9 deg. BTDC
	YJ, ZC (automatic)	On	TDC
1976	ZA, ZF	Off	9 deg. BTDC
	YN, YP, YT, YS, YU	On	TDC

On automatic transmission models a modified distributor is used which has vacuum advance and retard controls, the vacuum advance being switched off at coolant temperatures below about 58°C by means of a thermo-pneumatic valve.

This valve is fitted in one of the cooling system hoses and it is essential that it should be connected correctly as shown in **FIG 3:8**. The angled union is connected to the carburetter, the straight union to the distributor vacuum advance unit.

A defective valve may be the cause of such symptoms as poor progression, too high an idling speed and high fuel consumption. To test a suspect valve, try blowing through it; it must be closed below 45°C and open above 61°C.

3:7 Sparking plugs

Recommended types:

Plugs of Bosch manufacture are officially recommended and these, together with approved alternatives of other manufacture, are tabulated in **Technical Data** in the **Appendix**.

Cleaning and testing:

Every 5000 miles (8000 km), have the sparking plugs cleaned on an abrasive-blasting machine and tested under pressure with the gaps correctly set at .028 inch (.7 mm).

Prior to setting the gaps on used plugs, the electrodes should be filed until they are bright and parallel. The gaps must always be adjusted by bending the earth electrode. **Do not attempt to bend the centre electrode or the insulation will be damaged.**

Plugs as a tuning guide:

Inspection of the deposits on electrodes can be a helpful guide when tuning. Normally, from mixed periods of high and low speed driving, the deposits should be powdery and range in colour from brown to greyish tan. There will also be some slight wear of the electrodes. Long periods of fairly constant speed driving or low speed city driving will produce white or yellowish deposits. Dry, black fluffy deposits are due to incomplete combustion and indicate running with a rich mixture, excessive idling and, possibly, defective ignition. Overheated plugs have a white or light grey look round the centre electrode and the electrodes themselves will appear bluish and burnt. This may be due to weak mixture, poor cooling, incorrect ignition or sustained high speed running with a heavily loaded vehicle.

Black, wet deposits result from oil in the combustion chambers from worn pistons, rings, valve stems or guides or from worn and scored cylinder bores. Sparking plugs which run hotter may alleviate this problem temporarily but the cure is in an engine overhaul.

3:8 Emission control

This section is relevant only to USA Dasher models. It must be noted that, as stated in **Section 3:4**, distributor series numbers differ between vehicles which meet Californian requirements and those which meet the requirements of other States.

Since effective emission control depends to a great extent upon the special features being kept in first class order, maintenance must never be neglected and, in the ignition system, this will apply to distributor points, sparking plugs and ignition timing.

It is recommended that a new set of contact breaker points is fitted to the distributor every 10,000 miles (16,000 km) irrespective of the apparent serviceability of those in use.

Other emission control features are covered in **Chapter 1, Section 1:20** and **Chapter 2, Section 2:10**.

3:9 Fault diagnosis

(a) Engine will not fire

1 Battery discharged
2 Distributor points dirty, pitted or out of adjustment
3 Distributor cap dirty, cracked or 'tracking'
4 Centre contact not touching rotor arm
5 Faulty wire or loose connection in LT circuit
6 Rotor arm defective
7 Defective coil
8 Broken contact breaker spring
9 Contact breaker points stuck open
10 Defective ignition switch

(b) Engine misfires

1 Check 2, 3, 5 and 7 in (a)
2 Weak contact breaker spring
3 HT cables cracked or perished
4 Sparking plug(s) loose
5 Sparking plug insulation cracked
6 Sparking plug gaps incorrectly set
7 Ignition timing too far advanced
8 Fouled sparking plugs
9 HT cable(s) incorrectly connected

NOTES

CHAPTER 4

THE COOLING SYSTEM

4:1 Description

The cooling system is pressurized to 13 to 15 lb/sq in (.9 to 1.05 kg/sq cm) and is thermostatically controlled. The components and layout of the system are shown in **FIG 4:1**. Coolant circulation is assisted by centrifugal pump which is located on the lefthand side of the cylinder block and is belt driven from a pulley on the forward end of the crankshaft. This belt also drives the alternator. An electrically driven fan draws air intermittently through the radiator matrix as coolant temperature at the bottom of the radiator dictates and is cut in and out by a temperature controlled switch situated adjacent to the coolant outlet hose connection in the bottom of the radiator. Ambient air is ducted from the front grille to the radiator.

Refer to **FIG 4:1**. The pump takes coolant from the bottom of the vertical-flow radiator through hose 1 and delivers it directly to the cylinder block where it rises through internal passages to the cylinder head. The pump incorporates a thermostat which, at normal operating temperatures, closes the bypass hose 3 and coolant returns through hose 15 to the top of the radiator. At lower coolant temperatures, the thermostat closes the inlet to the pump from hose 1 and the pump draws coolant down hose 3.

This bypassing of the radiator provides a rapid warm-up not only to the engine but also to the external coolant circuit which is routed through the carburetter and the core of the air heater.

4:2 Maintenance

Check the coolant level at least every month and, if there is a steady loss, investigate and correct the cause. The level is best checked when the engine is cold. **If the engine is hot,** to avoid danger of being scalded and to prevent loss of coolant, place a cloth over the filler cap and release the pressure before removing the cap.

If antifreeze solution (see **Section 4:7**) is not in use, the cooling system should be drained and flushed to remove sediment every 6000 miles (10,000 km). If antifreeze solution is in use, it should be inspected every 12,000 miles (20,000 km) or every 12 months. If it is dirty or has a rusty appearance, drain the system, flush and refill with fresh solution. The solution should, in any case, be discarded after two winters. It is preferable that this maintenance be carried out immediately before the start of the winter.

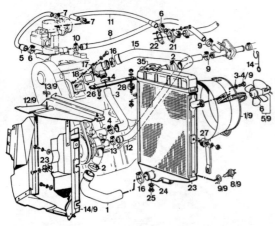

FIG 4:1 Components of the cooling system

Key to Fig 4:1 1 Bottom hose 2 Hose clamp 3 Bypass hose 4 Hose clamp 5 Choke chamber hose 6 Hose clamp 7 Hose clamp 8 Throttle housing hose 9 Hose clamp 10 Hose clamp 11 Choke chamber hose 12 Heater hose 13 Hose clamp 14 Clip 15 Top hose 16 Hose clamp 17 Outlet elbow 18 Gasket 21 Heater feed 22 Gasket 23 Radiator and fittings 24 Washer 25 Drain plug 26 Mounting strap 27 Mounting 28 Mounting 35 Filler cap 1/9 Fan duct 3/9 Washer 4/9 Bolt 5/9 and 6/9 Fan and motor assembly 8/9 Thermo switch 9/9 Washer 12/9 and 14/9 Radiator ducting 13/9 Clips

Draining:

Fully open the air heater control knob. Remove the radiator filler cap. Remove the hexagon headed plug from the side of the cylinder block adjacent to the starter motor. Remove the hexagon headed plug from the bottom of the radiator (25 in **FIG 4:1**). Coolant which contains antifreeze may be collected for re-use if it is not contaminated.

Certain operations (removal of the carburetter for example) do not require the system to be fully drained and, in these cases, the drain plugs should be refitted when the level has fallen sufficiently.

Flushing:

Drain the system. Remove the thermostat as described in **Section 4:6** and temporarily refit the water pump inlet elbow.

Use a water hose and allow water to run into the radiator filler orifice. Adjust the rate of flow to balance the rate of draining and, with the header tank full, run the engine at about 1000 rev/min to assist circulation until the drain water runs clear. Remove the pump inlet elbow and refit the thermostat as described in **Section 4:6**.

Filling:

Refit the drain plugs. Prepare the correct solution of antifreeze as described in **Section 4:7** and fill the system. Fit the filler cap and run the engine up to normal operating temperature. When the coolant is cold, check the radiator level and top up if necessary.

The capacity of the cooling system inclusive of the heater is approximately 11.4 pints (13.7 US pints, 6.5 litres). The radiator should be filled to the brim. The expansion chamber should be about half full.

4:3 The radiator

Removal:

1 Remove the bonnet as described in **Chapter 13, Section 13:2**.
2 Disconnect the wiring from the thermoswitch (8/9 in **FIG 4:1**) and from the cooling fan motor.
3 Drain the cooling system as described in **Section 4:2**. Loosen the hose clamps on the top and bottom hoses (1 and 15 in **FIG 4:1**) and remove these hoses.
4 Refer to **FIG 4:2**. Remove the air duct attachment screws which are arrowed. Remove the mounting bolt 1. Remove the nut from the side support 2 and the bolt from the mounting bracket 3.
5 Carefully lift out the radiator complete with its air duct and cooling fan assembly. Separate the radiator by removing the air duct and the fan assembly.

Keep the radiator in an upright position so that any scale or sediment in the bottom tank will not pass into the matrix and cause a blockage.

A radiator in which the matrix is leaking or which has a defective top or bottom tank should be passed to a specialist for repair. A radiator which is severely corroded or which has suffered damage should be rejected and replaced by a new unit.

Refitting:

The installation procedure is the removal sequence in reverse. Fit new hoses if their condition is doubtful. Fill the cooling system as described in **Section 4:2**. Run the engine up to normal temperature and check the hose connections for leaks.

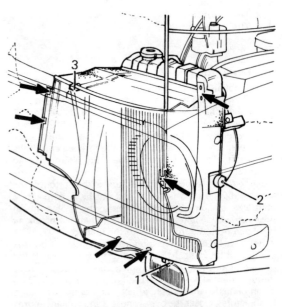

FIG 4:2 The radiator and ambient air ducting

Key to Fig 4:2 1 Mounting bolt 2 Side mounting 3 Mounting bolt Ducting attachments are arrowed

Restricted flow:

If poor flow through the radiator matrix is suspected, a proprietary radiator cleaning chemical may be used. Flush the system as described in **Section 4:2**, refill with the cleaning solution and, after the prescribed period of running, drain the system and repeat the flushing procedure. Use only a reputable cleaning chemical and adhere rigidly to the makers' instructions.

4:4 The cooling fan

The cooling fan and its motor are supported in a venturi duct which is mounted immediately behind the radiator. The electrical supply to the fan motor is via a relay which is switched in and out by the thermo switch 8/9 in **FIG 4:1** fitted in the bottom of the radiator. A defective fan motor cannot be repaired by an owner and should be exchanged for a new assembly.

Thermo switch:

A serviceable thermo switch should close at a temperature of between 90°C and 95°C (194°F and 203°F) and open between 85°C and 90°C (185°F and 194°F). If the serviceability of the switch is suspect, bridge the switch terminals and switch on the ignition briefly. The fan should operate. If it does not, refer to **Chapter 12, FIG 12:1** and check the relevant relay as described later. If the relay is operative, it must be assumed that the thermoswitch is defective or that there is a discontinuity in its wiring.

The cooling system must be drained as described in **Section 4:2** before a defective thermo switch can be renewed.

Do not omit the rubber grommet which is fitted to seal the switch on later models. On earlier cars the grommet was omitted, but one should be fitted if dismantling is undertaken.

Fan motor relay:

If the serviceability of the relay is suspect, refer to **Chapter 12, FIG 12:1** and withdraw the relevant relay. Bridge terminals 30 and 87 and switch on the ignition. The fan should operate. If it does, the relay must be suspect or there may be a wiring discontinuity. A relay that is suspect is best checked by substitution.

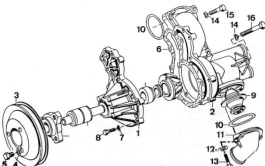

FIG 4:3   Components of the water pump

Key to Fig 4:3   1 Pump cover   **2** Pump body   **3** Drive pulley   **4** Washer   **5** Bolt   **6** Gasket   **7** Washer   **8** Bolt   **9** Thermostat   **10** Sealing ring   **11** Inlet elbow   **12** Washer   **13** Bolt   **14** Washer   **15** Bolt   **16** Bolt

FIG 4:4   Drive belt for pump and alternator

Key to Fig 4:4   a .4 to .6 inch (10 to 15 mm)

Wiring discontinuity:

Trace a suspected wiring fault with the aid of the relevant wiring diagram in the **Appendix.** In particular, ensure that the fan motor earth wire is providing a good connection.

4:5 The water pump

The components of the water pump are shown in **FIG 4:3.** It, together with the alternator, is belt driven from a pulley on the front end of the crankshaft.

Belt removal:

Loosen the alternator mounting bolts, swing the alternator towards the engine and disengage the belt from the pulleys.

Belt fitment and tension adjustment:

With the alternator mounting bolts loosened and the alternator swung towards the engine, engage the drive belt into the grooves in the pulleys. Swing the alternator away from the engine to tension the belt and tighten the alternator mounting bolts. The tension is correct when, under thumb pressure, the belt can be depressed by no more than .4 to .6 inch (10 to 15 mm) as at **a** in **FIG 4:4.**

Pump removal:

1 Drain the cooling system as described in **Section 4:2.**
2 Remove the drive belt as described earlier. Refer to **Chapter 12, Section 12:5** and dismount the alternator. Remove the camshaft drive belt cover.
3 Loosen the hose clamps and remove the hoses which are attached to the pump. Remove the four bolts (two of 15 and two of 16 in **FIG 4:3**) which attach the pump to the cylinder block and dismount the pump by pivoting it slightly upwards.
4 Remove and discard the sealing ring 10 in **FIG 4:3.**

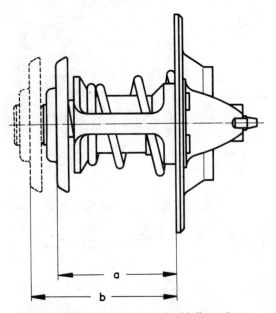

FIG 4:5 Thermostat hot and cold dimensions

Key to Fig 4:5   a 1.22 inch (31 mm)   b 1.50 inch (38 mm)

Dismantling and assembling the pump:

Refer to **FIG 4:3**. Remove the three bolts 5, collect the washers and pull off the drive pulley. Remove the bolts 8 which attach the cover 1 to the pump body 2. Using a soft hammer, separate the cover complete with the flange, shaft and impeller from the pump body. Remove bolts 13, remove the inlet elbow 11, withdraw the thermostat 9 and discard the sealing ring 10. Discard the gasket 6. The pump cover assembly cannot be dismantled and, if un-serviceable, must be replaced by a new assembly.

Assembly is the reverse of the dismantling sequence. Clean off old gasket and jointing compound from the cover and body joint faces. Use a waterproof jointing compound and a new gasket 6. Use a new sealing ring 10.

Pump refitment:

Follow the removal sequence in reverse. Use a new sealing ring 10. Tension the drive belt as described earlier. Refill the cooling system as described in **Section 4:2** and, after running the engine up to normal temperature, check for hose and joint leaks.

4:6 The thermostat

The function of the thermostat is described in **Section 4:1**. It is located in the water pump body immediately behind the coolant inlet elbow. A defective thermostat cannot be repaired and should be replaced by a new unit.

Removal and fitment:

Drain the cooling system as described in **Section 4:2**. Remove the inlet hose 1 in **FIG 4:1**. Refer to **FIG 4:3**. Remove the two bolts 13 and dismount the elbow 11. Withdraw the thermostat 9 and discard the sealing ring 10.

Refitment is the reverse of the removal sequence. Use a new sealing ring and, after running the engine up to normal temperature, check for hose and joint leaks.

Testing:

Remove the thermostat as described earlier. Clean it off and ensure that no scale or sediment is interfering with its operation. Immerse it in a container of cold water together with a 0°C to 100°C (32°F to 212°F) thermometer. Heat the water and, keeping it stirred, observe if the thermostat begins to 'open' at 80°C (176°F). Continue heating the water and check the maximum 'opening'. At 90°C (194°F) the increase in length should be .28 inch (7 mm) as shown in **FIG 4:5**.

4:7 Frost precautions

The use of antifreeze at all times is recommended, since, apart from it providing protection from frost in relevant conditions, the correct solution will inhibit corrosion in the cooling system. Use VW solution G10 if available. In the proportions of one volume of G10 to 1.5 volumes of water, protection down to −25°C (−13°F) is provided while in equal proportions, protection down to −35°C (−30°F) is provided. If G10 solution is not available, use an ethylene-glycol type of antifreeze of reputable make and use the proportions recommended by the maker for the degree of frost protection required.

Whether using G10 or a proprietary antifreeze the recommended proportions should be measured into a separate container and the cooling system filled from this and not by adding the chemical directly into the radiator. After two winters use, discard the antifreeze and, after flushing the system as described in **Section 4:2**, refill with fresh solution.

If antifreeze is not used, it must be remembered that the action of the thermostat will delay circulation of warm coolant to the radiator which may consequently freeze after the engine has been started.

4:8 Fault diagnosis

(a) Internal water leakage

1 Cracked cylinder block
2 Loose cylinder head bolts
3 Cylinder head cracked
4 Faulty head gasket

(b) Poor circulation

1 Radiator matrix blocked
2 Water passages restricted
3 Low coolant level
4 Pump drive belt loose or broken
5 Defective water pump
6 Defective thermostat
7 Perished or collapsed hose(s)

(c) Corrosion

1 Impurities in the water
2 Infrequent draining and flushing

(d) Overheating

1 Check (b)
2 Sludge in crankcase
3 Low oil level in sump
4 Tight engine
5 Faulty ignition timing
6 Retarded ignition
7 Incorrect valve timing
8 Mixture too weak
9 Choked exhaust system

10 Binding brakes
11 Slipping clutch
12 Electric fan inoperative

(e) Electric fan inoperative

1 Fuse blown
2 Thermo switch defective
3 Relay defective
4 Discontinuity in wiring
5 Fan motor defective

NOTES

CHAPTER 5

THE CLUTCH

5:1 Description
5:2 Maintenance
5:3 Removal and installation

5:4 Release mechanism
5:5 Adjustment
5:6 Fault diagnosis

5:1 Description

A cross-section through the single dry-plate clutch assembly is included in **FIG 6:1** in **Chapter 6**. The pressure plate assembly and the clutch driven plate are shown in **FIG 5:1**.

When the clutch is engaged the driven plate, which is splined to the gearbox drive shaft, is nipped between the pressure plate and the flywheel and therefore rotates with the flywheel and transmits the torque to the gearbox. The clutch is disengaged when the pressure plate is withdrawn from the driven plate by the clutch pedal being depressed. The clutch pedal operates the clutch release lever through a flexible cable assembly and the components of the mechanism are shown in **FIG 5:2**. When the clutch is disengaged, the driven plate ceases to transmit torque to the gearbox.

5:2 Maintenance

Every 5000 miles (8000 km), check the clutch pedal free play and adjust if necessary as described in **Section 5:5**. When the limit of adjustment is reached, a new release bearing and/or clutch plate must be fitted.

5:3 Removal and installation

Removal:

1 Remove the complete transmission as described in **Chapter 6, Section 6.3**.
2 Mark the pressure plate cover and the flywheel so that the assembly may be refitted in its original position.
3 Refer to **FIG 5:1** and loosen the six pressure plate cover attaching bolts 1 a turn at a time. Work diagonally and evenly to avoid distorting the cover and gradually release the spring load. Collect the spring washers 2 and dismount the pressure plate and clutch plate from the flywheel.
4 Refer to **FIG 5:2** and remove the release bearing 11 from the release bearing shaft 16.

Inspection:

Examine the clutch plate linings. A polished surface is normal but a very dark or a resinous surface results from burned or partially burned-off oil. This is a condition which cannot be rectified. Excessive wear of the linings or of the hub splines will also dictate the fitment of a new plate. Check that the hub springs are intact and that all

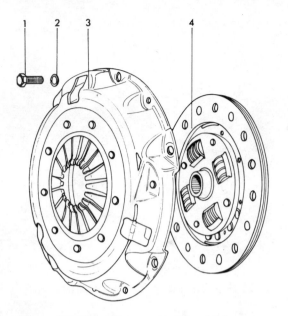

FIG 5:1   Components of the clutch

Key to Fig 5:1   1 Bolt   2 Spring washer   3 Pressure plate assembly   4 Clutch plate

rivets are secure. Runout measured at a radius of 3.45 inch (87.5 mm) should not exceed .016 inch (.4 mm).

Check the fingers of the diaphragm spring. Scores which are not deeper than .012 inch (.3 mm) may be ignored but cracked or broken fingers dictate that a new assembly should be fitted. Clean the surface of the pressure plate and check for wear. An inward taper of up to .012 inch (.3 mm) is acceptable. Check that all rivets are tight. An assembly with damaged or loose rivets should be renewed.

Refer to **Chapter 1, Section 1:11** and confirm that the flywheel is serviceable. Refer to **Chapter 1, Section 1:12** and check the pilot bearing in the end bore of the crankshaft.

Check the release mechanism for free movement and also for wear. **Do not wash the release bearing.** Wipe off only.

Installation:

1 Position the clutch plate and the pressure plate cover assembly (in the marked position) on the flywheel with the three dowels engaged. Fit the six attachment bolts but do not tighten them.
2 Align the clutch plate using a stub shaft inserted into the pilot bearing. Working diagonally, tighten the six retaining bolts evenly and finally torque them to 18 lb ft (2.5 kg m). Remove the stub shaft.

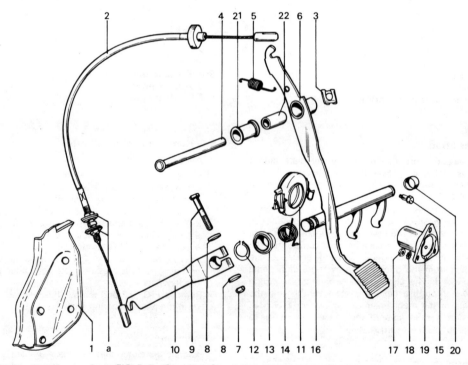

FIG 5:2   Components of the release mechanism

Key to Fig 5:2   1 Bracket   2 Clutch cable   3 Locking clip   4 Shaft   5 Spring   6 Pedal   7 Nut   8 Washer   9 Bolt   10 Clutch release lever   11 Release bearing   12 Circlip   13 Bush   14 Return spring   15 Shouldered bolt   16 Release bearing shaft   17 Nut   18 Locking washer   19 Sleeve   20 Release bearing shaft bush   21 Pedal outer bush   22 Bush   **a** Adjuster nuts

3 Lightly grease the external diameter of the release bearing guide (19 in **FIG 5:2**) with lithium base molybdenum disulphide grease. Clean the splines of the drive shaft and lubricate them with molybdenum disulphide **powder**.

4 Instal the transmission as described in **Chapter 6, Section 6:3** and adjust the clutch pedal free play as described in **Section 5:5**.

5:4 Release mechanism

Clutch cable:

Refer to **FIG 5:2**. A clutch cable 2 which is unserviceable is removed by loosening the nuts **a**, disengaging the adjuster from the bracket 1 and the ends of the inner cable from the release lever 10 and the clutch pedal 6. Fitment of a new cable is the reverse of this sequence and is followed by adjustment of the free play as described in **Section 5:5**.

Clutch release lever:

If the release lever 10 in **FIG 5:2** is to be removed, mark its position in relation to the release bearing shaft 16 so that it may be refitted in its original position. Only light lubrication should be applied to the shaft bushes.

5:5 Adjustment

Free play at the clutch pedal should be .6 inch (15 mm) and is adjusted by loosening nuts **a** in **FIG 5:2** and altering the position of of the threaded cable sleeve in relation to its retaining bracket 1. On completion of the adjustment ensure that both nuts are retightened.

5:6 Fault diagnosis

(a) Drag or spin

1 Oil or grease on clutch plate linings
2 Clutch plate hub splines binding
3 Distorted clutch plate
4 Distorted pressure plate or cover
5 Broken clutch plate linings
6 Dirt or foreign matter in clutch
7 Incorrect release cable adjustment

(b) Fierceness

1 Check 1 and 7 in (a)
2 Worn clutch plate linings

(c) Slip

1 Check 1 and 7 in (a)
2 Check 2 in (b)
3 Weak pressure plate spring load
4 Seized release cable

(d) Judder

1 Check 1, 5 and 6 in (a)
2 Pressure plate not parallel with flywheel face
3 Contact area of clutch plate linings not evenly distributed
4 Bent or worn splined shaft
5 Excessively worn clutch plate hub splines
6 Buckled clutch plate

(e) Rattle

1 Check 6 in (a)
2 Check 4 and 5 in (d)
3 Broken spring in clutch plate
4 Worn release mechanism
5 Release bearing loose
6 Wear in transmission

NOTES

CHAPTER 6

THE MANUAL TRANSMISSION

6:1 Description

The front wheel drive transmission incorporates a single dry-plate type clutch, a four forward speed and reverse gearbox and a differential and final drive assembly and a drive shaft to each front wheel hub. The clutch is covered in **Chapter 5** and the drive shafts are included in **Chapter 8**.

Gearbox ratios are identical for all models covered by this manual and are tabulated in **Technical Data** in the **Appendix**. Final drive ratios differ between models fitted with the 1297 cc engine and those fitted with the 1471 and 1588 cc engines and these are also listed in **Technical Data**.

A cross-section through the transmission is shown in **FIG 6:1**. The forward end of the main drive shaft is supported in a pilot bearing in the end of the crankshaft (see **Chapter 1, Section 1:12**). It is splined to the clutch driven plate. The gearbox provides four forward speeds and reverse. All forward gears have synchromesh engagement. The straight toothed reverse gear on the main drive shaft drives through an idler gear to a straight-toothed driven gear which is integral with the first/second synchro unit. Reverse gear is engaged and disengaged by the idler gear being put into and out of mesh with the driving and driven gears. The switch which operates the

reversing lights is automatically closed when the reverse gear is selected. All forward gears have helical teeth and are constantly in mesh. Engagement is by means of the synchro units. The first/second synchro hub which is splined to the primary shaft engages first gear when in its rearward position and second gear when in its forward position. The third/fourth synchro hub which is splined to the main shaft engages third gear when in its rearward position and fourth gear when in its forward position.

The drive pinion at the forward end of the driven shaft is integral with the shaft and meshes with a ring gear which is bolted to the differential case. The differential is of conventional design with two pinions and two side gears and is shown in cross-section in **FIG 6:2**. The output shafts are splined into the side gears. The flanges which engage with the driven shafts are integral with the output shafts. An exploded view of the final drive assembly is shown in **FIG 6:3**. The speedometer is driven from a spiral gear on the lefthand output shaft.

The fore and aft position of the pinion shaft is controlled by shim S3. This is item 11 in **FIG 6:1**. The pinion/ring gear backlash and also the taper roller bearing preload is controlled by shims S1 and S2. These are items 10 and 11 in **FIG 6:2** and 13 and 15 in **FIG 6:3**.

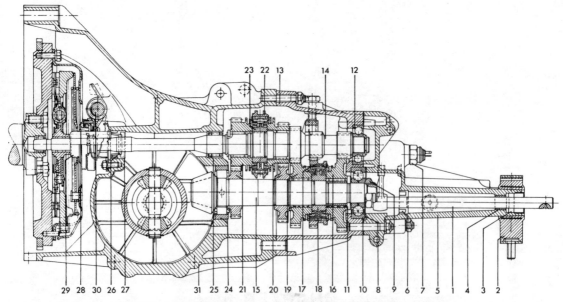

FIG 6:1 Cross-section through the clutch and manual gearbox

Key to Fig 6:1   1 Gearchange rod   2 Bonded rubber mounting   3 Oil seal   4 Bush   5 Gearchange housing   6 Bush
7 Reversing lights switch   8 Shim   9 Nut   10 Pinion ballbearing   11 S3 shim   12 Mainshaft ballbearing   13 Gearbox
casing   14 Mainshaft   15 Pinion shaft   16 First speed gear   17 First/second synchro sleeve   18 First/second synchro hub
19 Second speed gears   20 Third speed gears   21 Fourth speed gears   22 Third/fourth synchro sleeve   23 Third/fourth
synchro hub   24 Pinion roller bearing   25 Needle bearing   26 Oil seal   27 Bush   28 Clutch release bearing   29 Guide
sleeve   30 Clutch release shaft   31 Differential and final drive casing

Special measuring equipment is required for complete overhaul of the transmission assembly and the work may well therefore, be beyond the scope of the amateur.

There have been a number of revisions and modifications to the unit, so if overhaul work is to be carried out, care should be taken to ensure that any replacement parts obtained are appropriate to the particular assembly concerned.

6:2 Maintenance

Oil level:

Every 5000 miles (8000 km), check the transmission oil level and top up if necessary. The filler plug is socket-headed and is located in the lefthand side of the final drive casing. It is arrowed **A** in **FIG 6:3**.

Clean off around the filler plug before removing it. The correct level is when the oil is just up to the bottom of the filler plug orifice. It is inadvisable to mix oils of different brands and the oil used for topping up should be the same as that already in the transmission. If it is proposed to change the brand of oil, do so at a 30,000 mile (50,000 km) interval when, as described later, the old oil is being drained off and discarded. On refitment, the filler plug should be torque tightened to 18 lb ft (2.5 kg m).

Draining the transmission:

Every 30,000 miles (50,000 km), drain off and discard the transmission oil. This should preferably be carried out when the transmission oil is warm after a run. The socket-headed drain plug is in the bottom of the lefthand side of the final drive casing below the drive shaft centre line and

is arrowed **B** in **FIG 6:3**. Position a suitable tray below the drain plug, clean off round the drain plug and the filler plug, remove both plugs and allow the old oil to drain off thoroughly. The drain plug incorporates a magnet which will retain steel particles and these should be cleaned off. If, rather than particles, there should be evidence of debris, investigation of its source is indicated.

Filling the transmission:

When the old oil has completely drained, refit the drain plug and torque tighten it to 18 lb ft (2.5 kg m). Use an oil of reputable brand to specification SAE 80 and fill the transmission to the level of the bottom of the filler plug orifice. Fit and tighten the filler plug as described earlier.

The quantity of oil required is approximately $3\frac{1}{2}$ pints (2 litres).

From 1976 models no oil changes are required during the life of the gearbox. The small magnet in the drain plug is omitted and a larger magnet fitted in the final drive cover in order to deal with the possibility of increased metallic deposits.

Gearchange linkage:

No specific mileage intervals are prescribed for routine maintenance of the gearchange linkage and adjustments as described in **Section 6:8** should be made as indicated by any stiffness, jamming or difficulty in engaging gear.

6:3 Removing and installing the transmission

The transmission can be removed without disturbing the engine. As the transmission must be lowered out, the vehicle must be raised on stands or positioned over a pit.

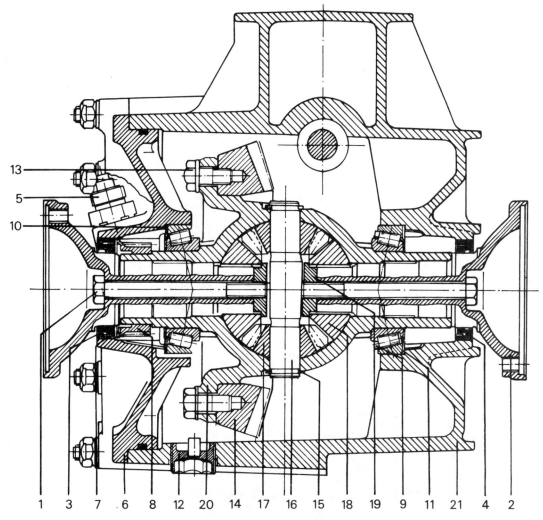

FIG 6:2   Cross-section through the differential and final drive

Key to Fig 6:2   1 Bolt   2 Drive flange   3 Lefthand oil seal   4 Righthand oil seal   5 Speedometer drive pinion   6 Cover
7 Bush   8 Speedometer drive gear   9 Taper roller   10 S1 shim   11 S2 shim   12 Drain plug   13 Bolt   14 Ring
gear   15 Circlip   16 Differential pinion shaft   17 Pinion   18 Side gear   19 Nut   20 Differential casing   21 Differential
and final drive casing

Two operators are required for the final removal and initial installation operations.

Removal:

The order of numbering in **FIG 6:4** indicates the sequence in which the removal operations should be performed.

1 With the vehicle raised on stands or positioned over a pit, disconnect the battery earth cable 1. Uncouple the exhaust pipe from the engine and at the bracket 2.
2 With the gearbox in neutral, remove the wire locking, remove the square-headed bolt 3 (the official T-spanner is VW 114) and press off the coupling. Remove bolt 4.

3 Refer to **Chapter 5, Section 5:4** and disconnect the clutch cable from the clutch release lever 5. Withdraw the speedometer cable 6.
4 Refer to **Chapter 8, Section 8:9** and remove the six socket-headed bolts which retain the drive shaft inner universal joint flanges to the transmission output shaft flanges (7 in **FIG 6:4**). Disengage and suitably support the inner ends of the drive shafts.
5 Refer to **Chapter 12, Section 12:4** and remove the starter motor 8. Remove the guard plate 9.
6 With a second operator supporting the transmission, remove the engine/transmission bolts 10. Remove two bolts and one nut and withdraw the crossbracket 11 which supports the transmission rear mounting.

7 Taking great care not to strain the main drive shaft, lever the transmission rearwards off the dowels and disengage the shaft from the crankshaft pilot bearing and from the splines of the clutch plate. When out of engagement and clear of the clutch, lower the transmission and withdraw it from beneath the vehicle.

Installation:

The installation sequence is the reverse of that described for the removal of the transmission. Torque tighten the engine/transmission bolts to 40 lb ft (5.5 kg m). Torque tighten the drive shaft to transmission flange socket-headed bolts to 25 lb ft (3.5 kg m). Torque tighten bolt 4 to 14.5 lb ft (2 kg m). Tighten the square-headed bolt 3 and wire lock it.

Refill the transmission with approved oil as described in **Section 6:2**. Refer to **Section 6:8** and check the adjustment of the gearchange linkage. Check the adjustment of the clutch as described in **Chapter 5, Section 5:5**. Test run the vehicle and check for oil

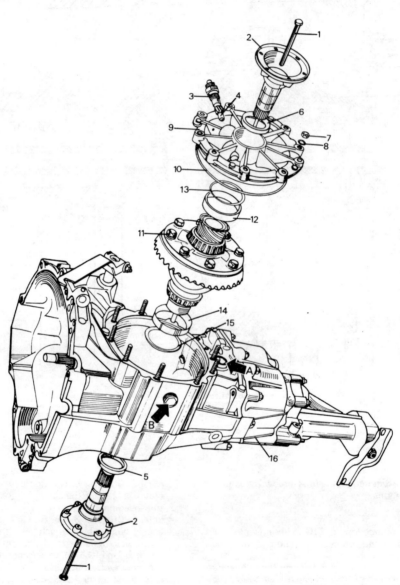

FIG 6:3 Exploded view of differential and final drive components

Key to Fig 6:3   **A** Lubrication filler plug   **B** Lubrication drain plug   1 Bolt   2 Drive flange   3 Speedometer pinion assembly   4 Speedometer pinion   5 Righthand oil seal   6 Lefthand oil seal   7 Nut   8 Washer   9 Cover   10 Oil seal   11 Differential and ring gear assembly   12 Taper roller bearing outer race   13 S1 shim   14 Taper roller bearing outer race   15 S2 shim   16 Gearbox and gearchange assembly

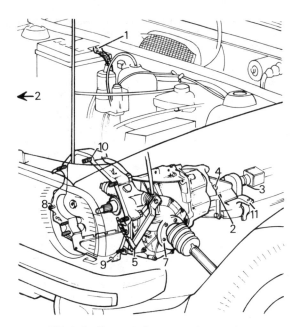

FIG 6:4 Transmission removal operations

Key to Fig 6:4 1 Battery earth connection 2 Exhaust pipe bracket 3 Square-headed bolt 4 Bolt 5 Clutch release cable 6 Speedometer drive cable 7 Drive shaft socket-headed bolts 8 Starter motor 9 Guard plate 10 Bolts 11 Transmission support crossmember

leaks. Check and, if necessary, top up the level of oil in the transmission assembly.

6:4 Dismantling the transmission

In view of the many special tools required for dismantling and reassembling this transmission, the home operator is strongly advised to read through the necessary operations described in this and the next three sections before commencing a task which he may consider more suitable for a VW service station.

Following removal of the transmission as described in **Section 6:3**, drain off the lubricating oil if this was not done earlier. Refer to **FIG 6:5**.

1 Remove the nuts and washers 1 and 2 and withdraw the complete gearchange housing 3. Collect the shim 4 and gasket 5 and retain them for thickness measurement (see **Section 6:5**).

2 Remove the eleven nuts and washers 6 and 7 and two dowels 8. Separate the gearbox assembly 9 from the differential and final drive assembly and, while withdrawing the mainshaft, take great care that the mainshaft splines do not damage the bore of the oil seal 26 in **FIG 6:1**.

The gearchange housing 3 and the gearbox 9 are dealt with in **Section 6:6**. Note that the fitment of certain new parts (see tabulation in **Section 6:7**) will necessitate the thickness of shim S3 (11 in **FIG 6:1**) being recalculated. If such replacements are a possibility, the position of the pinion in relation to the gearbox casing must be determined before the gearbox is dismantled. The procedure is covered in **Section 6:6**.

The differential and final drive unit are dealt with in **Section 6:7**.

6:5 Reassembly of the transmission

With the gearbox, gearchange housing and differential and final drive units serviced and assembled as described in **Sections 6:6** and **6:7**, reassembly of the transmission can proceed.

Refer to **FIG 6:6** and accurately measure **a, b** and **c**. Ensure that the mainshaft and pinion shaft bearings are fully into their locations otherwise false readings of **a** and **b** will be obtained. Add **a** and **c** and subtract **b**. This gives the desired thickness **s** of the shim (4 in **FIG 6:5**). The actual shim thickness which should be fitted will be one of seven thicknesses which are available and will closely approximate to the desired thickness. The following tabulation indicates the shim thickness which should be used. Thicknesses are given in inches with mm equivalents in brackets.

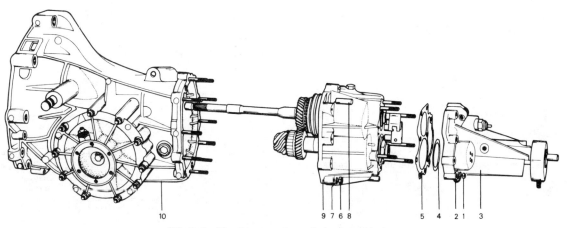

FIG 6:5 The three sections of the transmission

Key to Fig 6:5 1 Nut 2 Washer 3 Gearchange housing assembly 4 Shim 5 Gasket 6 Nut 7 Washer 8 Dowel 9 Gearbox assembly 10 Differential and final drive assembly

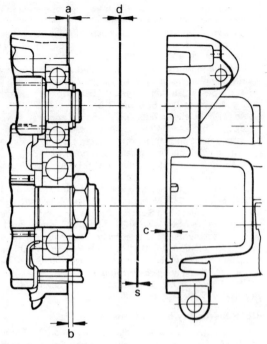

FIG 6:6 The gearbox/gearchange housing shim and gasket

Key to Fig 6:6   **a** Projection of mainshaft bearing   **b** Projection of pinion shaft bearing   **c** Depth of recess in gearchange housing   **d** Thickness of gasket   **s** Thickness of shim

Desired thickness a+c−b	Actual part S	Shim thickness No.
.017 to .019 (.44 to .48 mm)	.018 (.45 mm)	014 311 390
.019 to .021 (.49 to .53 mm)	.020 (.50 mm)	014 311 391
.021 to .023 (.54 to .58 mm)	.022 (.55 mm)	014 311 392
.023 to .025 (.59 to .63 mm)	.024 (.60 mm)	014 311 393
.025 to .027 (.64 to .68 mm)	.026 (.65 mm)	014 311 394
.027 to .029 (.69 to .73 mm)	.028 (.70 mm)	014 311 395
.029 to .031 (.74 to .78 mm)	.030 (.75 mm)	014 311 396

The thickness **d** of the gasket 5 in **FIG 6:4** depends upon the bearing projection as follows. Dimensions **a** and **d** are given in inches with mm equivalents in brackets.

Projection a	Gasket thickness d	Gasket part no.
.008 to .010 (.20 to .26 mm)	.012 (.30 mm)	014 301 235
.011 to .013 (.27 to .32 mm)	.016 (.40 mm)	014 301 237

If no critical new parts (see tabulation in **Section 6:7**) were used in rebuilding units 3 or 9, the original shim and gasket thicknesses will apply. A new gasket must however be used.

Assembly is now the reverse of the dismantling sequence. With the gearbox in neutral, ensure that the gearchange lever engages the selector rods. Refer to **FIG 6:5**. Torque tighten nuts 1 to 14 lb ft (2 kg m). Apply a thin coating of D3 jointing compound to the forward face of the gearbox casing on early cars, a gasket being used after 1975. Wrap protective tape round the splines of the mainshaft to preclude them damaging the oil seal (26 in **FIG 6:1**) in the differential and final drive casing. Fit the dowels and torque tighten nuts 6 to 14 lb ft (2 kg m).

6:6 The gearbox

Pinion location:

Before dismantling the gearbox, it will be prudent to determine the exact location of the pinion in relation to the axis of the final drive unit so that, on reassembly, it can, by means of the S3 shim (11 in **FIG 6:1**), be set again to its original relative position. If this is not done before dismantling and it is later found necessary to fit new components which affect the pinion location, the pinion shaft assembly will have to be refitted to the gearbox casing using the original components so that the pinion location may then be determined. The procedure is as follows and **FIGS 6:6** and **6:7** relate.

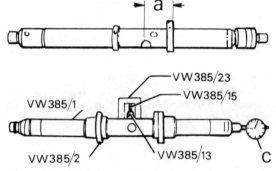

FIG 6:7   Preparing the gauging bar

Key to Fig 6:7   **a** = approximately 1.969 inch (50 mm)

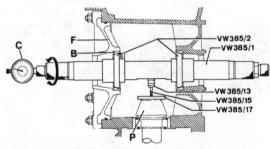

FIG 6:8   Determining the pinion location

Key to Fig 6:8   **B** Bearing outer race   **C** Dial indicator   **F** Differential and final drive cover   **P** Pinion

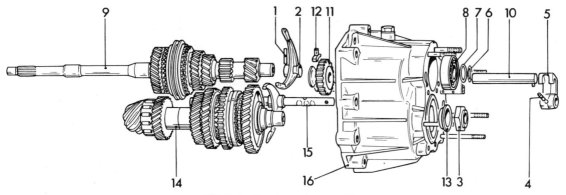

FIG 6:9   Gearbox sub-assemblies

Key to Fig 6:9   1 Spring pin   2 Third/fourth fork   3 Nut   4 Spring pin   5 First/second selector operating dog
6 Circlip   7 Washer   8 Mainshaft bearing   9 Mainshaft assembly   10 Reverse idler shaft   11 Reverse gear   12 Reverse
gear segment   13 Pinion shaft bearing inner race (outer half)   14 Pinion shaft assembly   15 First/second selector rod
and fork   16 Gearbox casing

1 Dismantle the differential and final drive unit as described in **Section 6:7**. The outer races of both taper roller bearings (**B** in **FIG 6:8**) must be left in position.

2 Refer to **FIG 6:7** and prepare the VW 385/1 mandrel as indicated. Position the setting gauge VW 385/23 with R_0 at 1.9173 inch (48.70 mm) and give the dial indicator a 'preload' of .0787 (2 mm).

3 Fit the prepared mandrel into the differential and final drive casing, place the measuring plate VW 385/17 onto the pinion **P**, fit the final drive cover **F** (6 in **FIG 6:2**) and torque tighten the retaining nuts to 18 lb ft (2.5 kg m).

4 Turn the mandrel to bring the dial indicator pin into contact with the measuring plate and oscillate to determine the maximum pin depression. Ensure that the pinion shaft does not move rearwards. Note the reading.

On final reassembly of the gearbox output shaft, the thickness of the S3 shim must be selected to reproduce this reading. There are fourteen thicknesses of shims which are available. These are tabulated in **Section 6:7**. The procedure to be adopted for the adjustment of the pinion (and the ring gear) when critical new parts are fitted is also described in **Section 6:7**.

Dismantling the gearbox:

The components shown in **FIG 6:9** are, substantially, numbered in the order in which they should be removed.

Use a pin punch to drift out pin 1 and disengage fork 2 from its selector rod. Engage reverse gear to lock the pinion drive and remove nut 3. Knock out pin 4 with a suitable pin punch. Press the mainshaft assembly out of bearing 8 and, if necessary, remove this bearing from the casing. Refer to **FIG 6:10** and press out the reverse gear shaft (arrowed). Press out the pinion shaft assembly complete with the first/second fork and selector rod. The selector rod may need to be tapped lightly if it begins to jam. **FIG 6:11** shows the selector interlock springs and plungers.

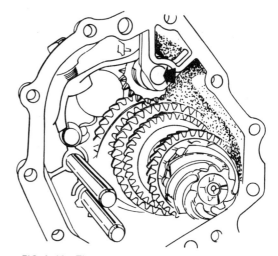

FIG 6:10   The reverse idler gearshaft is arrowed

Reassembling the gearbox:

On reassembly, follow, substantially, the reverse of the dismantling sequence.

When reassembling the interlocks, refer to **FIG 6:11** and note that parts 3 and 8 are fitted through the upper hole. When fitting 6, 9 and 15, the plungers must be held down from the opposite side with a screwdriver. Position the selector rods in neutral. Component 15 is not fitted until the gear train is inserted.

If the reverse selector rocker lever was removed, follow the following procedure when refitting. Fit the reverse gear and shaft. Insert the rocker lever and selector segment. Fit the bolt and washer. Refer to **FIG 6:12** and press the rocker in the direction of the arrow. Screw in the bolt until it touches the lever. Press the lever against the bolt and back off the bolt until the thread is heard to engage with the lever. Screw in the bolt fully and torque tighten it to 25 lb ft (3.5 kg m). Check the movement of the lever. The reverse gear and shaft may now be again removed.

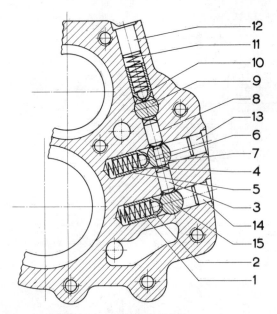

FIG 6:11   Selector rod interlocks

Key to Fig 6:11   1 Spring   2 Plunger   3 Plunger
4 Spring   5 Plunger   6 Third/fourth selector rod   7 Pin
8 Plunger   9 Reverse selector rod   10 Plunger   11 Spring
12 Plug   13 Plug   14 Plug   15 First/second selector rod

The gearchange housing:

The components of the gearchange housing are shown in **FIG 6:13** and are numbered in the order in which they should be removed.

On reassembly, follow the numerical sequence in reverse. The reversing lights switch 6 should be tightened to a torque of 14 lb ft (2 kg m).

The shaft assemblies:

The components of both the mainshaft and the pinion shaft are shown in **FIG 6:14.** When dismantling, make notes of which way round the components face if they are not symmetrical so that, on reassembly, they can be correctly fitted. Follow, substantially, the order in which the components are numbered when dismantling each shaft and, on reassembly, follow the inverse order.

Dismantling the mainshaft:

1 Remove circlip 1. Circlip pliers will be required. Withdraw the shim 2, the needle bearing 3, the fourth-speed gear 4 and the fourth-speed synchro ring 5.
2 Remove the circlip 6 using suitable circlip pliers. Press off the third/fourth syncrho hub, the third-speed synchro ring 5 and the third-speed gear. The press load is applied at the rear face of the third-speed gear.
3 Remove the third-speed gear needle bearing 9. Withdraw the spring pin 10. Wash off the mainshaft 11 and all other parts in petrol and, to prevent rusting, brush gearbox oil over all steel parts.

4 Inspect all components for wear and damage. Check that splines which engage with the clutch driven plate are not excessively worn and that the shaft is not bent. Confirm that the diameter on which the oil seal (26 in **FIG 6:1**) runs is free from scores.
5 Discard components which are unserviceable and obtain new replacements. Dismantling of the synchro units is described later in this Section.

Assembling the mainshaft:

On reassembly, make sure that the components which are not symmetrical are positioned the correct way round as noted during dismantling. Assembly of the synchro units is covered later in this Section. Note that, as shown in **FIG 6:15,** the spring pin registers in the slot in the shim.

Fit the circlip 1 temporarily and under a press load the third-speed gear and synchro ring against circlip 6. The load should be up to 4400 lb (2000 kg) maximum. Using feeler gauges between the hub of the fourth gear and the shim 2, measure the axial clearance of the fourth-speed gear. This should be between .004 and .016 inch (.10 and .40 mm) and, preferably, towards the lower limit. If the clearance is excessive, remove the circlip and fit a thicker shim or vice versa. Shims are available in thicknesses of .138, .142 and .146 inch (3,5, 3.6 and 3.7 mm).

Dismantling the pinion shaft:

1 Press off the first-speed gear 16, the S3 shim 13 and the bearing inner race together. Collect the inner race 15 and the needle bearing 14.
2 Press off the second-speed gear 19 together with the synchro hub 18 and the synchro rings 17. Collect the needle bearing 20.
3 Remove the circlip 21. Press off the third speed gear 22. Press off the fourth-speed gear 23. Remove the bearing roller assembly 24.
4 Wash the pinion shaft 25 and other components in petrol and, to prevent rusting, brush clean gearbox oil

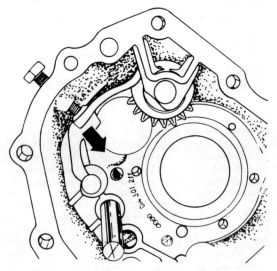

FIG 6:12   Refitting the reverse selector rocker

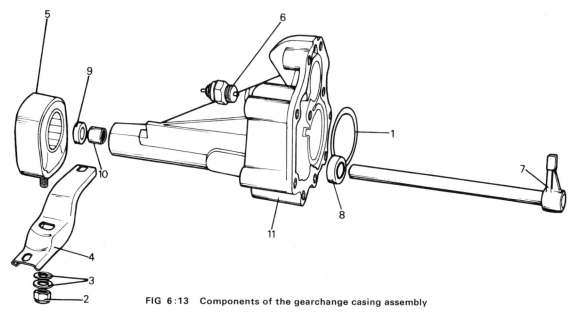

FIG 6:13   Components of the gearchange casing assembly

Key to Fig 6:13   1 Shim   2 Nut   3 Washers   4 Mounting support crossmember   5 Bonded rubber mounting
6 Reversing lights switch   7 Gearchange rod and lever   8 Bush   9 Oil seal   10 Bush   11 Gearchange casing

over all parts. Inspect the components for wear and damage, discard parts which are unserviceable and obtain new replacement parts. The pinion and final drive ring gear are matched and, should either be unserviceable, both must be renewed. Dismantling of the synchro unit is described later.

Assembling the pinion shaft:

On reassembly ensure that those components which are not symmetrical are positioned the correct way round. Assembly of the synchro unit is described later. The bores of the fourth- and third-speed gears and their registers on the pinion shaft must be dry (unoiled) when these gears

are pressed onto the shaft. Using feeler gauges as shown in **FIG 6:16,** measure the thickness of circlip which is required. If the feeler gauge measurement is less than .063 inch (1.6 mm), use a circlip of .059 inch (1.5 mm) thickness. If the measurement is .063 inch (1.6 mm) or greater, use a circlip of .063 inch (1.6 mm) thickness. Only these two thicknesses of circlip are available. The procedure for selecting the required thickness of the S3 shim 13 is described at the beginning of this Section.

Synchro units:

The components of the two synchro units are shown in **FIG 6:17.**

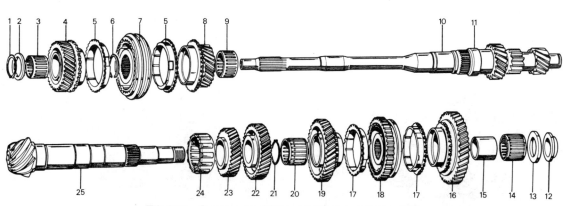

FIG 6:14   Components of the mainshaft and pinion shaft

Key to Fig 6:14   1 Circlip   2 Shim   3 Needle bearing   4 Fourth speed gear   5 Third/fourth speed synchro rings
6 Circlip   7 Third/fourth synchro unit   8 Third speed gear   9 Needle roller bearing   10 Pin   11 Mainshaft   12 Pinion
bearing inner race (inner half)   13 S3 shim   14 Needle bearing   15 Inner race   16 First speed gear   17 First/second
synchro rings   18 First/second synchro unit   19 Second speed gear   20 Needle roller bearing   21 Circlip   22 Third speed
gear   23 Fourth speed gear   24 Roller bearing   25 Pinion shaft

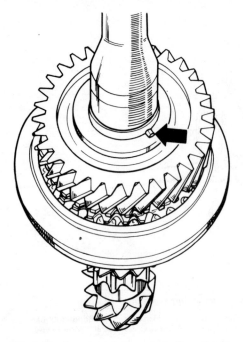

FIG 6:15   Location of the mainshaft spring pin

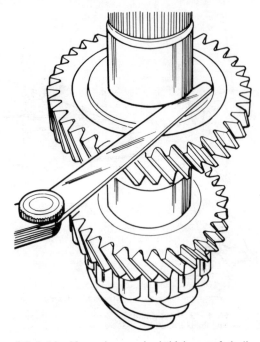

FIG 6:16   Measuring required thickness of circlip

Before dismantling a synchro unit, note the alignment marks and how the two springs on each unit are fitted offset to each other by 120 degrees. Note also that the angled end of each spring engages with a hollow key. Measure the gap **a** in **FIG 6:18**. When new, this gap was .043 to .067 inch (1.1 to 1.7 mm) in the case of a first/second-speed unit and .053 to .067 inch (1.35 to 1.9 mm) in the case of a third/fourth-speed unit.

To dismantle, remove the springs 4 and withdraw the hub 2 or 6 and the keys 3 from the operating sleeve 1 or 5.

Assembly is the reverse of this sequence.

6:7 The differential and final drive

Separation of the differential and final drive from and assembly to the gearbox is described in **Sections 6:4** and **6:5**. If necessary, however, the components of the differential and final drive may be stripped out of the casing without separating it from the gearbox. An exploded view of the unit is shown in **FIG 6:3** and components and sub-assemblies are removed in, substantially, the order in which they are numbered in that illustration.

Block the drive flanges 2 when removing bolts 1. Do not confuse oil seal 6 (lefthand) with oil seal 5 (righthand). The righthand seal 5 has an **unbroken groove** round the side. The lefthand seal 6 has a **broken groove** round the side. **Do not get them mixed.**

Inspect all parts for wear and damage. Discard components which are unserviceable and obtain new replacements. The ring gear and the pinion are matched and, should the ring gear be unserviceable, both components must be renewed. Ensure, particularly, that the oil seals are in good condition.

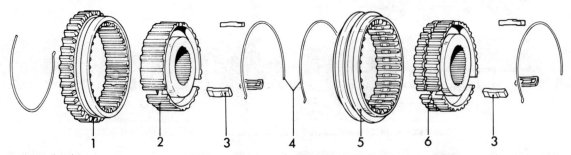

FIG 6:17   Components of the synchro units

Key to Fig 6:17   1 First/second speed synchro sleeve   2 First/second speed synchro hub   3 Key   4 Spring   5 Third/fourth speed synchro sleeve   6 Third/fourth speed synchro hub

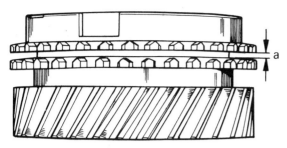

FIG 6:18 Checking synchro ring wear

Key to Fig 6:18 Gap **a** dimensions are given in the text

Assembly is the reverse of the dismantling sequence and, if no new critical parts have been fitted, it willl not be necessary to revise the thicknesses of the S1 and S2 shims. If, however, new critical parts have been required, refer to the instructions given later under the heading 'Adjusting the ring gear'. Torque tighten nuts 7 to 18 lb ft (2.5 kg m). Tighten bolts 1 to a torque of 14 lb ft (2 kg m).

The differential unit:

The components of the differential unit are shown in **FIG 6:19**. When completely dismantling the unit, follow, substantially, the order in which the components are numbered. The pinion and side gears may be stripped out, if necessary, without disturbing the ring gear and vice versa. On reassembly, tighten the eight bolts 5 to a torque of 40 lb ft (5.5 kg m). Ensure that the circlips are fully seated in their grooves.

Adjustment:

FIG 6:20 identifies the S1, S2 and S3 shims and indicates the R_o and **r** dimensions. The procedure for determining the pinion position is described in **Section 6:6**. If no new critical components are being renewed, it should not be necessary to revise the thicknesses of the S1, S2 or S3 shims.

The following tabulation lists the critical components and indicates the adjustment(s) required if it is found necessary to renew any of these components. The key to the adjustments **A**, **B**, **C** and **D** is listed below the tabulation.

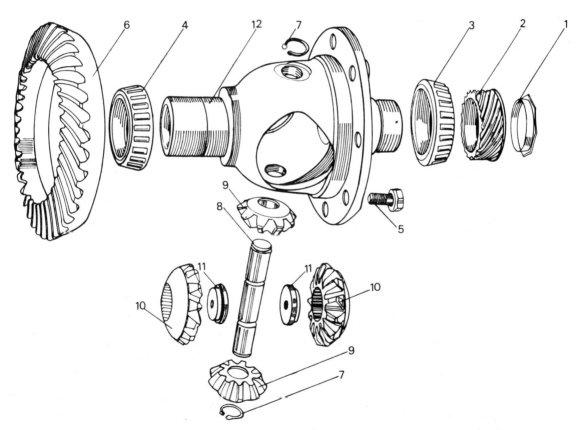

FIG 6:19 Components of the differential

Key to Fig 6:19 1 Speedometer drive gear bush 2 Speedometer drive gear 3 Tapered roller bearing 4 Tapered roller bearing 5 Bolt 6 Ring gear 7 Circlip 8 Shaft 9 Differential pinion 10 Side gear 11 Nut 12 Casing

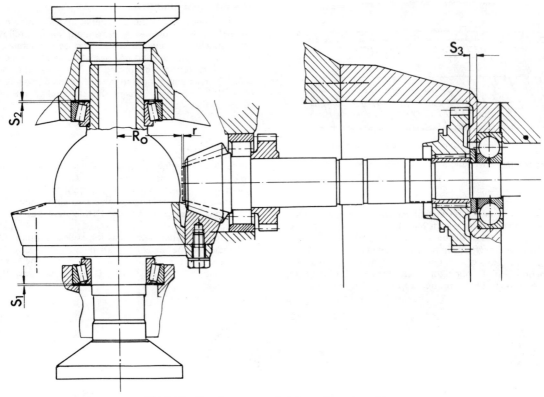

FIG 6 : 20   The ring gear and pinion adjustment shims

Key to Fig 6 : 20   S1 Shim in cover   S2 Shim in casing   S3 Shim on pinion shaft R_o Gauge dimension (48.70 mm)
r Deviation of pinion from standard

Critical component(s)	*Adjustments*			
	A	B	C	D
Differential and final drive casing	x		x	
Final drive cover			x	
Differential taper roller bearing			x	
Ring gear and pinion		x	x	
Differential unit casing			x	
Pinion bearing	x			x
Mainshaft bearing				x
Gearbox casing	x			x
Gearchange housing				x
First-speed needle bearing	x			

A Set pinion to position determined before dismantling.
B Revise thickness of S3 shim.
C Revise thicknesses of S1 and S2 shims.
D Revise thickness of gearbox/gearchange housing shim (4 in **FIG 6:5**).

Adjusting ring gear and pinion:

Careful adjustment of the ring gear and pinion (which must always be renewed as a set) is essential for satisfactory service and quiet running. During manufacture, each ring gear and pinion are matched and run on special testing machines to ensure proper tooth contact pattern. Each set of ring and pinion gears are then marked with a 'deviation' dimension **r**. The optimum position is obtained by moving the pinion axially by means of the S3 shim and, at the same time, moving the ring gear by means of the S1 and S2 shims to the point where the backlash is within a specified range. The deviation **r** is quoted in units of .01 mm and, for example, a marking of 25 means that **r** =.25 mm.

Although, in the following descriptions of the procedures, dimensions are given in inches, it will probably be found most convenient to work in mm units. Manufacturer's shim thicknesses are officially quoted in mm units.

Adjusting the pinion:

As a datum, an S3 shim of .157 inch (4 mm) in thickness is required. The part no. of this shim is 014 311 400. Proceed as follows.

1 Assemble the pinion shaft with the datum shim and tighten nut 9 in **FIG 6:1** to 14 to 22 lb ft (2 to 3 kg m). Fit the gearbox to the unassembled differential and final drive casing and secure it with four nuts. Ensure that the bearing 10 is fully home in its gearbox location.
2 Carry out operations 1, 2 and 3 of the procedure described under 'Pinion location' at the beginning of **Section 6:6**. Let the reading obtained from the dial indicator be **e**.

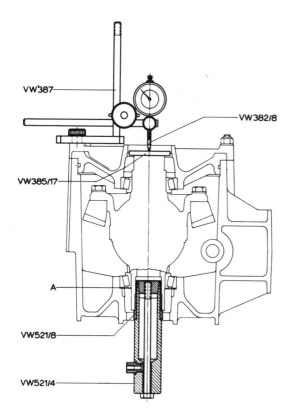

Fit the required thickness of shim(s) and recheck the pinion position by repeating the procedure described earlier. The selected thickness is correct if the dial indicator shows the marked **r** dimension ±.0016 inch (+.04 mm).

Adjusting the ring gear:

Readjustment of the S1 and S2 shim thicknesses is only necessary when the relevant critical component(s) tabulated earlier have been renewed. A shim of .047 inch (1.20 mm) thickness is required as a datum. The part no. of this shim is 113 517 211A. The procedure allows for the fact that a 'preload' of .016 inch (.40 mm) must be applied to the taper roller bearings. Proceed as follows.

1 Dismantle the differential and final drive assembly as described earlier. The oil seals 3 and 4 in **FIG 6:2** must be removed. The taper roller outer races must also be removed so that the S1 and S2 shims 10 and 11 can be withdrawn.

2 Refer to **FIG 6:20**. Fit the datum shim **A** into the casing (into the S2 shim position). Fit the bearing outer race. In the second bearing position, fit the outer race directly into the casing (no shim in the S1 shim position).

3 Fit the new ring gear to the differential and torque tighten the eight retaining bolts to 40 lb ft (5.5 kg m). Install the differential without the speedometer drive gear. Fit the drive cover and, working diagonally, torque tighten the ten retaining nuts to 18 lb ft (2.5 kg m).

FIG 6:21   Measuring the differential casing axial play

Key to Fig 6:21   A Datum shim of .047 inch (1.2 mm) thickness

3 Obtain a new S3 shim of thickness equal to **e − r** + .157 inch (4 mm). This last figure is the thickness of the datum shim.

Fourteen thicknesses of shims are available. One or more shims may be used together to build up to the required thickness as calculated above. Note that if the .006 inch (.15 mm) thick shim has to be included, it must be fitted between the thicker shim(s) and the race of the pinion shaft bearing. The following tabulation lists the thicknesses and part nos. of the fourteen available S3 shims.

Shim part no.	Shim thickness
019 311 391	.006 inch (0.15 mm)
014 311 400	.157 inch (4.00 mm)
014 311 401	.161 inch (4.10 mm)
014 311 402	.165 inch (4.20 mm)
014 311 403	.169 inch (4.30 mm)
014 311 404	.173 inch (4.40 mm)
014 311 405	.177 inch (4.50 mm)
014 311 406	.181 inch (4.60 mm)
014 311 407	.185 inch (4.70 mm)
014 311 408	.189 inch (4.80 mm)
014 311 409	.193 inch (4.90 mm)
014 311 410	.197 inch (5.00 mm)
014 311 411	.201 inch (5.10 mm)
014 311 412	.205 inch (5.20 mm)

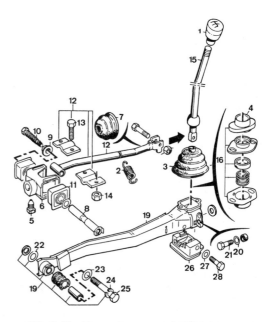

FIG 6:22   The early type gearchange linkage

Key to Fig 6:22   1 Knob   2 Spring   3 Boot (upper)
4 Boot (lower)   5 Square-headed bolt   6 Housing   7 Boot
8 Pin   9 Cap   10 Screw   11 Bearing   12 Gearchange rod
and weights   13 Bolt   14 Nut   15 Lever   16 Bearing
assembly (lever ball)   17 Nut   18 Housing   19 Bush
assembly   20 Washer   21 Bolt   22 Washer   23 Washer
24 Washer   25 Bolt   26 Selector gate   27 Washer
28 Bolt

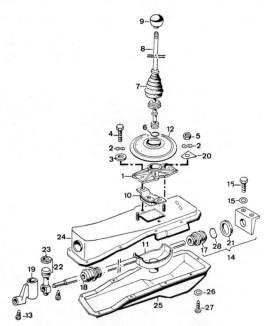

FIG 6:23   The 1973-74 type gearchange linkage

Key to Fig 6:23   1 Bearing shell   2 Washer   3 Washer
4 Bolt   5 Nut   6 Damping ring   7 Boot   8 Lever   9 Knob
10 Stop plate   11 Selector rod   12 Cover   13 Bolt
14 Rear bush and bracket assembly   15 Washer   16 Bolt
17 Bush (rear)   18 Bush (front)   19 Connecting link
20 Washer   21 Ring   22 Gearchange finger   23 Damping
ring   24 Housing   25 Cover   26 Washer   27 Screw
28 Bush ring

4 Fit the dial indicator setup at the cover end as shown
in **FIG 6:21** and, to enable the differential to be
pressed towards or away from the indicator, fit
VW 521/8 and 521/14 (or an equivalent 'handle') at
the outer end.

5 **Without turning the differential,** move the assembly towards and away from the dial indicator and
note the total movement.

6 Shim(s) which in thickness equal this free play plus the
bearing preload of .016 inch (.40 mm) must now be
fitted behind the bearing outer race (the S1 position) in
the drive cover. Remove the cover, press out the outer
race, fit the shim(s) of this thickness, refit the race,
lubricate the bearings with gear oil, refit the cover and
torque tighten the retaining nuts as before.

7 Check that the torque required to turn the differential is,
with new bearings, at least 1.5 lb ft (.21 kg m). If the
original bearings are being re-used, this turning torque
check is not required.

Adjusting final drive backlash:

The thickness of the shim(s) selected at operation 6 of
the 'Adjusting ring gear' procedure (the measured free play
plus the preload of .016 inch (.40 mm) plus the thickness
of the datum shim fitted in the S2 shim position at
operation 2) in total equal the thickness of the final S1 plus
S2 shims. This total thickness is now divided between the
two shim locations. The thickness which is fitted in each

position must be such that the pinion/ring gear backlash is
within a specified range and the proportioning procedure
is as follows.

1 Assemble the gearbox to the differential and final drive
casing, mesh the pinion with the ring gear and retain
with four nuts.

2 Transfer the dial indicator setup to the 'handle' in **FIG
6:21**. Use measuring stalk VW 388 in VW 521/4
(set to 2.677 inch (68 mm) from the VW 521/4 flat)
and block the pinion shaft so that it cannot turn.

3 Measure the backlash at the end of the measuring stalk.
By releasing and relocking the 'handle' and the pinion
shaft block, measure the backlash three further times at
90 degree intervals round the ring gear. These backlash
measurements should not differ by more than .0024
inch (.06 mm). If they do, the installation of the pinion
and/or ring gear is incorrect. Calculate the average of
the four backlash measurements.

4 The final thickness of the S2 shim(s) will be the
thickness of the datum shim (see 'Adjusting the ring
gear') less the average backlash just calculated plus an
allowance which is .006 inch (.15mm).

5 The final thickness of the S1 shim(s) will be the total
thickness of the shims temporarily fitted in the S1 and
S2 positions less the newly determined final thickness
of the S2 shim.

The following tabulation lists the eleven thicknesses of
shims which are available for fitment to the S1 and S2
positions.

Shim part no.	Shim thickness
113 517 201A	.006 inch (.15 mm)
113 517 202A	.008 inch (.20 mm)
113 517 203A	.012 inch (.30 mm)
113 517 204A	.016 inch (.40 mm)
113 517 205A	.020 inch (.50 mm)
113 517 206A	.024 inch (.60 mm)
113 517 207A	.028 inch (.70 mm)
113 517 208A	.031 inch (.80 mm)
113 517 209A	.035 inch (.90 mm)
113 517 210A	.039 inch (1.0 mm)
113 517 211A	.047 inch (1.2 mm)

Install the final thicknesses of S1 and S2, the
speedometer drive and the drive flange oil seal and recheck
the backlash in four places. The backlash readings should
be between .004 and .008 inch (.10 and .20 mm) and
should not differ by more than .002 inch (.05 mm) one to
another.

6:8 Gearchange linkage

The components of the gearchange linkage fitted to
earlier Passat models are shown in **FIG 6:22**. The
components of the linkage fitted to Dasher models and to
some later Passat models in 1973 are shown in **FIG
6:23**, while **FIG 6:24** shows the gearchange mechanism
fitted for 1975. **FIG 6:25** shows the components of the
latest type gearlever assembly. Unless the linkage
has been disturbed, adjustment will not normally
be required but, if difficulty in engaging gear is
experienced, follow the adjustment sequence described
for the relevant type of linkage.

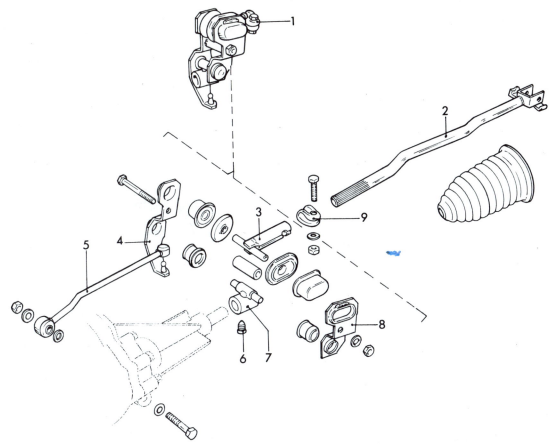

FIG 6:24   Components of the gearchange mechanism as fitted for 1975 models

Key to Fig 6:24   1 Shift rod coupling assembly   2 Shift rod   3 Shift finger   4 Right side plate   5 Support   6 Square head bolt   7 Adaptor   8 Left side plate   9 Clamp

Adjusting early type linkage:

Refer to **FIG 6:22**. Disengage the upper boot 3 and slide it up the gearchange lever. Similarly bring the lower boot 4 out of the way to allow access to loosen the two screws which retain the bearing assembly 16. Press the lever to the right (third and fourth gear plane) as far as it will go and retighten the two screws. Move the lever left and right across neutral. If the lever catches or jams, adjust the selector gate.

To adjust the selector gate, proceed as follows. From beneath the vehicle, loosen the two bolts 28 which retain the selector gate 26. Move the gate forwards or backwards until, by trial and error, a position is found in which the gearchange lever will move smoothly and freely. Retighten the two bolts.

Return the lower and upper boots to their normal positions.

Adjusting 1973 type linkage:

Refer to **FIG 6:23**. Loosen the two nuts 5 which retain the bearing shell 1. Move the bearing shell fore or aft until the gearchange lever has an inclination rearwards of about

5 degrees when in neutral. Retighten the nuts.

Engage second gear (left and rearwards) and loosen the two bolts 4 which retain the stop plate 10. Adjust the plate to allow the knob of the gearchange lever a lateral free play of .40 to .60 inch (10 to 15 mm). Moving the plate towards the right will increase the free play and vice versa. Retighten the two bolts.

Adjustment of the gearchange rod assembly may be required after removal and installation of the transmission. Install the connecting link, slide the rod forwards and move the guide in the elongated holes until the rod is laterally in centre of the hole in the connecting link. Tighten the bolts which secure the rod guide. In the vertical direction, the rod must not be more than .08 inch (2 mm) offcentre in the hole in the connecting link. The rod may now be pulled back to allow the gearchange finger and other parts to be fitted.

Adjusting the 1975 type gearlever:

Place the lever in the neutral position and loosen the clip just forward of the rubber boot, which secures the shift finger to the shift rod.

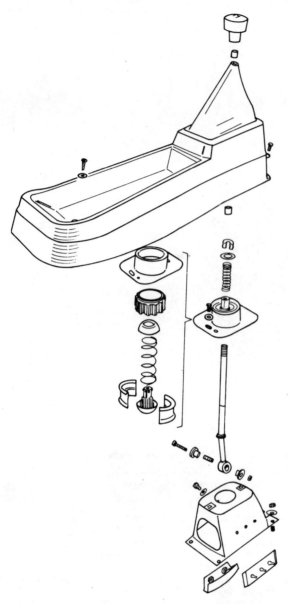

FIG 6:25 The console and gearchange lever components (1975)

Remove the console and then align the two centring holes on the top of the lever housing with those in the lever bearing plate and tighten the two bolts. See **FIG 6:26**.

Place the tool 3009 in position as shown, with the locating pin in the front centring hole and lightly tighten the knurled screw.

With the gearbox selector in neutral, line up the shift rod and the shift finger and secure the clip. Remove the tool 3009.

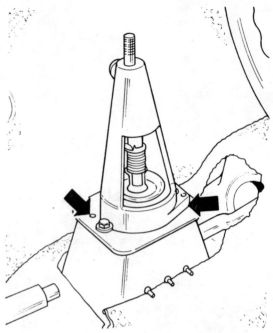

FIG 6:26 Using the jig tool 3009 to adjust the gear-lever position. The arrows indicate the two centring holes

Select all the gears and check for full and easy engagement. Check also the operation of the reverse gear catch. It is permissible at this stage to move the lever bearing plate a little to one side on the housing if necessary.

6:9 Fault diagnosis

(a) Jumping out of gear

1 Gearchange linkage requires adjustment
2 Gearchange linkage worn
3 Interlock parts worn
4 Interlock spring broken
5 Selector rod bore worn
6 Selector fork worn
7 Synchro unit fork groove worn
8 Excessive end play in gearbox
9 Excessively worn synchro unit(s)

(b) Noisy transmission

1 Check (a)
2 Worn or damaged gears
3 Insufficient oil
4 Worn or damaged bearings
5 Worn splines
6 Worn differential components

(c) Difficulty in engaging gear

1 Check 1, 2, 4 and 5 in (a)
2 Synchro rings worn or damaged
3 Defective clutch release cable
4 Clutch requires adjustment
5 Defective clutch

(d) No drive when gear engaged

1 Check 5 in (c)
2 Stripped mainshaft splines
3 Stripped pinion shaft splines

4 Stripped gear teeth
5 Broken mainshaft or pinion shaft

(e) Oil leaks

1 Defective oil seal
2 Defective gasket
3 Damaged joint face(s)
4 Oil level too high
5 Loose drain or filler plug
6 Loose interlock plug
7 Cracked casing or cover

NOTES

CHAPTER 7

THE AUTOMATIC TRANSMISSION

7:1 Description

The front wheel drive transmission incorporates a hydraulic torque converter, a three forward speed and reverse automatic gearbox and a differential and final drive unit. These assemblies are shown in **FIG 7:1**. An exploded view of the differential and final drive unit is shown in **FIG 7:2**. Final drive ratios are given in **Technical Data** in the **Appendix**. A drive shaft connects each final drive flange with a front wheel hub. The drive shafts are covered in **Chapter 8, Sections 8:9** and **8:10** and it should be noted that they are of different lengths.

There are two quite separate lubrication systems and they must not be confused. That for the differential and final drive uses a hypoid gear oil and that for the gearbox and the torque converter uses an automatic transmission fluid. The specification of approved lubricants is covered in **Section 7:2**.

The three forward speeds and reverse are provided by combinations of multi-disc clutches, planetary gears, brake bands and a one-way clutch. These sub-assemblies are shown in **FIG 7:3**. Gear ratios of the gearbox are common to all models and are tabulated in **Technical Data** in the **Appendix**.

Gear selection is by a floor mounted manual control.

Up to September 1975 the gearbox used is the type 003 and this will be described in some detail, although it must be stressed that these units are not suitable for servicing other than by a qualified service station. For 1976 a new gearbox, the 010, and final drive were introduced and those items of interest to the home operator which differ from the earlier type will be described in **Section 7:11**.

Transmission operation:

The selector is a **P, R, N, D, 2, 1** arrangement. A starting inhibitor switch precludes the engine from being started unless the selector lever is in either the **P** or the **N** position. With **D** selected all forward speeds are available and upward and downward gear changes will automatically occur depending upon road gradients and the amount of throttle applied. Kick-down (see later) is available. With **2** selected, the vehicle will move off in first gear and will, depending upon road gradients and the amount of throttle applied, automatically change to second gear or down again to first gear. Kick-down is available. Irrespective of road conditions or throttle position, third gear will not be engaged. With **1** selected, the vehicle will move off in first gear. No gearchanges will occur. Kick-down will not apply. With **R** selected, only reverse drive is available.

With either **N** or **P** selected, the starter inhibitor switch is closed and the engine can be started. In both positions the gearbox is in neutral but, with **P** selected, the front wheels are blocked mechanically by a 'sprag' arrangement within the gearbox.

When the accelerator pedal is depressed beyond the full throttle position, the contacts of the kick-down switch are closed, a solenoid is energized and, subject to the road speed, an immediate gearchange occurs and provides maximum acceleration performance. The road speed at which both normal and kick-down upwards and downwards gear changes should occur are tabulated in **Section 7:3.**

7:2 Maintenance

Lubrication:

There are two lubrication systems. HD90 hypoid gear oil of a reputable brand is used in the differential and final drive and automatic transmission fluid ATF Dexron B10 of

reputable brand is used in the torque converter and automatic gearbox. There is normally no intercommunication between the two systems and should the level in one rise and in the other fall, it will be evident that leakage from one to the other is occuring. A defective gasket 12 in **FIG 7:1** or a defective seal 39 in **FIG 7:2** will be found to be the reason for this leakage.

Final drive oil level:

Every 5000 miles (8000 km), check the final drive oil level and top up if necessary. The filler plug is socket-

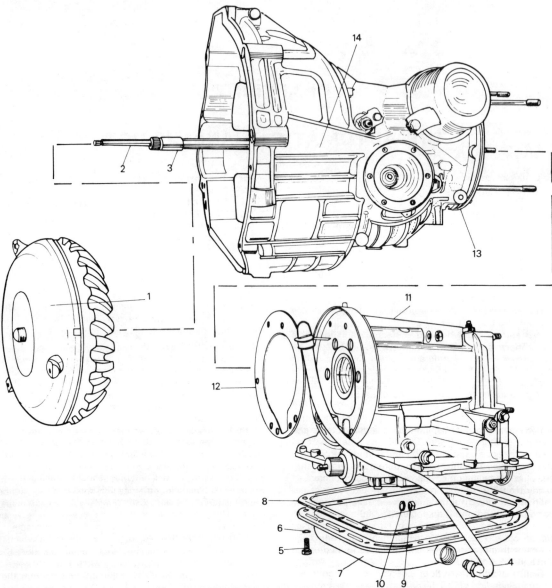

FIG 7:1   The main sections of the automatic transmission

Key to Fig 7:1   1 Torque converter   2 Impeller shaft   3 Turbine shaft   4 Dipstick/filler tube   5 Bolt   6 Washer
7 Sump   8 Gasket   9 Nut   10 Washer   11 Gearbox   12 Gasket   13 'O' ring   14 Differential and final drive

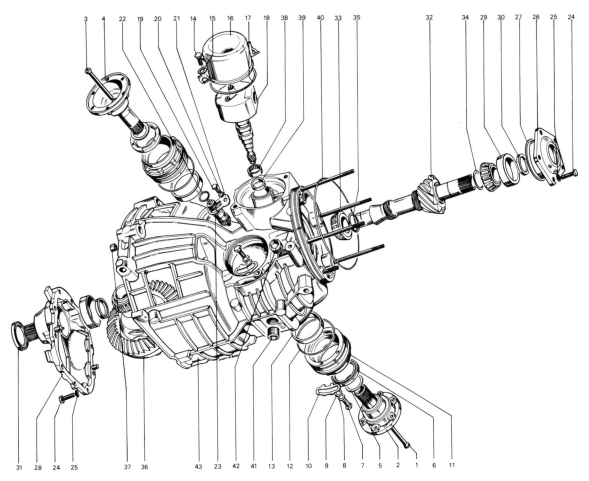

FIG 7:2 Exploded view of differential and final drive

Key to Fig 7:2 1 Bolt 2 Drive flange 3 Bolt 4 Drive flange 5 Shim 6 Seal 7 Bolt 8 Washer 9 Washer 10 Lockplate 11 Adjusting ring 12 'O' ring 13 Outer race 14 Bolt 15 Washer 16 Cap 17 'O' ring 18 Governor 19 Bolt 20 Washer 21 Lockplate 22 'O' ring 23 Speedometer pinion assembly 24 Bolt 25 Washer 26 Rear cover plate 27 'O' ring 28 Front cover plate (with one-way clutch support) 29 Outer race 30 Seal 31 Seal 32 Pinion shaft 33 Inner race 34 S3 shim 35 S4 shim 36 Differential sub-assembly 37 Bush 38 Needle bearing 39 Seal 40 'O' ring 41 Drain plug 42 Filler plug 43 Final drive casing

headed and is located in the lefthand side of the final drive casing. It is 42 in **FIG 7:2.**

Clean off around the filler plug before removing it. The correct level is when the oil is just up to the bottom of the filler plug orifice. It is inadvisable to mix oils of different brands and the oil used for topping up should be the same brand as that already in the final drive. If it is proposed to change the brand of oil, do so at a 30,000 mile (50,000 km) interval when, as described later, the old oil is being drained off and discarded. On refitment, the filler plug should be torque tightened to 18 lb ft (2.5 kg m).

Draining the final drive:

Every 30,000 miles (50,000 km), drain off and discard the oil from the final drive. This should preferably be carried out when the oil is warm after a run. The socket-headed drain plug is in the bottom of the final drive casing

and is 41 in **FIG 7:2.** Position a suitable tray below the drain plug, clean off round the drain plug and the filler plug, remove both plugs and allow the old oil to drain off thoroughly. The drain plug incorporates a magnet which will retain steel particles and these should be cleaned off. If, rather than particles, there should be evidence of debris, investigation of its source is indicated.

Filling the final drive:

When the old oil has completely drained off, refit the drain plug and tighten it to a torque of 18 lb ft (2.5 kg m). Use a hypoid HD90 gear oil of reputable brand and fill the final drive to the level of the bottom of the filler plug orifice. Fit and tighten the filler plug as described earlier.

The quantity of oil required is approximately $1\frac{3}{4}$ pints (1 litre).

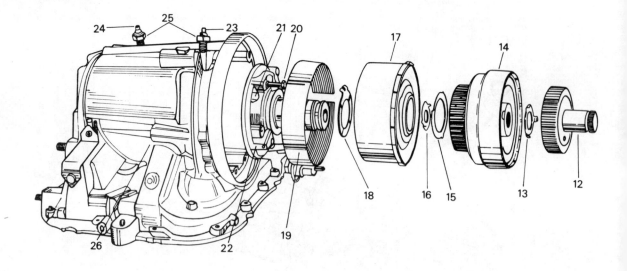

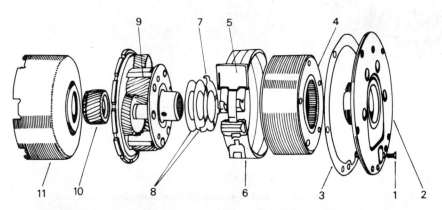

FIG 7:3 Exploded view of gearbox mechanical parts

Key to Fig 7:3 1 Screw   2 Bearing flange   3 Gasket   4 Annulus gear with one-way clutch   5 Fork   6 First gear brake band   7 Thrust washer   8 Shim   9 Planetary gear set   10 Sun gear   11 Driving shell   12 Clutch hub   13 Thrust washer   14 Forward clutch   15 Thrust washer   16 Thrust washer   17 Direct and reverse clutch   18 Thrust washer   19 Second gear brake band   20 Bolt   21 Washer   22 Pump   23 First brake band adjusting screw   24 Second brake band adjusting screw   25 Locknut   26 Gearbox casing

Transmission fluid level:

The fluid level should be maintained between the two marks on the dipstick. The quantity of fluid which is required to raise the level from the lower to the upper mark is approximately 1 pint (.6 litre).

Carry out the following fluid level check when the transmission is warm. The fluid temperature should be between 40°C and 60°C (100°F and 140°F).

With the selector lever in the **N** position, apply the handbrake firmly. With the engine running at idling speed, withdraw and wipe off the dipstick. Re-insert it fully and check the level. Use a clean funnel and a length (approximately 24 inches (50 cm) will be required) of hose to top up the level through the dipstick tube. Use only approved fluid, ATF Dexron B10 of reputable brand.

Transmission fluid draining:

Every 30,000 miles (50,000 km) drain off and discard the transmission fluid. This should be carried out when the transmission is warm after a run. Refer to **FIG 7:1**, position a tray and uncouple the dipstick/filler pipe 4 from the gearbox sump. When the fluid has drained off, remove the twelve retaining bolts 5 and washers 6 and drop the sump 7. Discard the gasket 8. Remove the screw and washer which retains the gauze strainer to the transfer plate and dismount the strainer. Clean the strainer and the interior of the sump with petrol and dry off with compressed air. Refitment of the sump is described in **Section 7:6**. A new gasket 8 is essential.

Pour $4\frac{1}{2}$ pints (2.5 litres) of ATF into the dipstick/filler tube. Run the engine to warm up the fluid. With the vehicle stationary and the handbrake firmly applied, engage, successively, all positions of the selector lever. Check the fluid level and, if necessary, top up as described earlier.

Since some $4\frac{1}{2}$ pints (2.5 litre) of fluid remain in the torque converter and about 1 to $1\frac{3}{4}$ pints (.5 to 1 litre) remain in the gearbox, the volume required for this refilling procedure differs from the quantity required when the torque converter has been emptied as described in **Section 7:7** and the gearbox has been dismantled.

7:3 Tests

Before proceeding with either the stationary or the road testing of the vehicle, check and if necessary, top up the fluid level as described in **Section 7:2**. Confirm that the idling speed is within the limits specified in **Chapter 2, Section 2:2** for the relevant model. Check, as described in **Chapter 3, Sections 3:2, 3:6** and **3:7,** that the sparking plugs are in good condition, that their gaps are correctly set, that the ignition distributor points gap is also correctly set and that the ignition timing is in order. Poor engine condition must not be allowed to confuse the following tests.

Stationary tests:

The following tests are carried out with the vehicle stationary. An engine operated tachometer is essential for stall speed testing.

Kick-down switch:

Switch on the ignition but do not start the engine. Depress the accelerator pedal fully (beyond the full throttle position). The kick-down solenoid in the gearbox should be heard to click as its armature is energized. If no engagement can be heard, refer to **Section 7:4.**

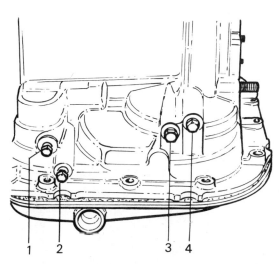

FIG 7:4 Pressure take-off points

Key to Fig 7:4   1 Main pressure   2 Primary throttle pressure   3 Main pressure release side of second brake band   4 Main pressure apply side of second brake band

Starting inhibitor switch:

1 With the selector lever in the **P** position, confirm that the starter motor will operate when the ignition key is turned to the start position.
2 Repeat this check with the selector lever in the **N** position.
3 Successively select each drive position, turn the ignition key to the start position and, in each case, confirm that the starter motor will not operate.

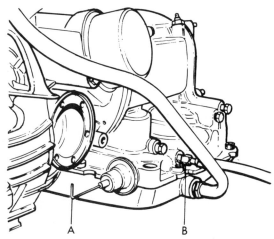

FIG 7:5   Primary throttle pressure adjustment

Key to Fig 7:5   A Allen key in vacuum unit adjuster   B Primary throttle pressure take-off point

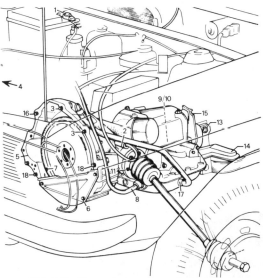

FIG 7:6   Transmission removal operations

Key to Fig 7:6   1 Battery earth connection   2 Speedometer drive cable   3 Bolts   4 Exhaust pipe flange   5 Starter motor   6 Cover plate   7 Bolts   8 Vacuum hose   9 Selector cable   10 Kick-down solenoid connection   11 Drive shaft socket-headed bolts   12 Lefthand ball joint   13 Exhaust pipe bracket   14 Transmission carrier   15 Transmission support   16 Bolt   17 Dipstick/filler pipe   18 Bolt

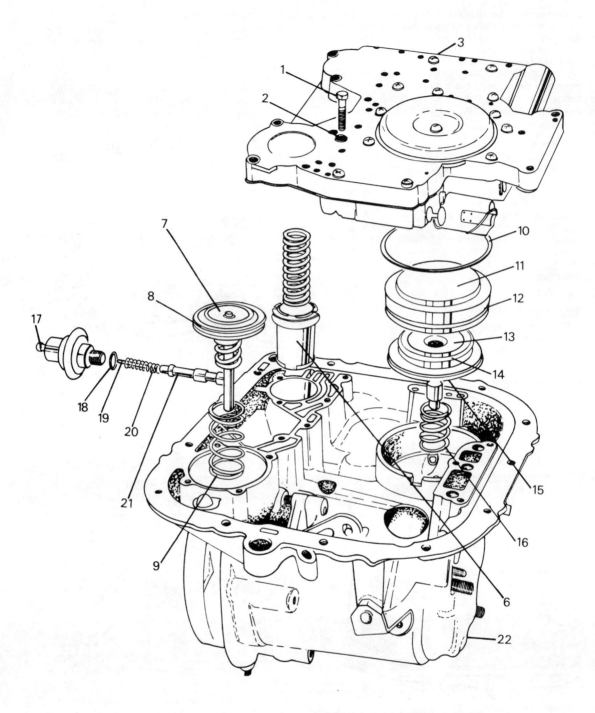

FIG 7:7   Exploded view of valve and piston assembly

Key to Fig 7:7   1 Bolt (see **FIG 7:9**)   2 Washer   3 Valve assembly plate   4 Accumulator spring   5 Accumulator piston
6 Seal   7 First band brake piston and spring   8 Seal   9 First band brake return spring   10 Circlip   11 Cover   12 'O' ring
13 Piston   14 Second band brake piston seal   15 Second band brake piston seal   16 Second band brake return spring
17 Vacuum unit   18 Ring (aluminium)   19 Pin   20 Primary throttle pressure valve spring   21 Primary throttle pressure valve
22 Gearbox casing

If the starting operation is not as specified in these tests, refer to the adjustment procedure which is described in **Section 7:4**.

Selector lever settings:

1 Select **N** and start the engine. With the engine running at fast idling (1000 to 1200 rev/min), apply the footbrake firmly, move the lever to the **R** position and notice if there is transmission of power and a drop in engine speed.

2 Move the lever to the **P** position. Engine speed should increase as an indication that reverse drive has disengaged. Press the lever against the stop in the direction of **R**. An indication of premature reverse drive engagement will be shown if the engine speed drops.

3 Repeat operation 1. Move the lever to the **N** position. Engine speed should increase as an indication that reverse drive has disengaged.

4 Move the lever to the **D** position. Transmission of power and a drop in engine speed must be noticeable.

5 Move the lever to the **1** position. The lever must engage without first having to overcome any resistance.

6 Refer to **Section 7:10** for any adjustment which may be indicated by these tests.

Stall speed:

If not already fitted, a tachometer must be wired into the ignition circuit temporarily and positioned so that it can be read from the driver's seat.

The stall speed is the maximum rev/min at which the engine can drive the torque converter impeller while the turbine is held stationary. Stall testing provides an indication of both engine and transmission efficiency.

With the engine oil and the transmission fluid levels correct, select **P** and run the engine until the converter fluid is at normal operating temperature (see **Section 7:2**). Chock the road wheels, apply the handbrake firmly and, while carrying out stall tests, apply the brakes with the left foot.

1 Select **D** and gradually depress the accelerator pedal until full throttle is reached. As soon as a steady engine speed is obtained, quickly note the rev/min. **Do not hold the stall speed for more than 5 seconds without carrying out operation 2.**

2 Release the accelerator pedal, select **N** and run the engine at approximately 1200 rev/min for some minutes to allow the torque converter to cool.

If the stall speed recorded is within the range of 1900 to 2200 rev/min, the engine and transmission are in good order. Note, however, that per 3000 ft (1000 m) of test location altitude, there will be a reduction of 125 rev/min in the acceptable stall speed. Note also that if the ambient temperature is high there will be a slight additional reduction in the acceptable stall speed. If, on the other hand, the ambient temperature is low, a slight increase in the stall speed should be anticipated.

If the stall speed is low by about 200 rev/min (after making allowance for altitude and ambient temperature), poor engine performance is indicated.

If the stall speed is low by about 400 rev/min (after making allowance for altitude and ambient temperature), a defective one-way torque converter clutch is indicated.

If the stall speed is high, either a slipping forward clutch or a slipping first speed one-way clutch is indicated.

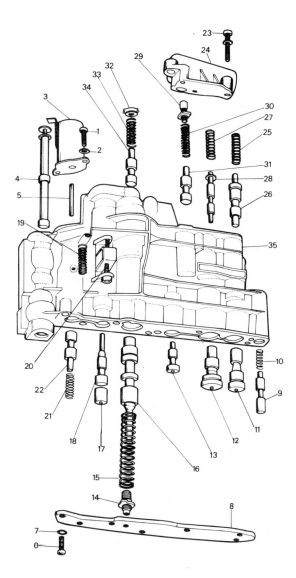

FIG 7:8 **Exploded view of valve body assembly**

Key to Fig 7:8   1 Screw   2 Washer   3 Solenoid
4 Manual valve   5 Plunger   6 Screw   7 Washer   8 Rear end plate   9 Part throttle valve **3-2**   10 Part throttle valve spring   11 Plug **2-3**   12 Plug **1-2**   13 Control valve **3-2** 14 Adjusting screw with spring seat   15 Main regulating spring   16 Main regulating valve   17 First gear plunger/ secondary throttle pressure valve   18 Secondary throttle pressure valve   19 Secondary throttle pressure spring 20 Adjusting screw (**do not disturb setting**)   21 Kick-down valve spring   22 Kick-down valve   23 Screw and washer   24 **3-2** accumulator   25 **2-3** valve spring   26 **2-3** valve   27 **1-2** valve spring   28 **1-2** valve with spring seat 29 Adjusting screw with spring seat (**do not disturb setting**) 30 Throttle pressure limiting spring   31 Throttle pressure limiting valve   32 Spring cup, converter pressure valve 33 Converter pressure spring   34 Converter pressure valve 35 Valve body

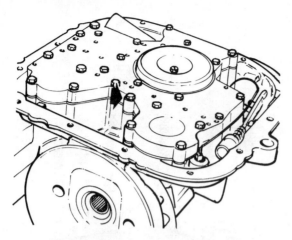

FIG 7:9   Removing valve assembly plate

lb/sq in (0 to 10 kg/sq cm) pressure gauge will be required together with suitable connectors and flexible hoses (the official tool set is Matra V-90). The two pressure take-off points are identified in **FIG 7:4**. Connect the zero to 350 lb/sq in (0 to 25 kg/sq cm) gauge to point 1 and the zero to 140 lb/sq in (0 to 10 kg/sq cm) gauge to point 2. Proceed as follows.

1 Refer to **FIG 7:5** and remove the vacuum hose. Blank off the open end of the hose with a suitable plug.
2 Run the engine at 1000 rev/min and note both pressure readings. The primary throttle pressure should be 42 lb/sq in (3 kg/sq cm) and the main pressure should be 85 lb/sq in (6 kg/sq cm).
3 If necessary, adjust the primary throttle pressure to 42 lb/sq in (3 kg/sq cm) as described in **Section 7:4** before proceeding with further pressure tests.
4 Reconnect the vacuum hose. The primary throttle pressure should increase to 50 to 60 lb/sq in (3.5 to 4.5 kg/sq cm).
5 Engage **R** and maintain the idling sped at 1000 rev/min. The main pressure should be between 153 and 167 lb/sq in (10.7 and 11.7 kg/sq cm) with the vacuum hose on.
6 Engage **D**. Proceed as for stall speed testing (see earlier in this Section) and, with the vacuum hose on, run at full throttle for the minimum time required to record the primary throttle pressure which should be between 38 and 42 lb/sq in (2.7 and 3 kg/sq cm) and the main pressure which should be 85 lb/sq in (6 kg/sq cm). Allow the torque converter to cool off before proceeding.
7 Engage **R**. Proceed as for stall speed testing and note the main pressure. This should be between 234 and 305 lb/sq in (16.5 and 21.5 kg/sq cm).
8 If the main pressures are not in line with the figures quoted, refer to **Section 7:11**.

Unless the owner has experience of fault diagnosis in automatic transmissions, he should, if stall tests appear to indicate serious trouble, consult an Agent before proceeding further.

Pressure tests:

Pressure tests should only be carried out if other diagnosis tests have failed to determine the cause of a fault. All other stationary vehicle tests and road testing should first be performed and only if after completing them without being able to diagnose the fault should the following pressure tests be carried out. A zero to 350 lb/sq in (0 to 25 kg/sq cm) pressure gauge and a zero to 140

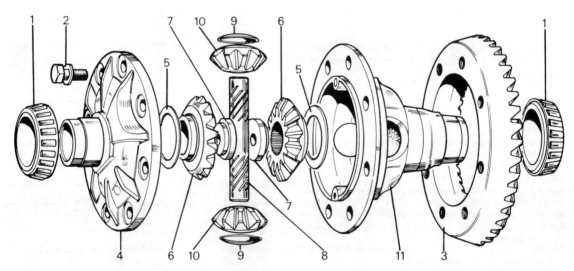

FIG 7:10   Components of the differential

Key to Fig 7:10   1 Bearing inner race   2 Bolt and washer*   3 Crown wheel   4 Differential housing cover   5 Washer
6 Side gear   7 Nut   8 Shaft   9 Washer   10 Pinion   11 Differential housing

Note: Special toothed bolts without the spring washer are used on later cars. These must also be used after any dismantling and tightened to a torque of 50 lb ft (7 kg m)

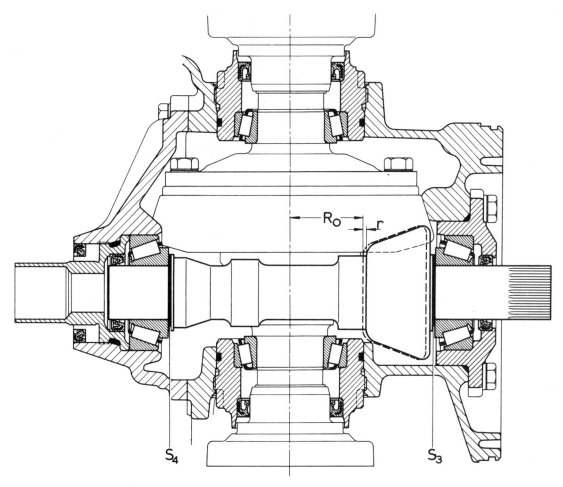

FIG 7:11 The pinion adjusting shims and the ring gear adjusting rings

Key to Fig 7:11 S4 Pinion positioning shim   S3 Bearing preload shim R_o Gauge dimension (40.55 mm)   r Deviation of pinion from standard

Road tests:

Unless an owner has experience in the diagnosis of automatic transmission faults he may have difficulty in interpreting test results. Reference should be made to the tabulation in **Section 7:11** and, if the fault(s) cannot be readily defined, the advice of an Agent should be sought. Road testing of the vehicle should cover all speed ranges and a full variety of uphill and downhill gradients.

Note gearchange points for both upward and downward changes. Changes should take place smoothly but smartly and without interruption of power flow. Note any lack of smoothness, irregular drive or absence of drive. Listen for any indication of the engine speeding up during changes as this implies slipping clutches or brake bands. In addition to normal driving right up to full throttle conditions, check downward and upward kick-down points. Check that, when the throttle is released, engine braking occurs on downhill gradients and that there is no 'free wheeling'.

With an engine of normal performance, changes should occur within the speed ranges given in the following tabulations.

Passat S and LS models

Gearchange	Full throttle miles/hr	Kick-down miles/hr
1 to 2	19 to 21	28 to 35
2 to 3	50 to 55	57 to 62
3 to 2	33 to 38	55 to 59
2 to 1	14 to 15	27 to 34
Passat TS models		
1 to 2	20 to 22	32 to 40
2 to 3	55 to 60	62 to 68
3 to 2	37 to 42	60 to 65
2 to 1	15 to 16	31 to 38
Dasher models		
1 to 2	19 to 22	31 to 40
2 to 3	53 to 61	60 to 68
3 to 2	34 to 42	58 to 64
2 to 1	13 to 16	29 to 37

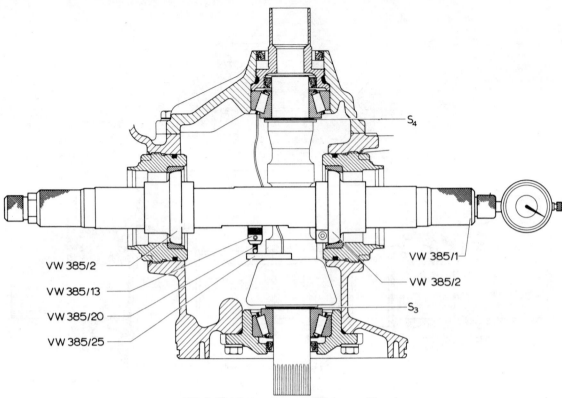

FIG 7:12   Determining the pinion position

7:4 Adjustments

Kick-down switch:

The switch is attached to a bracket under the accelerator pedal. To remove a defective switch, disconnect the pedal from its lever, detach the bracket from the floor plate, disconnect the wiring and remove the switch from the bracket. Fitment of a new switch is the reverse of this sequence. Confirm that, when the pedal is depressed fully, the switch operates.

Inhibitor switch:

Access to the switch requires removal of the selector lever console as described in **Section 7:10**. The contact plate is retained by two screws. Loosening these screws allows the plate to be moved in its elongated holes. Adjustment is by trial and error until only with the selector lever in **N,** or **P** will the starter operate. A defective switch should be removed and a new replacement fitted.

Selector lever settings:

Refer to **Section 7:10**.

Primary throttle pressure:

Refer to 'Pressure tests' in **Section 7:3**, fit the pressure gauge and carry out operations 1 and 2. Refer to **FIG 7:5**

and, with the engine running at 1000 to 1200 rev/min, use an Allen key (2.5 mm size) as shown at **A** to adjust the primary throttle pressure to 42 lb/sq in (3 kg/sq cm). Proceed with the pressure tests as described in **Section 7:3**.

Throttle cable adjustment:

When the throttle valve is in the fully open position the cable should be so adjusted that there is a clearance of 5 to 8 mm ($\frac{3}{16}$ to $\frac{5}{16}$ inch) between the accelerator pedal and the kick-down switch.

7:5 Removing and installing the transmission

The transmission can be removed without disturbing the engine. As the transmission must be lowered out, the vehicle must be raised on stands or positioned over a pit. At least two (preferably three) operators are required for the final removal operations and for the initial installation operations.

Removal:

The order of numbering in **FIG 7:6** indicates the sequence in which the removal operations should be performed.

1 With the vehicle raised on stands or positioned over a pit, disconnect the battery cable 1. Withdraw the speedometer cable drive 2. Remove the two upper engine/transmission bolts 3.

2 Detach the exhaust pipe from the engine manifold. Refer to **Chapter 12, Section 12:4** and remove the starter motor 5. Remove the converter cover plate 6.

3 Remove the three bolts 7 which retain the torque converter to the drive plate. Remove hose 8 from the transmission vacuum unit.

4 Refer to **Section 7:10** and disconnect the control cable from the selector lever 9. Disconnect the kick-down wiring 10.

5 Refer to **Chapter 8, Section 8:9** and remove the six socket-headed bolts which retain the drive shaft inner flanges (11 in **FIG 7:6**). Disengage and suitably support the inner end of the righthand drive shaft.

6 To give clearance for the lefthand drive shaft, refer to **Chapter 8, Section 8:9** and carry out operation 4 of the shaft removal procedure. Swing the wheel hub assembly outwards. This covers 12 in **FIG 7:6**.

7 Remove bolt 13 which attaches the exhaust pipe bracket to the transmission support. Detach the bonded rubber mounting and floor plate from the transmission carrier 14. The assembly will drop at the rear but no support is necessary.

8 Remove three nuts 15 and dismount the transmission support. Remove bolt 16. Drain the transmission 17 as described in **Section 7:2** (if this was not done earlier).

9 With the transmission supported and the torque converter secured from separating from the assembly either by tool 32-200 or by a third operator, remove the two remaining engine/transmission bolts 18 and lower and withdraw the complete transmission assembly.

Installation:

The installation sequence is the reverse of that described for removing the assembly. Torque tighten all engine/transmission bolts (18, 16 and 3 in **FIG 7:6**) to 40 lb ft (5.5 kg m). The nut which retains the transmission support floor plate should be tightened to a torque of 22 lb ft (3 kg m) and those which attach the floor plate should be torque tightened to 29 lb ft (4 kg m). Tighten the exhaust/transmission bracket bolt to 14 lb ft (2 kg m). Refer to **Chapter 8, Section 8:9** when refitting the righthand drive shaft and to **Sections 8:4** and **8:9** and, if necessary, to **Section 8:11** when refitting the lefthand drive shaft. Tighten the torque converter drive plate bolts to a torque of 10 lb ft (1.5 kg m). Refer to **Chapter 12, Section 12:4** when refitting the starter motor. Tighten the exhaust pipe to engine manifold nuts to a torque of 18 lb ft (2.5 kg m). Adjustment of the selector linkage is covered in **Section 7:10**.

7:6 Dismantling and reassembling the transmission

Following the removal of the complete transmission assembly as described in **Section 7:5**, the sections of the transmission are separated into separate assemblies by following the numerical order of the numbering of the parts shown in **FIG 7:1**.

Dismantling:

1 Take great care not to damage the bore of the torque converter hub when withdrawing it from the turbine and impeller shafts 2 and 3. Withdraw the shafts.

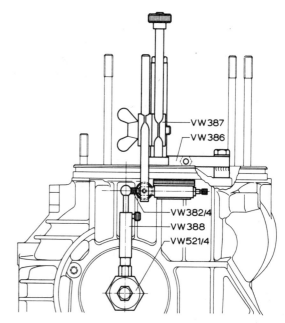

FIG 7:13   Measuring the pinion/ring gear backlash

2 Remove the dipstick/filler tube 4 if this was not done earlier and drain off the transmission fluid. Drain off the final drive oil also if this was not done earlier. Remove twelve bolts and washers 5 and 6, remove the sump 7 and discard the gasket 8.

3 Remove five nuts and washers 9 and 10 which retain the gearbox to the differential and final drive casing. One nut and washer is located inside the gearbox casing.

4 Separate the gearbox 11 from the final drive casing 14. Remove the O-ring 13. Remove and discard the gasket 12.

Reassembly:

The procedure for reassembling the units ready for reinstallation of the transmission follows the separation sequence in reverse. Note the following points however.

Use a new gasket 12 and, if there is any doubt about its condition, fit a new O-ring 13. Working diagonally, torque tighten the sump retaining nuts to 7 lb ft (1 kg m) and, after intervals of five to ten minutes, repeat this torque tightening at least three times. This is necessary because the new gasket settles. **Do not attempt to speed up this process by increasing the tightening torque.** Ensure that the impeller shaft is inserted fully.   Ensure also that, when fitting the torque converter, the pump shaft is inserted to the full depth of the pump splines.

7:7 The torque converter

The converter is a sealed unit and cannot be repaired by an owner. An internally defective converter must be removed and replaced by a new unit.

Hub bush:

The internal diameter of the bush in a new converter is 1.347 to 1.375 inch (34.025 to 34.095 mm) and the recommended wear limit is 1.436 inch (34.25 mm) dia. with an ovality limit of .0012 inch (.03 mm).

An unserviceable bush may be extracted and a new bush pressed in. The bore of the new bush is factory finished and does not require to be finally machined in position. It is important that the chamfer for the seal is rounded, free of sharp edges and burrs and that the face where the seal is in contact with the hub is undamaged. Take great care when fitting the silicone seal. It is very soft and easily damaged. **On no account should the seal be allowed to come in contact with petrol or any other cleaning agent.** Dip the seal in transmission fluid and, using mandrel VW 192, drive it in as far as it will go.

Draining off fluid:

The draining procedure described in **Section 7:2** leaves about $4\frac{1}{2}$ pints (2.5 litre) of fluid in the converter. If a gearbox failure or a burnt clutch has contaminated the fluid, some $3\frac{1}{2}$ to 4 pints of this can be siphoned off using a suitable bung (fitted with two tubes) in the hub bore. Lay the converter on a bench with its front face downwards. Use compressed air to start the siphon and let the converter drain for at least twelve hours.

7:8 The gearbox

Unless an owner has experience of automatic gearboxes, he should not attempt to strip down, repair and rebuild a defective gearbox himself but should pass it to a competent Agent for rectification. The information given in this Section is, consequently, intended to assist an experienced automobile engineer with knowledge of automatic gearboxes to investigate internal faults.

The components shown in **FIG 7:3** are numbered in the order in which the mechanical parts and sub-assemblies should be dismantled. Similarly, **FIGS 7:7** and **7:8** are numbered in the order in which the control components shown should be removed. Supplement this general sequence rule by making notes and sketches as advised in Hints on Maintenance and Overhaul in the **Appendix**. In each case the reassembly order is, substantially, the dismantling sequence in reverse.

The multi-disc clutches, oil pump, one-way clutch, brake band clutches, etc. are, for their type, all of conventional design and construction. Clearances and end play figures are typical for gearboxes of this type.

Identification of springs may be troublesome and, in case of difficulty, reference should be made to the tabulation given at the end of this section. The number after each spring title corresponds with the component numbers in **FIG 7:8**.

When adjusting the brake bands, keep the gearbox horizontal or jamming of the bands may occur. Except for the amount by which the adjuster is backed off, the procedure for adjusting is the same for both bands. Tighten each band to a torque of 7 lb ft (1 kg m), slacken off, retighten to half this torque and, in the case of the second gear adjuster, back off by exactly $2\frac{1}{2}$ turns. In the case of the first gear band, back off by $3\frac{1}{4}$ to $3\frac{1}{2}$ turns. Tighten the locknuts to 14 lb ft (2 kg m).

Spring identification:

Description	Part No.	Coils	Wire diameter mm (inch)	Free length mm (inch)	Inner diameter of coil mm (inch)
Main pressure valve spring 15	003 325 131 A	16.5	1.5 (.059)	71.6 (2.819)	11.9 (.468)
Secondary throttle pressure valve spring 19	003 325 157 B	11.5	.85 (.033)	27.7 (1.091)	7.35 (.288)
Kick-down valve spring 21	003 325 175	10.5	.63 (.024)	23.8 (.936)	7.7 (.302)
2–3 valve spring 25	003 325 207	10.5	.8 (.031)	29.2 (1.150)	8.2 (.323)
1–2 valve spring 27	003 325 207	10.5	.8 (.031)	29.2 (1.150)	8.2 (.323)
Throttle pressure limiting valve spring 30	003 325 227 B	12.5	1.0 (.039)	31.0 (1.220)	7.7 (.302)
Converter pressure valve spring 33	003 325 247	9.5	1.25 (.048)	27.3 (1.073)	8.13 (.319)
Spring·Part throttle valve 10	003 325 129	6.5	.4 (.015)	18.1 (.713)	6.1 (.240)
Pressure relief valve spring (between valve body and separator plate)	003 325 267	15.5	.8 (.031)	27.7 (1.064)	4.7 (.184)
Spring 2–3 and valve 3–2	003 325 269	4.5	.2 (.007)	5.8 (.227)	4.3 (.168)
Primary throttle pressure valve spring	003 325 295	10.5	.63 (.024)	36.3 (1.428)	9.0 (.354)
3–2 accumulator spring	003 325 233 B	14.0	2.0 (.079)	61.7 (2.429)	11.6 (.457)

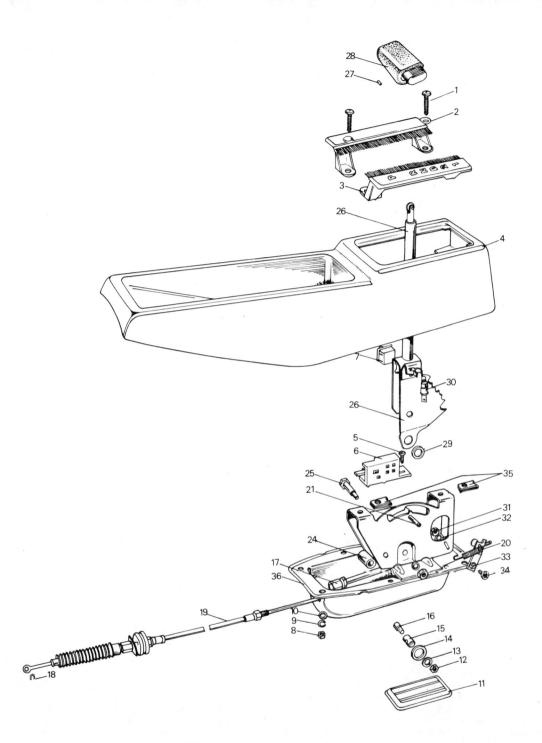

FIG 7:14 The selector linkage

Key to Fig 7:14   1 Screw   2 Washer   3 Strip   4 Console   5 Screw   6 Starter inhibitor switch   7 Contact bridge
8 Nut   9 Washer   10 Washer   11 Cover plate   12 Nut   13 Washer   14 Rubber washer   15 Sleeve   16 Pin
17 Nut   18 Retainer   19 Cable   20 Spring   21 Threaded pin   22 Nut   23 Spring   24 Sleeve   25 Bolt   26 Lever
and segment   27 Socket-headed pin   28 T-grip   29 Bush   30 Bulb (strip illumination)   31 Nut   32 Washer   33 Pawl
34 Screw   35 Nut   36 Bracket

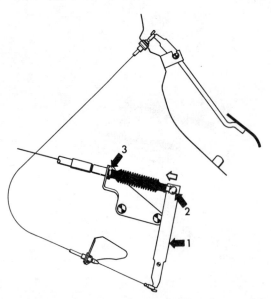

FIG 7:15 Adjusting the accelerator cable on 1976 models

Key to Fig 7:15 1 Operating lever 2 Ball joint 3 Nut

Where relevant, a range of shims of different thicknesses are available and, in the case of the multi-plate clutches, different thicknesses of retaining circlips.

When removing the valve assembly plate 3 in **FIG 7:7**, refer to **FIG 7:9** and leave the arrowed bolt until after the other fourteen have been removed. On reassembly, fit the arrowed bolt first.

7:9 Differential and final drive

Because of the number of special tools and fixtures which are required and because certain components have to be heated to provide shrink fits, it is recommended that an owner should entrust a competent Agent with major rectifications and should not himself attempt more than minor dismantling operations for the fitment of items (such as, for example, seal 39 in **FIG 7:2**) which do not require extensive stripping down. If, however, an owner has to go further than this, the following points should be noted.

The order in which components should be removed when the differential and final drive assembly is to be completely dismantled is the sequence in which the components are numbered in **FIG 7:2** and, for the differential subassembly, in **FIG 7:10**. The two adjusting rings (the righthand ring is 11 in **FIG 7:2**) position the differential subassembly 36 in relation to the pinion gear 32 and it is essential that their settings are precisely recorded so that, on reassembly, it will not be necessary (unless critical new components have had to be fitted) to carry out the backlash adjustment procedure.

When new critical components have had to be fitted, it will be necessary to adjust the position of the pinion and to reset the backlash. Reference to **FIG 7:11** will show that the pinion position is controlled by the S3 shims while the bearing preload and setting allowance is applied by the S4

shims. **FIG 7:12** shows the setup for measuring the pinion setting. It will be seen from **FIG 7:11** that the position of the differential subassembly (and therefore the meshing of the ring gear with the pinion) is adjustable by repositioning the two adjusting rings which carry the bearings on which this subassembly runs. **FIG 7:13** shows the setup for measuring the backlash. The measuring stalk VW 388 must be set to 2.441 inch (62 mm) from the flat of VW 521/4. The procedure is similar to that described in **Chapter 6, Section 6:7**.

Pinion bearing preload should be .007 inch (.18 mm) and the setting allowance to be added is .004 inch (.10 mm). From zero backlash, turn the righthand adjusting ring back by $\frac{1}{2}$ tooth division. Screw the lefthand adjusting ring in by 2 tooth divisions (this also applies to the bearing preload). Check the backlash (see **FIG 7:13**). It should be between .006 and .010 inch (.15 and .25 mm) dial indicator measurement and four measurements round the ring gear should not differ by more than .002 inch (.05 mm).

7:10 The selector linkage

A Bowden type cable links the manual selector lever with the control lever on the gearbox. The components of the linkage are shown in **FIG 7:14** and are numbered in the order in which they should be removed if the complete linkage is being dismounted.

Access to the starter inhibitor switch requires the console to be lifted away after first removing screws 1, washers 2 and strips 3.

Adjust the cable, when necessary, with the manual selector lever in the **P** position. Check that the lever is correctly engaged and loosen the cable clamp nut at the bottom of the lever. Press the gearbox lever fully rearwards against the spring load and up to the stop (pliers should be used). Hold the gearbox lever in this position and tighten the cable clamp nut at the selector lever. Check all lever positions as described in **Section 7:3**.

Later (1975) models:

In early 1975 the transmission tunnel was widened and this necessitated a modification to the selector linkage in which the cable clamp can be reached only inside the car. To adjust this linkage, one operator must be under the car pressing the transmission selector lever to the P position while another holds the manual lever in P and secures the cable.

7:11 Later (1976) type transmission

On this later type of automatic transmission the differences likely to interest the home operator are in the gear selector linkage and the throttle cable adjustments. In place of the vacuum controlled selection of gear ratios in the box a mechanical linkage is used, and a mechanical actuation of the kick-down takes the place of the electrical system on the earlier models.

Selector lever linkage:

The selector quadrant no longer has a toothed segment for the positive location of the selector lever and no pawl and ratchet mechanism is necessary as the function

Fault or defective part — *Selector lever position* — *Gear or defect*

Probable cause of fault. Numerals relate to key list

Fault or defective part	Selector lever position	Gear or defect	1	2	3	4	5	6	7	8	9	10	11	12	13	14	15	16	17	18	19	20	21	22	23	24	25	26	27	28	29	30	31	32	33	34	35	36	37	38	39	40	41	42	43	44	45	46	47	48	49	50	51	52	53	54	55	56
No drive	R, D, 2, 1	All gears			●					*																*																			*														
	D, 2, 1	Forward gears																																																					×	×			×	×
	D, 2	1st gear																																												×										×	×			×
	1	1st gear (deceleration)																														×	×	×																									
	D	3rd gear																																																										
	R	Reverse																														×	×									*								×	×					×			
	R, D, 2, 1	Wheels locked																																							*									×	×								
Irregular drive	D, 2	All forward gears			●																			*		*																																	
	1	1st gear			●																			*		*																																	
	R	Reverse			●																			*		*																																	
No upward gearchange	D, 2	Into 2nd gear				●										*	*	*	*				*	*	*	*		*		*		×				×	×															*						
	D	Into 3rd gear				●												*							*		*		*			×				×	×															*						
	D	Kick-down into 2nd and 3rd gear													*	*	*	*	*	●																																							
No downward gearchange	D	Into 2nd gear																	*							*		*		*		×																											
	1	Into 1st gear																	*							*		*		*			×																										
Gearchange takes place	D, 2	Below normal speeds														*	*			●		*				*																																	
	D, 2	Above normal speeds													*	*	*	*	*	●		*				*																			×														
	D	Delayed on part throttle																		*																																							
Downward changes	2, 1	Delayed and bumpy													*																																												
Gear engagement	D, R	Jerky on selection from N													*	*						*				*																	×																
	D, 2	Delayed upward 1 to 2															*					*				*									×	×	×	×																					
	D, 2	Delayed upward 2 to 3															*					*				*									×	×	×	×													×	×	×						
Kick-down	D, 2	Does not work									*	*	*	×																													×																
Parking lock	P	Does not work							●																														*	*																			
Acceleration	D, 2, 1 and R	Below standard				●																																																					
Maximum speed	D	Not reached					●																																																					
Moving off	D, 2	Squeals in C and 2 only																																												×													
Excessive creep	D, 2, 1 and R	Gear selected, no throttle							●																				*																															
Converter		Bush worn									●																																																	
ATF		Loss, not visible externally														*												×																				×	×										
		Loss, visible externally					*	*																																								×	×										
		Dirty, smells burnt																																		×	×														×	×					×	
Forward clutch		Burnt			●																															×	×									×	×					×					×	
D and R clutch		Diaphragm spring broken			●																								*																														
		Burnt			●																					*										×	×	×								×	×	×		×	×	×						×

previously served by these items is now carried out at the transmission itself. The use of this type of selector makes its correct adjustment of prime importance and the following procedure is specified.

First check to ensure that the inner cable and its outer casing are thoroughly clean and lightly lubricated with grease, make sure also that the cable has a straight run without any twists or bends. Loosen the cable clamp nut.

Hold the selector lever firmly in the P position and at the same time move the transmission lever to the P position, pressing it rearwards and making sure that it contacts its stop. Secure the cable to the selector lever in this position.

Start up the engine and let it run at about 1000 to 1200 rev/min. To make sure that the car will not move, chock the wheels and apply the brakes. Select N position.

1 Move the selector lever to R and note that the engine speed should be noticeably reduced and there should be a straining towards the rear.
2 Move the lever to P and the engine speed should immediately increase, indicating that reverse has disengaged. Pull the lever back towards R up to the detent and there should be no change in engine speed.
3 Repeat check item No. 1.
4 Move the selector to N and note that the engine speed increases again and the rearward straining is no longer felt.
5 Move the selector to D and again there should be a drop in engine speed and a slight forward movement.

Accelerator cable:

Refer to **FIG 7:15**. Close the throttle to its idling position and press the lever 1 on the transmission in the direction of the arrow to its end position. Hold it in this position and adjust the cable at the throttle lever so that all play in the cable is eliminated.

It should now be possible to engage the cable ball socket on to the lever ball joint 2 without any straining or slackness on the cable.

Transmission cable:

Loosen the locknut securing the cable lever to the upper end of the accelerator pedal.

Place a block 10 mm (.4 inch) thick between the pedal and the pedal stop and press the pedal down hard against it.

Press the operating lever on the transmission in to the kick-down position and hold it there. Pull up the cable lever on the pedal to the full throttle position and secure the locknut.

Remove the spacing block and press the pedal down to the kick-down position. Check that there is no play at the operating lever on the transmission.

Lubrication:

The automatic transmission should be drained every 28,000 miles (45,000 km) and refilled with ATF Dexron B. The total capacity of the unit is $10\frac{1}{2}$ pints (6 litres) but only half this quantity should be needed to replace the fluid drained off.

The final drive should also be drained at the same intervals and approximately $1\frac{1}{4}$ pints ($\frac{3}{4}$ litre) of SAE 90 hypoid oil will be required to refill it.

7:12 Fault diagnosis

This section indicates the checks and actions relevant to an extensive list of possible faults. Although an owner will be in a position to deal with only some of these himself, the list will assist him to consult more knowledgeably with the specialist whose services will have to be enlisted to deal with the remainder of these possible faults.

(a) Incorrect primary throttle pressure

1 Adjust as described in **Section 7:4**
2 Vacuum unit bent
3 Primary throttle valve sticking
4 Vacuum hose leaking or disconnected

(b) Incorrect main pressure

1 Check (a)
2 Defective pump
3 Internal fluid leaks
4 Sticking control valve

(c) Tabulation of faults

The table overleaf relates faults to 56 possible causes which are listed below and on page 97. Note that those faults which can be dealt with by adjustment with the transmission installed in the vehicle are identified ● in the tabulation; those which require repairs which can be carried out with the transmission installed in the vehicle are identified ★ and those which can only be rectified after removing the transmission from the vehicle are identified **X**.

Key to probable cause of fault

1 Poor engine performance
2 Idling speed too high
3 Fluid level low
4 Selector lever linkage requires adjustment
5 Incorrect driver action (see Owner's Handbook)
6 Defective fluid seal
7 Torque converter bush worn
8 Drive plate incorrectly installed
9 Drive plate to converter bolts not fitted
10 Defective kick-down solenoid where fitted
11 Defective kick-down switch where fitted
12 Discontinuity in wiring between kick-down switch and solenoid where fitted
13 Kick-down valve sticking where fitted
14 Fluid in vacuum unit where fitted
15 Defective vacuum unit diaphragm where fitted
16 Vacuum hose leaking or disconnected where fitted
17 Vacuum unit damaged externally where fitted, check 2 in (a)
18 Wrong type vacuum unit where fitted
19 Vacuum connection at engine defective where fitted

20 Check 1 in (a)
21 Check 3 in (a)
22 Defective governor drive
23 Governor dirty
24 Governor incorrectly assembled
25 Governor drive shaft seal defective
26 Selector cable not connected to gearbox lever
27 Dirty valve assembly
28 Fluid strainer dirty
29 1 to 2 valve sticking
30 2 to 3 valve sticking
31 1 and R brake band incorrectly adjusted where fitted
32 1 and R brake band defective
33 Piston seal defective where fitted
34 2 brake band incorrectly adjusted
35 2 brake band defective
36 2 brake band piston defective
37 2 brake band piston sealing rings defective
38 Parking pawl defective or lever broken

39 Parking pawl damaged
40 Parking pawl not engaging
41 O-ring and/or gasket between final drive casing and gearbox defective
42 Internal leakage
43 Paper gasket defective
44 1 one-way clutch not holding
45 Pump drive defective (shaft/drive plate)
46 Fluid passage plug missing
47 Pump sealing rings broken
48 Wrong type pump installed
49 D and R clutch defective
50 D and R clutch piston seal defective
51 Wrong D and R clutch installed
52 D and R clutch fitted with wrong plates
53 Forward clutch plates defective
54 Forward clutch seized
55 Forward clutch diaphragm spring broken
56 Forward clutch piston seal defective

NOTES

CHAPTER 8

THE DRIVE SHAFTS AND FRONT SUSPENSION

8:1 Description

The front suspension, drive shafts and steering gear are shown diagramatically in **FIG 8:1**. A lefthand drive model is illustrated but, except for the handing of the steering column, the illustration is representative of a righthand drive vehicle.

Suspension:

Integral with the subframe 1 (this also carries the engine mountings) are two brackets at each side which carry the pivots of the suspension arms 5. The suspension arms are of triangular form and, at the apex of each, a ball joint is attached by two nuts and bolts. Each wheel hub carrier 10 is attached to a ball joint. A tubular strut 11 which is integral with each hub carrier carries a damper and a road spring. The upper end of each damper inner member is attached to the vehicle through a ballbearing and spring seat.

Steering:

Note that the steering arms which are part of the strut assemblies point forward. The steering axis is through the ball joint at each lower end and the ballbearing pivot at each upper end. An unusual aspect of the geometry of the steering axis and the reasons for its adoption are described in **Chapter 10, Section 10:1** and **Chapter 11, Section 11:1**.

Dampers:

A double-acting hydraulic telescopic damper is incorporated into each strut. The dampers are sealed assemblies (as also are the rear dampers) and cannot be serviced by an owner.

Road springs:

A single coil road spring surrounds each damper. Spring characteristics are not the same for all models and, when new springs are required, it is important that those of the correct colour code are obtained. Colour codes are covered in **Section 8:6**.

Stabilizer bar:

Beneath the subframe 1 to which it is attached by two brackets is a stabilizer bar 2. This straddles the vehicle and each of its outer ends is attached to a suspension arm.

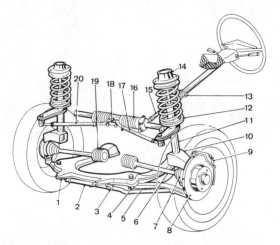

FIG 8:1 Diagrammatic layout of front suspension, drive shafts and steering gear

Key to Fig 8:1   1 Subframe   2 Stabiliser bar   3 Stabiliser bar retaining clip   4 Suspension arm pivot   5 Suspension arm   6 Drive shaft   7 Rubber boot   8 Brake disc   9 Brake caliper   10 Hub bearing carrier   11 Strut   12 Spring   13 Steering column   14 Strut top assembly   15 Steering shaft   16 Steering unit   17 Tie rod   18 Tie rod slide assembly   19 Rubber boot   20 Tie rod

Wheel hubs:

Each wheel runs on an angular contact twin row ballbearing. The external diameter of each bearing is carried in hub carrier 10 and is retained by circlips. A hub, to which the brake disc is attached, runs in the bearing internal diameter and is splined to take torque from the front wheel drive shaft.

Drive shafts:

The inboard end of each shaft is bolted to the flange of a differential drive shaft and is splined to a hub at its outboard end. Two constant velocity universal joints are incorporated into each drive shaft assembly and are protected by convoluted rubber boots. Drive shaft lengths differ for different models depending upon whether a manual or an automatic gearbox is fitted. The differences are covered in **Section 8:9.**

8:2 Maintenance

Wheels and tyres:

Regularly check and re-inflate the tyres to the pressure tabulated in **Technical Data** in the **Appendix.**

Every 5000 miles (8000 km), interchange the wheels to even out tyre wear. An interchange sequence is given in

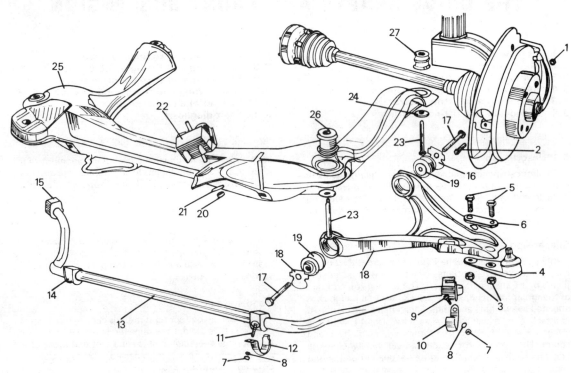

FIG 8:2   Components of the front suspension

Key to Fig 8:2   1 Ball joint retaining nut   2 Ball joint retaining bolt   3 Ball joint retaining nuts   4 Ball joint   5 Ball joint retaining bolts   6 Plate   7 Nut   8 Washer   9 Bolt   10 Clip   11 Bolt   12 Clip   13 Stabiliser bar   14 Inner rubber bush   15 Outer rubber bush   16 Plate   17 Bolt   18 Suspension arm   19 Bonded rubber bush   20 Nut   21 Washer   22 Bonded rubber engine mounting   23 Bolt   24 Washer   25 Subframe   26 Bonded rubber subframe mounting bush   27 Bonded rubber subframe mounting bush

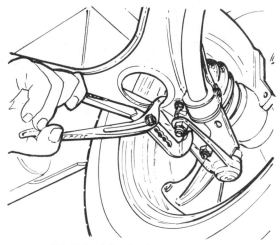

FIG 8:3 Adjusting ball joint position

Chapter 9, Section 9:2. At this same mileage interval have the wheel balance checked and corrected as necessary.

Suspension:

Every 5000 miles (8000 km), check over the suspension generally. Ensure that the springs are intact, that the dampers are securely mounted and that ball joints and bonded rubber bushes are serviceable.

Drive shafts:

No routine maintenance is required to the drive shafts except for checking that the rubber boots are serviceable.

8:3 Removing and fitting the stabilizer bar

Removal:

Refer to **FIG 8:2.** Remove the nut, bolt and washer 7, 8 and 11 from both clips 12 and release the stabilizer from the subframe 25. Collect the clips. Remove the bolt, nut and washer 7, 8 and 9 from each end of the stabilizer. Collect the clips and dismount the bar.

Inspection:

Check that the two inner rubber bushes 14 and the two outer rubber bushes 15 are serviceable. Fit new if necessary. If the stabilizer bar is damaged or distorted, fit a new replacement. Do not attempt to salvage it or to correct its contour.

Fitment:

The fitment procedure is the reverse of the removal sequence, using new self-locking nuts on M6 bolts and tightening to a torque of 7 lb ft (1 kgm). If the later M8 bolts are used, tighten to 18 lb ft (2.5 kgm).

8:4 Removing and fitting a suspension arm

Removal:

1 Remove the stabilizer bar as described in **Section 8:3.** Jack-up the front of the vehicle and remove the relevant road wheel.

2 Refer to **FIG 8:2.** Mark the position of the ball joint flange on the suspension arm so that it may be refitted without disturbing the camber angle setting.

3 Remove nuts, bolts and locking plate 3, 5 and 6 and disengage the flange of the ball joint from the arm.

4 Remove bolts 17 and locking plates 16. Withdraw the suspension arm.

Inspection:

Do not attempt to salvage a damaged suspension arm. If distortion is suspected, have the arm checked on gauge VW 527 with supplementary parts VW 527/4, /5 and /6. If the arm is serviceable, check that the bonded rubber bushes 19 are in acceptable condition. If necessary these may be removed and new bushes pressed in. Check the condition of the ball joint and renew if necessary.

Fitment:

Fitment is the reverse of the removal procedure. If a new arm or ball joint has been fitted or if the original positioning of the ball joint as marked before removal has been lost, the camber angle must be reset as described in **Section 8:11.** The operation of positioning the ball joint to its original position before finally tightening nuts 3 to 47 lb ft (6.5 kg m) is shown in **FIG 8:3.**

Ball joint:

If excessive wear in a ball joint is suspect, check the axial play as shown in **FIG 8:4.** Use a vernier to straddle the assembly and compare the measurement in the free state with one taken after all play has been eliminated by applying leverage with tool VW 281a or an equivalent. A

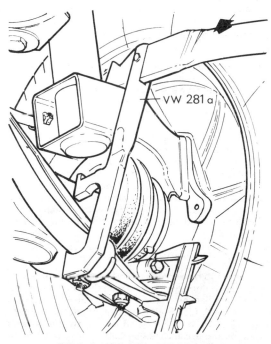

FIG 8:4 Measuring ball joint play

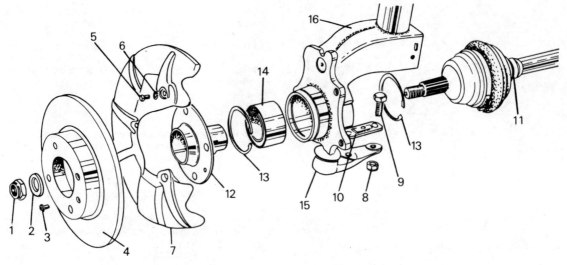

FIG 8:5 Components of a front wheel hub

Key to Fig 8:5   1 Drive shaft nut   2 Washer   3 Screw   4 Brake disc   5 Bolt   6 Washer   7 Splash plate   8 Nut
9 Bolt   10 Plate   11 Drive shaft   12 Hub   13 Circlip   14 Hub ballbearing   15 Ball joint   16 Hub carrier

new joint will have a play of .04 inch (1 mm). The wear limit is when the play reaches .1 inch (2.5 mm).

To remove a ball joint, proceed as described earlier and remove nuts, bolts and locking plate 3, 5 and 6 and also remove the pinch bolt and nut 1 and 2 from the hub carrier. On fitment, torque tighten nut 1 to 25 lb ft (3.5 kgm).

8:5 Removing and fitting a strut

Removal:

1 Before jacking up the vehicle, refer to **FIG 8:5** and loosen the self-locking drive shaft nut 1.
2 Refer to **Section 8:4** and carry out operatio s 1, 2 and 3 of the suspension arm removal procedure.
3 Dismount the brake caliper as described in **Chapter 11, Section 11:3** but do not uncouple the brake hydraulic pipe. Hang the caliper, without straining the pipe, conveniently on the chassis.
4 Remove the drive shaft as described in **Section 8:9.** Uncouple the steering tie rod from the strut steering arm as described in **Chapter 10, Section 10:6.**
5 From inside the engine compartment, remove the two nuts, washers and retaining cups which attach the top of the strut assembly to the body. Withdraw the strut assembly.

Fitment:

To install a strut assembly, follow the removal procedure in reverse. Tighten nuts and bolts to the torques given in the relevant Section. Tighten the two nuts in the engine compartment which retain the top of the strut assembly to a torque of 18 lb ft (2.5 kg m) and, **with the wheels again on the ground,** torque tighten the drive shaft nut to 180 to 216 lb ft (25 to 30 kg m).

8:6 Removing and fitting a spring

A hub carrier, damper, spring and retaining parts are shown in **FIG 8:6**.

Removal:

1 Remove the relevant strut assembly as described in **Section 8:5.**
2 Fit spring compressing tool VW 340 with adaptor VW 340/5 as shown in **FIG 8:7** or use a Matra W161 spring compressing tool or an equivalent.
3 Compress the spring and remove nut 2 in **FIG 8:6** while holding the damper shaft from turning with a suitable Allen key socket.
4 Remove parts 3 to 10. Detension the spring and lift it off. Check the condition of parts 3 to 10 and also that of parts 12 and 13. Renew as necessary. Check the action of the damper and, if it is unserviceable, renew it as described in **Section 8:7.**

Springs, Passat models:

Front suspension springs are available in eight tolerance groups and are identified by a colour coding. Specific groups are specified for different models and these are tabulated later. Springs must not only be of an appropriate group for the relevant model but must be of the same group on both the lefthand and the righthand suspension struts. If, on renewing a spring, a spare of the same (exact) coding as that removed is not available, fit springs of the same alternative coding to **both suspension struts.** This requirement does not apply to Dasher models.

In the following tabulations, x indicates availability and Estate models, Passat Variants, are shown as 5 door models.

Model	Passat and Passat L		
Transmission	Manual		
Number of doors	2	4	5
1 yellow mark	x		
2 yellow marks	x		
3 yellow marks	x	x	x
1 green mark	x	x	x
2 green marks		x	x

Model	Passat S and Passat LS					
Transmission	Manual			Auomatic		
Number of doors	2	4	5	2	4	5
1 yellow mark	x	x	x			
2 yellow marks	x	x	x			
3 yellow marks		x	x			
1 green mark		x	x			
2 green marks	x	x		x	x	x
3 green marks	x	x			x	x
3 white marks				x		
1 red mark				x		

Model	Passat TS					
Transmission	Manual			Automatic		
Number of doors	2	4	5	2	4	5
1 yellow mark		x	x			
2 yellow marks		x	x			
3 yellow marks		x	x			
1 green mark		x	x			
2 green marks		x	x	x	x	x
3 green marks		x	x		x	x
3 white marks	x	x	x	x	x	x
1 red mark	x	x	x	x	x	x

Springs, Dasher models:

During factory assembly, front springs from one of three tolerance groups will have been fitted (coded 1, 2 or 3 paint marks). Spare replacement springs are available in one group only (coded 2 paint marks) and, when a replacement has to be fitted, it is not necessary to renew both front springs. **This divergence does not apply to Passat models.**

Fitment:

The spring fitment procedure is the reverse of the removal sequence. Position and tension the spring before attempting to fit other parts. Dust the damping ring 7 with talcum powder. Tighten nut 2 to a torque of 43 lb ft (6 kg m) while holding the damper shaft from turning by the use of an Allen key socket as shown in **FIG 8:7**.

8:7 Removing and fitting a damper

Removal:

1 Remove the relevant strut assembly as described in **Section 8:5**. Remove the spring from the strut assembly as described in **Section 8:6**.

2 Refer to **FIG 8:6.** Remove the stop buffer 12 and the boot 13. Using special tool 40-201, unscrew the threaded cap 14. This frees the damper.

3 If, as is probable due to corrosion, dirt etc., the damper cannot be pulled out of the hub bearing carrier tube, proceed as follows.

4 Pull the damper shaft out to the full extent of its travel and fit nut 2. Clamp the carrier in a vice and hold an

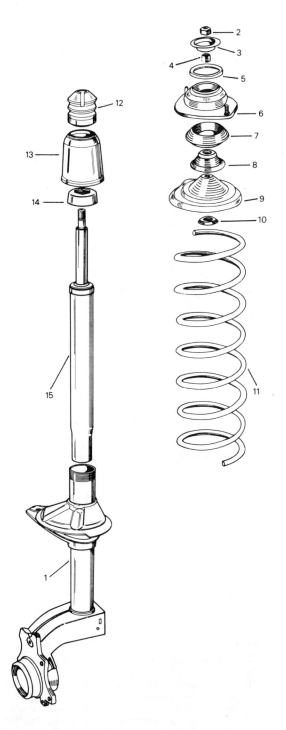

FIG 8:6 Damper, spring and their retaining components

Key to Fig 8:6 1 Strut and hub carrier 2 Nut 3 Stop 4 Distance piece 5 Collar 6 Cup 7 Damping ring 8 Strut bearing 9 Cup 10 Plate 11 Spring 12 Stop buffer 13 Boot 14 Threaded cap 15 Damper

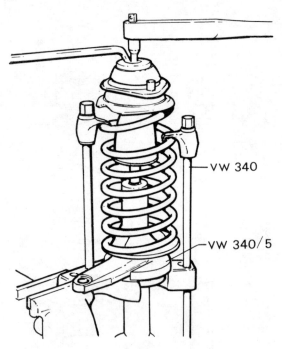

FIG 8:7 Compressing a spring

open-ended spanner immediately under the nut. Hammer gently on the spanner as close as possible to the damper and gradually force it out of the carrier tube.

5 Inspect the condition of the buffer stop and boot and, if they are worn or perished, renew them.

Fitment:

Ensure that the bore of the bearing carrier tube is thoroughly clean before inserting the damper body. Using special tool 40-201, tighten the threaded cap 14 to a torque of 108 lb ft (15 kg m). The remaining operations are the removal sequence in reverse.

8:8 Removing and fitting a hub bearing

The hub, hub bearing, hub bearing carrier and associated parts are shown in FIG 8:5. A hub bearing which has been removed from a hub and hub carrier cannot be used again.

Removal:

1 Remove the strut assembly as described in Section 8:5.
2 Remove the brake disc 4 and splash plate 7 as described in Chapter 11, Section 11:3.
3 Support the hub carrier under a press with its outer projection facing downwards and, using a suitble mandrel, press out the hub and bearing inner race. This operation is shown in FIG 8:8.
4 Using a two arm puller, withdraw the inner race from the hub stub shaft.
5 Remove the inner and outer circlips 13. Using a similar setup to that shown for operation 3 but with a mandrel

of slightly less diameter than the bore of the hub carrier, press out the bearing from the hub carrier. Discard the bearing.

Fitment:

1 Fit the outer circlip and ensure that it is correctly seated in its groove.
2 Press in the bearing using a mandrel of diameter only slightly less than the carrier bore until it seats against the circlip. Fit the second circlip.
3 Support the hub on the press with its stub shaft upwards. Position the hub carrier onto it (outer projection downwards) and, using a suitable mandrel, press the carrier onto the mandrel. **Ensure that this mandrel presses only on the inner race of the bearing.**
4 Refit the splash guard and the brake disc. Install the strut assembly as described in Section 8:5.

8:9 Removing and fitting a drive shaft

The components of a dismantled drive shaft are shown in FIG 8:9.

Removal:

1 **Before jacking up the front of the vehicle,** loosen the drive shaft nut (1 in FIG 8:5) of the relevant wheel. Jack-up the vehicle and remove the road wheel. Remove the drive shaft nut which was loosened earlier.
2 When a **righthand drive shaft** is to be removed, the exhaust pipe must be detached from the exhaust manifold and from the bracket on the transmission.

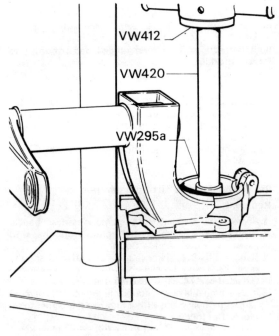

FIG 8:8 Pressing out the hub

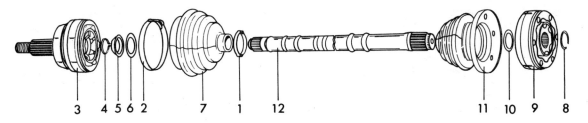

FIG 8:9   Components of a drive shaft

Key to Fig 8:9   1 Clip (34 mm diameter)   2 Clip (88 mm diameter)   3 Outer universal joint   4 Circlip   5 Spacer
6 Dished washer   7 Boot   8 Circlip   9 Inner universal joint   10 Dished washer   11 Boot protector cap   12 Shaft (see text for
lengths)

3 Remove the six socket headed bolts which retain the inner universal joint flange (9 in **FIG 8:9**) to the transmission drive flange.

4 When an **automatic transmission lefthand drive shaft** is to be removed, mark the position of the ball joint (see operation 2 of the suspension arm removal procedure in **Section 8:4**), remove the two retaining nuts, disengage the ball joint from the suspension arm and swing the hub assembly outwards as shown in **FIG 8:10** to give extra clearance for the shaft removal.

5 Disengage the drive shaft from the drive flange and from the hub splines. Withdraw the shaft.

Fitment:

This is the reverse of the removal sequence. Apply molykote paste to the wheel hub splines. Use a **new** self-locking nut, but do not tighten it to its final torque of 166 lb ft (23 kg m) until the car is standing on its wheels. Torque tighten the six socket headed bolts to 25 lb ft (3.5 kg m).

8:10 Dismantling and reassembling a drive shaft

The components of a dismantled drive shaft are shown in **FIG 8:9**. A cross-section through an outer universal joint is shown in **FIG 8:11**.

Dismantling a shaft assembly:

1 Refer to **FIG 8:9**. Cut and remove clip 1. Remove clip 2. Remove circlip 4 (this is 1 in **FIG 8:11**). It will be necessary, while holding this circlip open, to tap sharply with a soft hammer on the outer end of the drive shaft to make the circlip jump out of its groove. Discard the circlip.

2 Withdraw the outer universal joint. Note which way round the spacer 5 and the dished washer 6 (these are 2 and 3 in **FIG 8:11**) are fitted before removing them.

3 Remove boot 7. Using pliers VW 161a or their equivalent, remove and discard circlip 8. Press the protective cap off the inner joint using VW 402 and VW 408a.

4 Remove the dished washer 10 (note which way round it is fitted) and the boot 11 from the shaft 12.

Shaft lengths:

Refer to **FIG 8:9** and note that the shaft 12 is not the same overall length in all cases. If a new shaft is required, ensure that one of the appropriate length is obtained.

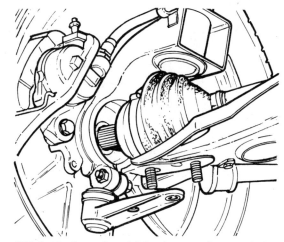

FIG 8:10   Removing a lefthand automatic transmission drive shaft

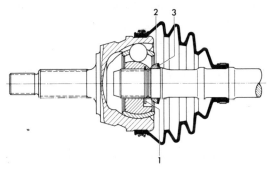

FIG 8:11   Cross-section through an outer universal joint

Key to Fig 8:11   1 Circlip   2 Spacer   3 Dished washer

Manual transmission lefthand and righthand shafts are equal in length and may be 506 mm or 508.4 mm according to model. For **automatic transmission** the two shafts are of unequal lengths and there have been a number of variations.

Dismantling an inner universal joint:

Pivot the ball hub and cage out of the joint body towards the smaller outside diameter of the joint and press the balls

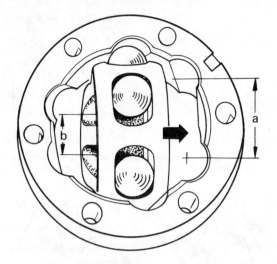

FIG 8:12 Hub and cage, inner universal joint

Key to Fig 8:12 **a** Wide groove in outer ring   **b** Narrow groove in hub

out of the cage. Align the two grooves and extract the hub from the cage.

Do not mix the balls or any other parts with those from another joint. If any part is unserviceable, a complete new joint will be required.

Dismantling an outer universal joint:

Before dismantling, mark the position of the ball hub in relation to the ball cage and housing so that, on reassembly, the parts may be installed in their original positions.

Pivot the ball hub and cage until the balls can be extracted. Turn the cage until the larger openings are level with the joint faces and remove the cage complete with the hub. Swing the hub until one segment can be pushed into the large rectangular opening in the cage and tilt the hub out of the cage.

Do not mix the balls or other parts with those from another joint. If any part is unserviceable, a complete new joint will be required.

Reassembling the outer and inner joints:

A total of 4 oz (90 grams) of molybdenum disulphide grease must be packed into each joint (half this amount into each side of each joint). The reassembly procedure is the reverse of the dismantling sequence in each case. Fit new circlips 4 and 8. Note that in the inner joint there is a wide groove **a** and a narrow groove **b** as shown in **FIG 8:12**.

Reassembling a shaft:

The reassembly sequence is the reverse of that described for dismantling. Fit new boots if those removed were cracked or perished. Use clip pliers ASE 000 049 to tighten clips 1 and 2.

8:11 Camber and castor angles

Of these two components of the front suspension geometry only the camber angle is adjustable, but in view of the special measuring equipment required for accurate assessment of the angles concerned it is recommended that the car be taken to a service station for any necessary work to be carried out. The need for such attention may be indicated by poor handling or irregular tyre wear, probably after a heavy impact against the front wheels.

8:12 Fault diagnosis

(a) Wheel wobble

1 Incorrect tyre pressure
2 Wheel(s) out of balance
3 Uneven tyre wear
4 Loose wheel attachment nuts
5 Incorrect wheel alignment
6 Worn hub bearings
7 Worn suspension arm pivot bushes
8 Weak or broken front road spring

(b) 'Bottoming' of suspension

1 Check 8 in (a)
2 Damper(s) inoperative

(c) Heavy steering

1 Ball joint(s) defective
2 Suspension arm(s) distorted
3 Damper seized
4 Defective steering gear (see Chapter 10)

(d) Excessive tyre wear

1 Check 1, 2, 5 and 7 in (a) and 2 in (c)
2 Defective brake (see Chapter 11)

(e) Noise and rattles

1 Check 6, 7 and 8 in (a)
2 Defective damper(s)
3 Loose strut mounting
4 Loose subframe
5 Worn or loose ball joint
6 Worn steering linkage (see Chapter 10)

(f) Excessive rolling

1 Check 1 and 8 in (a), 2 in (b) and 3 in (e)
2 Broken or loose stabilizer bar

(g) Excessive drive shaft backlash

1 Worn universal joints
2 Worn splines
3 Worn transmission (see Chapter 6 or Chapter 7)

(h) Abnormal steering 'kickback'

1 Check 4 in (c)
2 Universal joint(s) partially seized
3 Suspension arm twisted
4 Strut bent

CHAPTER 9

THE REAR AXLE AND SUSPENSION

9:1 Description

A diagramatic layout of the rear suspension is shown in **FIG 9:1.** The assembly is pivoted at the forward ends of the two radius arms 4 which are rigidly attached to the axle beam. The assembly is controlled laterally by the diagonal arm 1 and vertically by a telescopic damper and a coil spring at each road wheel. The coil springs are located immediately above the axle beam while the dampers are mounted slightly forward of the axle axis. A torsion bar is incorporated within the axle beam which is of inverted **U** profile. This feature is shown in **FIG 9:1** at **A.** The stub axles are bolted to rectangular flanges which are welded to the axle beam and are shown in **FIG 9:1** at **B.** A bump stop is incorporated within each coil spring. These bump stops limit road wheel vertical travel to approximately 7.9 inch (200 mm). Each wheel hub runs on two taper roller bearings. They are lubricated with multi-purpose grease which is retained by an oil seal inboard and by the hub cap. The wheel hub is integral with the brake drum.

9:2 Maintenance

Wheels and tyres:

Regularly check and re-inflate the tyres to the pressure recommended and tabulated in the **Technical Data** section of the **Appendix.**

Every 5000 miles (8000 km) have the wheel balance checked and corrected as necessary.

Suspension:

Every 5000 miles (8000 km), check over the suspension generally. Check that the dampers are securely mounted and that all bonded rubber bushes are serviceable.

Wheel hubs:

Every 30,000 miles (50,000 km), refer to **Section 9:3,** remove the hubs and repack the bearings with multipurpose grease.

9:3 Removing and fitting hub bearings

The components of a rear hub and brake assembly are shown in **FIG 9:2** for a lefthand wheel.

Bearing removal:

1 Chock the front wheels, jack-up and remove the relevant road wheel. Release the handbrake and back off the brake shoe adjustment.
2 Remove the hub cap 1 (the official tool is VW 637/2), extract and discard the splitpin 2, remove the

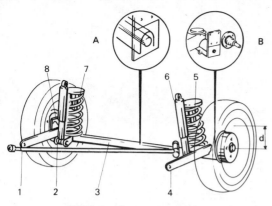

FIG 9:1 The rear suspension

Key to Fig 9:1 1 Diagonal arm 2 Lower mounting, right-hand damper 3 Axle beam 4 Radius arm 5 Spring 6 Damper 7 Bump stop 8 Stub axle mounting flange **A** Section through axle beam **B** Stub axle and mounting flange **d** Wheel vertical travel

locking ring 3 and the nut 4. Lift out the thrust washer 5.
3 Remove the hub/brake drum assembly using, if necessary, a suitable puller. It will not normally be necessary to remove the brake backplate assembly or the stub axle.
4 Extract and discard oil seal 8. Withdraw the inner race assemblies and clean off all old grease.
5 If new bearings are to be fitted, knock out the outer races using a copper drift. Otherwise, clean out all old grease. It will not normally be necessary to extract circlip 10.

Bearing fitment:

1 If new bearings are being fitted, press in the new outer races and ensure that they butt against the circlip 10.
2 Fill the space between the outer races with about $\frac{3}{4}$ oz (20 grams) of multi-purpose grease. Clean the inner diameter of the brake drum thoroughly.
3 Reassemble the inner races and fit a new oil seal 8. Fit the assembly to the stub shaft, fit the thrust washer 5 and tighten nut 4 until it is just possible, with a screwdriver, to move the thrust washer. This corresponds approximately to an assembly end float of .0012 to .0028 inch (.03 to .07 mm). Check this with a suitably mounted dial gauge and adjust, if necessary, until the float is within these limits.
4 Fit the locking ring and a new splitpin. Fill the hub cap with about $\frac{3}{8}$ oz (10 grams) of multi-purpose grease and, using a soft hammer, knock it into position.

Stub axles:

If, due to wear or accident damage, new stub axles have to be fitted, tighten their retaining bolts to a torque of 47 lb ft (6.5 kg m), but replace the lockwashers with double spring washers if these are not already used.

9:4 Removing and fitting a damper

The components of a lefthand rear suspension assembly are shown in **FIG 9:3**.

Removal:

1 Chock the front wheels, jack-up the rear of the vehicle and fit the spring compressing tool VW 655/3 (or an equivalent tool) as shown in **FIG 9:4**.
2 By means of this tool, lift the rear axle towards the

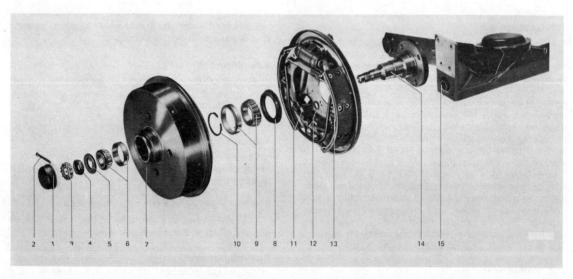

FIG 9:2 Components of a rear hub

Key to Fig 9:2 1 Hub cap 2 Splitpin 3 Locking ring 4 Nut 5 Thrust washer 6 Outer bearing 7 Brake drum 8 Oil seal 9 Inner bearing 10 Circlip 11 Bolt 12 Spring washer 13 Brake backplate assembly 14 Stub axle 15 Axle beam

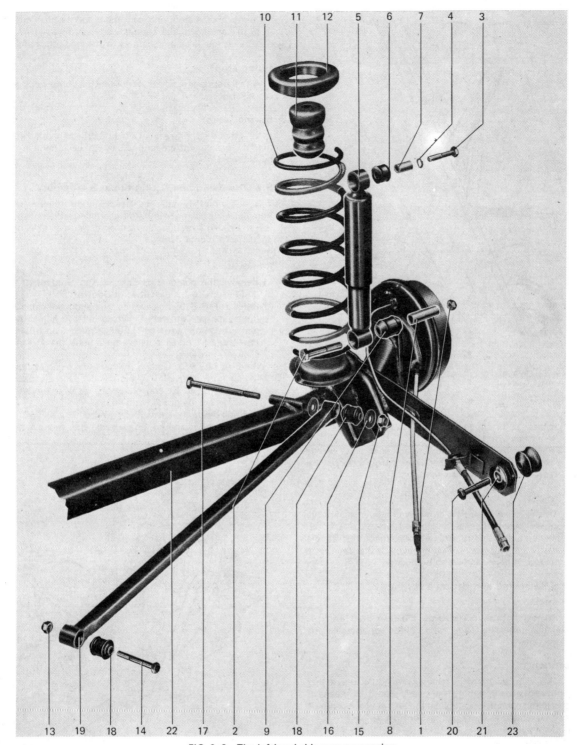

FIG 9:3 The lefthand side rear suspension

Key to Fig 9:3   1 Nut   2 Bolt   3 Bolt   4 Spring washer   5 Damper   6 Rubber bush   7 Sleeve   8 Sleeve
9 Rubber bush   10 Coil spring   11 Bump stop   12 Spring seat   13 Nut   14 Bolt   15 Nut   16 Washer   17 Bolt
18 Rubber bush   19 Diagonal arm   20 Bolt   21 Spring washer   22 Axle beam   23 Rubber bush

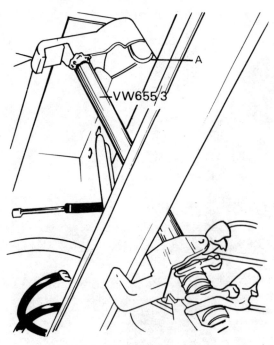

FIG 9:4   Spring compressing tool

Key to Fig 9:4   **A** Hook made from $\frac{5}{16}$ inch (8 mm)
diameter steel rod

chassis sufficiently to allow the damper **lower** attachment bolt 2 to be removed.
3 Remove the damper upper attachment bolt. **Never remove the upper attachment bolt before the lower.** Lift out the damper.

Fitment:

This is the reverse of the removal sequence. Torque tighten attachment bolts 2 and 3 to 43 lb ft (6 kg m). When renewing a damper, use only a replacement of the same manufacture and type as that removed. If this cannot be arranged, fit new dampers to both sides.

9:5 Removing and fitting a spring
Removal:

Remove both dampers as described in **Section 9:4.** Detension the axle lifting tool until the spring(s) can be dismounted.

Fitment:

This is the reverse of the removal procedure. Ensure that both ends of each spring are correctly seated. By means of the spring compressing tool, lift the axle until the dampers can be refitted as described in **Section 9:4.**

Springs:

On Passat models three colour codes of spare springs are available. **Ensure that springs of the same code are fitted to each side.** On Dasher models only one colour code of spare spring is available and this may differ from the coding of the springs originally fitted. This is acceptable and it is not necessary to change both springs.

Bump stop:

With the springs removed, check that the bump stops are serviceable.

Spring seats:

Note that the spring seats 12 in **FIG 9:3** are handed and that, if replacements are required, one of each hand must be obtained.

9:6 Removing and fitting the axle assembly

It will normally only be necessary to remove the complete axle beam assembly if the bonded rubber bushes 23 in **FIG 9:3** require renewal or if the rear axle has sustained accident damage.

Removal:

1 Remove the dampers as described in **Section 9:4** and the springs as described in **Section 9:5.**
2 Refer to **FIG 9:5.** Disconnect the handbrake cable at the equalizer (arrowed 1). Press out the handbrake plastic bushing (arrowed 2) from its retainer and, using tool VW 811 or an equivalent, unhook the forward silencer (arrowed 3).
3 Refer to **FIG 9:6.** Detach the handbrake cables from the chassis (arrowed 4). Uncouple the hydraulic brake hoses (arrowed 5) and blank off the open ends to preclude escape of fluid and entry of dirt.
4 Unhook the rear silencer. Remove bolts 14 and 17 in **FIG 9:3** and dismount the diagonal arm. Remove the

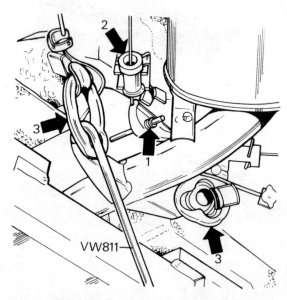

FIG 9:5   Removing the axle assembly

Key to Fig 9:5   1 Handbrake equaliser   2 Plastic bushing
3 Unhooking forward silencer

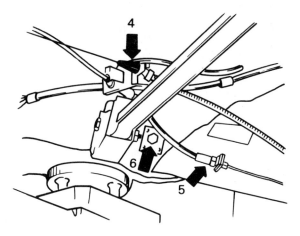

FIG 9:6 Removing the axle assembly

Key to Fig 9:6   4 Detach handbrake cables   5 Hydraulic brake hose connection   6 Axle arm pivot bolt

bolts (arrowed 6 in **FIG 9:6**, 20 in **FIG 9:3**) which retain the arms of the axle assembly to the chassis and withdraw the assembly from beneath the vehicle.

Refitting:

This is a reversal of the removal procedure, but it is important to position the axle in the centre of its travel before tightening the bolts securing the trailing arms to the body. This reduces the strain on the bonded rubber bushes.

Lift the axle beam until the centre of the stub axle is 2.75 inch (70 mm) higher than the centre of the bushes for the trailing arm. This corresponds to a distance of 10.6 inch (270 mm) between the stub axle centre and the lower edge of the wheel arch.

Holding the axle in this position, tighten the bolt securing the trailing arm to the body to 42 lb ft (6 kg m).

Fit the springs and complete the operation by bleeding the braking system and adjusting the handbrake as described in **Chapter 11**.

Bonded rubber bushes:

Bushes which are in any way damaged or deteriorated must be pressed out and renewed. If new bonded bushes with slots on each side are being fitted, make sure that the slots are in line with the horizontal axis of the trailing arm.

9:7 Camber and toe-in

Neither camber nor toe-in are adjustable at the rear but, in the event of accident damage, their measurement provides a check on possible deformation of the axle and/or stub axles.

Professional experience and equipment will be required. With the axle beam precisely horizontal, with a full fuel tank, with the spare wheel in position but without passengers, the camber angle should be $-30' \pm 15'$ and the deviation, one side to the other, should not exceed 30'. Total toe-in should be within $\pm 50'$.

9:8 Fault diagnosis

(a) Rattles

1 Worn pivot bushes
2 Defective damper
3 Loose damper mounting(s)
4 Broken coil spring
5 Defective hub bearings
6 Worn handbrake guides
7 Loose brake hydraulic piping
8 Loose bump stop

(b) 'Settling'

1 Check 1 and 4 in (a)
2 Spring seatings

(c) 'Bottoming' of suspension

1 Check 4 in (a) and 2 in (b)
2 Bump stops worn or missing
3 Dampers inoperative

(d) Excessive tyre wear

1 Check 1 in (a)
2 Incorrect tracking (distorted axle assembly)
3 Wheel(s) out of balance
4 Incorrect tyre pressure

NOTES

CHAPTER 10

THE STEERING GEAR

10:1 Description

The steering gear, linkage and column are included in the diagramatic layout in **Chapter 8, FIG 8:1.** A lefthand drive assembly is shown. The righthand drive assembly is a mirror version. The steering unit is a rack and pinion type which is designed for eventual replacement and not for overhaul by an owner. A damper, not shown in **FIG 8:1** is fitted between the steering unit and the chassis. The steering column shaft actuates the pinion and, through it, the rack moves the tie rod slide to which the two tie rods are attached. The steering column is, in the event of accident, 'collapsible' in that, at the lower end it is not rigidly connected to the steering unit and, at its upper end, it is supported by an expanded metal deformable bracket.

It will be seen, from reference to **Chapter 8, Section 8:1,** that the front suspension/steering design does not incorporate a kingpin. What would be the kingpin inclination is the inclination of the line through the strut top support and the suspension arm ball joint and this is illustrated in **FIG 10:1.** It will be noted that this geometry gives a steering axis which passes outboard (by the amount a) of the tyre contact patch and unequal forces on the front tyres apply a self-correcting moment to the steering. This geometry is necessary with the diagonal twin line braking system (see **Chapter. 11**) but the advantage of self-correcting characteristic is not confined to braking but also to any unequal drag situation such as that which results from a front wheel puncture or a deep puddle through which only one wheel passes.

10:2 Maintenance

General:

Every 5000 miles (8000 km), look over the steering gear generally and check the tightness of the steering unit attachments. Check the condition of the convoluted rubber boots. Check that the tie rod ball joints are secure.

Wheel alignment:

Every 10,000 miles (16,000 km), check and adjust if necessary wheel alignment. The procedure is described in **Section 10.7.**

10:3 Removing and fitting the steering wheel

Disconnect the battery earth cable. Set the wheels in the straight ahead position. Refer to **FIG 10:2** and pull off the padded horn bar 1. Disconnect the horn switch wiring.

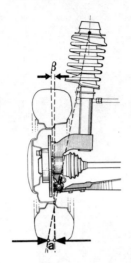

FIG 10:1   Steering axis geometry

Key to Fig 10:1   a Amount by which axis passes outboard of the tyre contact patch   **B** Camber angle

Remove the retaining nut 2 and the locking washer 3. Pull off the steering wheel.

Fitment is the reverse of this sequence. Ensure that the wheels and the steering wheel are both in the straight ahead position. Torque tighten nut 2 to 36 lb ft (5 kg m).

10:4 Removing and fitting the steering column

Removal:

1 Remove the steering wheel as described earlier. Remove the steering column switch assembly. Dismount the dashboard as described in **Chapter 13, Section 13:8.**
2 Refer to **FIG 10:2.** Drill out the two shear screws 13 and remove the steering lock. Use a drill of 8.5 mm diameter.
3 Unscrew the flange tube clip 20 and, using a soft drift, drive the flange tube 19 off the steering unit pinion shaft.
4 Detach the column tube mounting 26 and withdraw the steering column assembly into the interior of the car.
5 If necessary, the steering shaft 25 may be separated from the column tube 24 after removing the circlip 9, washer 10 and spring 11.

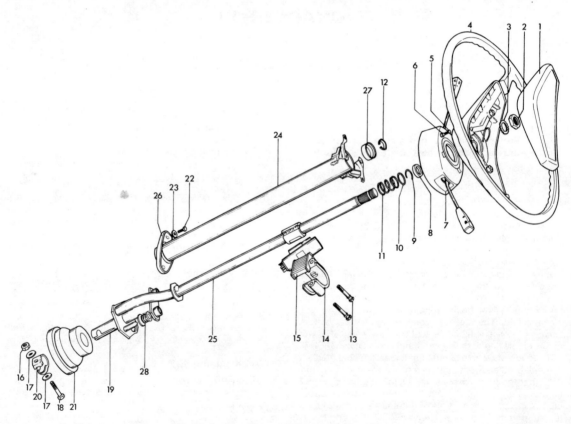

FIG 10:2   Components of the steering column

Key to Fig 10:2   1 Horn bar   **2** Nut   **3** Locking washer   **4** Steering wheel   **5** Screw   **6** Washer   **7** Switch assembly   **8** Stop ring   **9** Circlip   **10** Washer   **11** Spring   **12** Ring   **13** Shear screws   **14** Steering lock   **15** Bush   **16** Nut   **17** Washer   **18** Bolt   **19** Flange tube   **20** Clip   **21** Grommet   **22** Bolt   **23** Washer   **24** Column tube   **25** Steering column shaft   **26** Mounting flange   **27** Ballbearing   **28** Bush

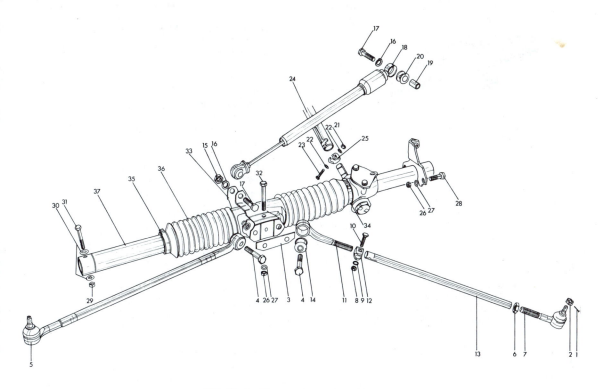

FIG 10:3   The steering unit and linkage

Key to Fig 10:3   1 Splitpin   2 Castellated nut   3 Locking plate   4 Bolt   5 Tie rod ball joint   6 Nut   7 Tie rod outer end   8 Nut   9 Spring washer   10 Bolt   11 Tie rod inner end   12 Clip   13 Tie rod tube   14 Bonded rubber bush   15 Nut   16 Spring washer   17 Bolt   18 Steering damper   19 Liner for bonded rubber bush   20 Bonded rubber bush   21 Nut   22 Washer   23 Bolt   24 Flange tube   25 Clip   26 Nut   27 Spring washer   28 Bolt   29 Nut   30 Washer   31 Bolt   32 Bolt   33 Tie rod slide   34 Clip   35 Clip   36 Boot   37 Steering unit

Fitment:

Reassembly and fitment is the reverse of the removal procedure. Tighten the new shear screws until their heads break off. Torque tighten the clip nut 16 to 22 lb ft (3 kg m).

10:5 The steering unit

Neither the steering unit nor the steering damper can be repaired by an owner and, if either is unserviceable, it should be replaced by a new unit.

Removal:

Loosen off the steering column clamp bolt 18 in **FIG 10:2.** Refer to **FIG 10:3.** Unlock and remove the two bolts 4 and disengage the tie rods from the tie rod slide assembly 33. Remove bolts 28 and 31 which attach the steering unit to the body. Remove bolt 17 which attaches the damper unit to the body. Jack-up the front of the vehicle, remove the relevant road wheel and withdraw the steering and damper units. Remove bolt 17 which attaches the damper unit to the tie rod slide and separate the damper, slide and steering unit.

Fitment:

Refer to **FIG 10:4** and screw in the two tie rod attachment bolts (arrowed). When the steering unit has been installed, remove one bolt and fit its tie rod then remove the second bolt and fit the second tie rod. Bolts 4 should be torque tightened to 40 lb ft (5.5 kg m). The remaing operations are the reverse of the removal sequence. Torque tighten attachment nuts 26 and 29 to 14 lb ft (2 kg m). If bolt 32 was removed, tighten it, on refitment, to a torque of 14 lb ft (2 kg m) also. Use a new locking plate 3.

10:6 The steering linkage

The steering linkage comprises two tie rods. One is adjustable for length to allow of adjustment of toe-in as described in **Section 10:7.** If either tie rod is unserviceable, it should be removed and a new replacement fitted.

Use a ball joint extractor when disconnecting a tie rod from its steering arm. Torque tighten the bolts which attach the tie rods to the steering unit slider to 40 lb ft (5.5 kg m) and torque tighten the ball joint nuts to 29 lb ft (4 kg m). Use new splitpins to lock these nuts.

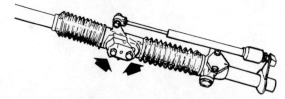

FIG 10:4 Steering unit refitment. Arrows show tie rod bolts fitted temporarily

10:7 Wheel alignment

The toe-in angle should be 10′±15′ or, when the wheels are pressed together under a load of 22 lb (10 kg), 25′±15′. First class optical equipment is essential when checking and adjusting the toe-in angle.

Adjustment:

Refer to **FIG 10:3**. Loosen clip bolt 10. Loosen locknut 6. Turn the tie rod tube 13 in the appropriate direction. On completion of the adjustment, tighten the clip bolt nut. Torque tighten the locknut 6 to 29 lb ft (4 kg m).

10:8 Fault diagnosis

(a) Wheel wobble

1 Incorrect tyre pressure
2 Wheel(s) out of balance
3 Uneven tyre wear
4 Loose wheel attachment bolts
5 Incorrect wheel alignment
6 Worn hub bearing(s)
7 Worn or loose tie rod ball joint(s)
8 Weak or broken front road spring
9 Inoperative steering damper unit

(b) Wander

1 Check 1, 3 and 7 in (a)
2 Uneven tyre pressures
3 Excessive play in rack and pinion
4 Worn suspension arm pivots
5 Deformed wheel

(c) Heavy steering when driving

1 Check 5 in (a)
2 Very low tyre pressure
3 Ball joint seized
4 Steering damper seized
5 Suspension damper seized
6 Steering unit seized
7 Steering shaft/column bearing binding
8 Deformed steering linkage

(d) Steering wheel play excessive

1 Check 6 and 7 in (a); 3 and 4 in (b)
2 Steering unit attachments loose
3 Defective steering unit to column coupling

(e) Rattles, noisy operation

1 Check 4, 6, 7 and 8 in (a); 3 and 4 in (b)
2 Excessively worn steering unit
3 Loose steering damper

(f) Vehicle pulls to one side

1 Drive shaft universal joint(s) defective
2 Low tyre pressure on one side
3 Accident damage to wheel or suspension

CHAPTER 11

THE BRAKING SYSTEM

11:1 Description

Front brakes:

Single piston, floating frame caliper, disc brakes are fitted to the front wheels of all models covered by this manual. Compensation for wear of the renewable friction pads is automatic. Friction pad linings may be either .4 inch (10 mm) or .55 inch (14 mm) in thickness depending upon the type of caliper fitted. Brake discs may be .4 inch (10 mm) or .47 inch (12 mm) thick. The 10 mm thick pads operate only on 10 mm thick discs. The 14 mm thick pads operate only on 12 mm thick discs.

Rear brakes:

Drum brakes are fitted to the rear wheels of all models covered by this manual. Drums may be 7.087 inch (180 mm) or 7.787 inch (200 mm) in diameter and compensation for friction lining wear may, for both sizes, be either manual or automatic. Wheel hubs are integral with the brake drums.

Hydraulic system:

Foot brake operation is by diagonally linked dual lines. Each hydraulic line applies one front brake and one rear brake. To avoid steering bias in the event of one line failing, the steering geometry is designed so that the pivot axis passes outboard of the tyre contact patch (see **Chapter 10, FIG 10:1**). The normal effect of unequal drag of one wheel against the other is precluded since this geometry automatically compensates for such imbalance.

Servo assistance of foot brake pressure is incorporated on certain models.

Handbrake:

The handbrake is mechanically actuated and operates on the rear brakes only. Routine adjustment is required to compensate for wear of the rear brake friction linings.

Regulators:

Except on early models, braking effort is biased towards the front wheels by a pressure sensitive regulator which is fitted into each of the dual hydraulic lines. These regulators limit the hydraulic pressure to the rear brake cylinders and prevent premature locking of the rear wheels when emergency braking effort is applied.

On some later cars, those fitted with automatic transmission and variant models, a single load-sensitive regulator is used.

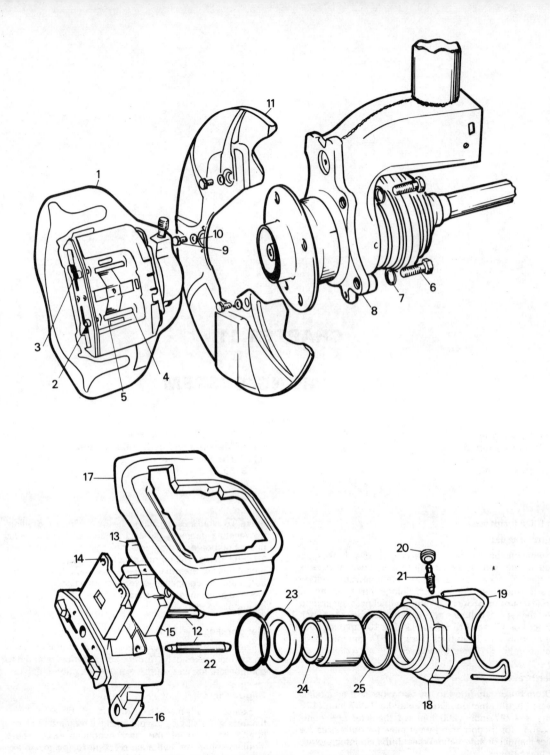

FIG 11:1   Components of a front brake caliper

Key to Fig 11:1   1 Caliper assembly   2 Lower retaining pin   3 Upper retaining pin   4 Inner pad   5 Outer pad   6 Bolt   7 Washer   8 Hub carrier   9 Bolt   10 Washer   11 Splash guard   12 Retaining pins   13 Anti-rattle spring   14 Outer pad   15 Inner pad   16 Mounting frame   17 Floating frame   18 Cylinder   19 Guide spring   20 Cap   21 Bleed screw   22 Circlip   23 Boot   24 Piston   25 Seal

11:2 Maintenance

Brake warning lights:

Ensure that the brake warning lights are, at all times, operating. Renew blown bulbs. If serviceable bulbs do not light up, check the serviceability of the switch (7 in **FIG 11:10** or 8 in **FIG 11:11**) and the wiring continuity.

Hydraulic fluid:

Check the fluid level in the master cylinder reservoir regularly and top up as necessary. Use the same approved fluid as that already in the system. This should be heavy duty brake fluid of reputable brand to specification SAE J1703a.

Every two years, drain the hydraulic system completely and refill with fresh fluid. The procedure is described in **Section 11:6**.

Brake pedal free play:

Every 5000 miles (8000 km), check that the brake pedal free play is within .16 to .27 inch (4 to 7 mm) in the case of models not fitted with servo assistance and that it is zero in the case of models which are fitted with servo assistance. The procedures are described in **Section 11:5**.

Adjustments:

Every 5000 miles (8000 km), to compensate for wear of brake shoe friction linings, the non-automatic adjustment type rear brake shoes must be reset as described in **Section 11:4**.

No corresponding action is required on automatic adjustment type rear brakes nor on front brakes.

Adjustment of the handbrake is required on all models to compensate for wear of rear brake linings. The procedure should be carried out every 5000 miles (8000 km) and is described in **Section 11:7**.

Friction linings:

Every 5000 miles (8000 km), check the thickness of the front brake pads and renew as necessary as described in **Section 11:3**. The wear limit thickness is .23 inch (6.0 mm).

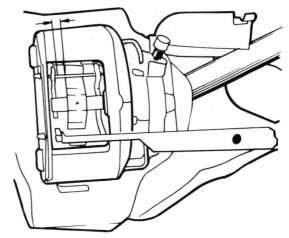

FIG 11:2 Measuring and gauging pad thickness

Some later cars have a pad wear warning device consisting of a small lug on the brake disc which comes into contact with an extension of the brake pad when the lining is worn down to the critical limit. This causes a pulsation which may be felt at the brake pedal.

Every 15,000 miles (25,000 km), check the thickness of the rear brake shoe linings as described in **Section 11:4** and renew if necessary. The wear limit thickness is .10 inch (2.5 mm) for riveted linings or .04 inch (1.0 mm) for bonded linings.

Hydraulic system:

Every 30,000 miles (50,000 km), overhaul the front brake calipers, the rear brake wheel cylinders and the master cylinder. The procedures are described in **Sections 11:3, 11:4** and **11:5** respectively. Also check the operation of the rear brake pressure regulators.

11:3 Front brakes

The components of a front wheel caliper are shown in **FIG 11:1**. The caliper assembly 1 is attached, through the mounting frame 16, by two bolts and washers 6 and 7 to

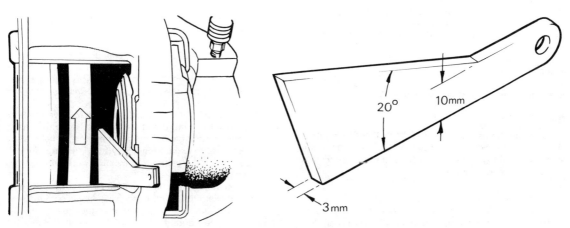

FIG 11:3 Checking piston 20 deg. position

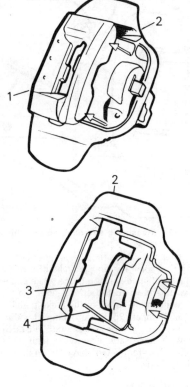

FIG 11 : 4   Dismantling a caliper

Key to Fig 11 : 4   1 Mounting frame   2 Floating frame
3 Cylinder sub-assembly   4 Guide spring

the hub carrier 8. The piston and cylinder assembly 18 to 25 is located within the floating frame 17. This sub-assembly, together with the pads, retaining pins and anti-rattle spring 12 to 15, can slide within the mounting bracket. When the brakes are applied, the piston acts directly on the inner pad and forces it against the inner face of the disc. By reaction, the outer pad is pulled inwards against the outer face of the disc. Compensation for wear of the pads is automatic. The floating frame and cylinder sub-assembly takes up a gradually more 'inward' position in relation to the mounting frame as the pads wear and the piston projects from a cylinder by a gradually increasing distance. There are two types of retaining pin; those shown in **FIG 11:1** and those which are locked by a retaining spring as in **Chapter 8, FIG 8:10**.

Girling calipers:

Some later cars are fitted with Girling caliper assemblies in place of the Teves units described above. There are some small differences in construction, but servicing procedures are very similar.

Pad wear measurement:

The pad wear limit thickness is .23 inch (6.0 mm). Refer to **FIG 11:2**. The actual pad thickness (between the arrows) may be checked visually after removing the road wheels or the minimum thickness may be gauged by using tool VW 136 without removing the wheels. Slide the gauge into position, turn it through 90 degrees and rest it on the lower retaining pin. If the gauge cannot be turned into this position, the anti-rattle spring to pad backing plate dimension is less than the gauge dimension indicating that the pad has reached or is less than the wear limit thickness.

Pad renewal:

1 Raise the front of the vehicle and remove the road wheels. Refer to **FIG 11:1**. Remove the lower retaining pin 2 using, if necessary, a suitable pin punch. Remove the anti-rattle spring 13. Remove the upper retaining pin 3.
2 Withdraw the inner friction pad using, if necessary, wire hooked into the retaining pin holes.
3 Press the floating frame and cylinder inwards, disengage the recess in the outer face of the outer pad and withdraw the outer pad. Discard the pads, the anti-rattle spring, both pins and, if fitted, their retaining spring. **Do not now operate the brake pedal until the new pads have been fitted.**
4 Empty some fluid from the master cylinder reservoirs and, keeping a watch on the fluid level to ensure that it does not overflow, press the piston back into the cylinder.
5 Using piston setting gauge 3.9314.2400.1 or an equivalent (see **FIG 11:3**), check that the piston 20 degree setting is correct as shown in **FIG 11:3**. Adjust if necessary. The official tool for rotating a piston is 3.9314.1500.2.
6 Fit the new pads, retaining pins and, if applicable, their locking spring. Operate the brake pedal a number of times to adjust the position of the pads.
7 Repeat the procedure on the other front wheel and lower the vehicle.

Caliper overhaul:

1 Carry out operations 1, 2 and 3 of the friction pad renewal procedure described earlier.
2 Disconnect the hydraulic flexible pipe from the caliper and blank off the open end to prevent loss of fluid and entry of dirt.
3 Remove the two bolts and washers 6 and 7 and dismount the caliper.
4 Refer to **FIG 11:4**. Press the floating frame and cylinder (see direction of arrows in upper illustration) from the mounting frame. Use a hammer and soft drift (see arrows in lower illustration) and press the piston assembly 3 from the floating frame 2. Remove the guide spring 4.
5 Refer to **FIG 11:1**. Remove circlip 22 followed by boot 23. Apply compressed air to the hytdraulic pipe connecion and blow the piston from the cylinder. Use a plastic rod to extract seal 25. Discard the boot and the seal. Clean the piston and cylinder bore with methylated spirits.
   On assembly, apply brake cylinder paste to the cylinder bore and seal and to the piston diameter. The remaining operations are the dismantling sequence in reverse. Torque tighten bolts 6 to 43 lb ft (6 kg m). Bleed the hydraulic system as described in **Section 11:6**.

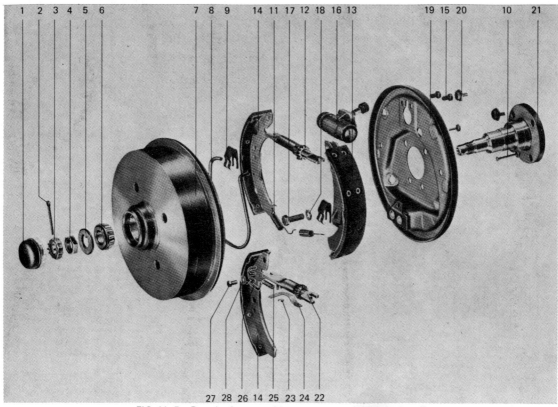

FIG 11 : 5   Rear brake assembly components (180 mm drum)

Key to Fig 11 : 5   1 Hub cap   2 Splitpin   3 Locking ring   4 Nut   5 Thrust washer   6 Outer bearing   7 Drum
8 Spring   9 Spring   10 Retaining pin   11 Spring   12 Adjuster (manual)   13 Brake shoe   14 Brake shoe   15 Bolt
16 Wheel cylinder (14.29 mm diameter)   17 Bolt   18 Washer   19 Backplate   20 Plug   21 Stub axle   22 Adjuster
(automatic)   23 Circlip   24 Automatic adjuster   25 Spring   26 Lever   27 Bolt   28 Washer

Dismounting a caliper:

Carry out operations 1 and 3 of the caliper overhaul sequence. Carry out operation 2 only if the caliper must be disconnected. **Do not operate the brake pedal until refitment has been completed.** Torque tighten bolts 6 to 43 lb ft (6 kg m).

Brake disc:

To remove a brake disc, dismount the caliper as described earlier. Refer to **Chapter 8, FIG 8:5** and remove the single countersunk screw. If necessary, use a soft hammer to separate the disc from the hub. Discs may be either .4 inch (10 mm) or .47 inch (12 mm) in thickness. If scored, discs may be salvaged by regrinding provided that the thickness is not reduced by more than .04 inch (1 mm) from the original. The minimum wear limit thickness is .06 inch (1.5 mm) below the original.

Splash guard:

To dismount the splash guard, remove the three bolts and washers 9 and 10 in **FIG 11:3**.

11:4 Rear brakes

Drum brakes with either 7.087 inch (180 mm) or 7.874 inch (200 mm) internal diameter drums are fitted to vehicles covered by this manual and their components are shown in **FIGS 11:5** and **11:6**. For each drum size there are two variants; those which require manual adjustment to compensate for wear of shoe linings and those in which the compensation is automatic. Differing components for these variants are included in the illustrations. It will be noted that the wheel hubs are integral with the brake drums.

When the brakes are applied, two hydraulically actuated pistons housed in each fixed cylinder expand the shoes against the internal diameter of the drums. This gives a leading and trailing shoe arrangement. The shoes are withdrawn by return springs.

Adjustment:

Chock the front wheels, raise the rear of the vehicle and release the handbrake. Refer to **FIGS 11:7** and **11:8** and, depending upon the type, rotate the toothed adjuster or turn the eccentric adjuster (in the **a** direction) on both brakes until the rear wheels cannot be turned by hand. Turn the adjusters in the opposite direction until the wheels turn freely. Depress the foot brake pedal a number of times and recheck. Adjust the handbrake as described in **Section 11:7**. Lower the vehicle. Top up the brake fluid level.

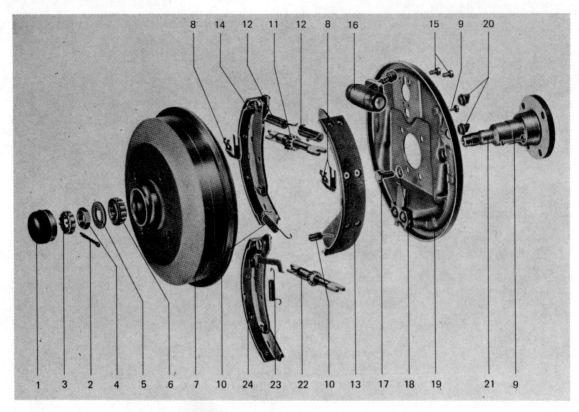

FIG 11:6   Rear brake assembly components (200 mm drum)

Key to Fig 11:6   1 Hub cap   2 Splitpin   3 Locking ring   4 Nut   5 Thrust washer   6 Outer bearing   7 Drum
8 Spring   9 Retaining pin   10 Spring   11 Adjuster (manual)   12 Spring   13 Brake shoe   14 Brake shoe   15 Bolt
16 Wheel cylinder (17.46 mm diameter)   17 Bolt   18 Washer   19 Backplate   20 Plug   21 Stub axle   22 Adjuster
(automatic)   23 Spring   24 Brake shoe with automatic adjuster

FIG 11:7   Rear brake shoe adjustment

Backing off the brake shoe adjustment:

This operation is only required if the brake drum is to be removed. Refer to **FIG 11:7** or **FIG 11:8** and turn the adjuster to increase the shoe to drum clearance. In the case of brakes with automatic adjustment, the pinion automatic adjuster must be disengaged by using a wire hook through the wheel bolt hole before the adjuster can be backed off and the shoe to drum clearance increased.

Brake shoe linings:

The wear limit thickness of shoe linings is .10 inch (2.5 mm) for riveted linings or .04 inch (1 mm) for bonded linings. On some cars removal of the brake drum is necessary for checking the thickness, on others an inspection hole is provided in the backplate for this purpose. The type of lining is indicated by a white stripe, straight for riveted or waved for bonded linings.

Linings which have become contaminated with oil or grease must also be renewed as they cannot be satisfactorily cleaned.

Although, with riveted linings, it is possible to reline the old shoes, it is always advisable to obtain readly lined shoes from the VW agent. Always renew the shoes in axle sets of four in order to ensure balanced braking.

Overhauling a rear brake assembly:

In **FIGS 11 : 5** and **11 : 6**, the components are numbered in the order in which they are to be removed. It will not normally be necessary to dismount the backplate or the stub axle. Removal and refitment of the drums is covered in **Chapter 9., Section 9:3**. After disconnecting the hydraulic pipe, blank off the open end to prevent loss of fluid and entry of dirt.

The components of a wheel cylinder assembly are shown in **FIG 11:9**. To dismantle, remove boots 1, withdraw the pistons 2 and spring 4. Remove seals 3. Discard the rubber parts 1, 2 and 3. Clean the remaining parts in methylated spirits. On reassembly, fit new boots and seals and coat the pistons and cylinder bores with brake cylinder paste.

Reassembly is the reverse of the dismantling sequence and must be followed by bleeding of the hydraulic system as described in **Section 11:6**, by manual adjustment (if relevant) as described earlier and by adjusting the handbrake as described in **Section 11:7**.

11:5 The hydraulic system

Observe scrupulous cleanliness when working on any part of the hydraulic system and use only fluid of reputable brand and to specification SAE J1703a. Note that **brake fluid will damage paintwork.**

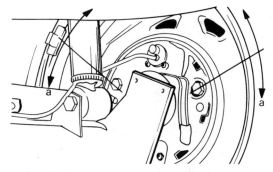

FIG 11:8   Rear brake shoe adjustment

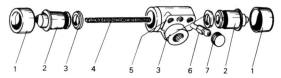

FIG 11:9   Components of a wheel cylinder

Key to Fig 11:9   1 Boot   2 Piston   3 Seal   4 Spring
5 Cylinder   6 Bleed screw   7 Cap

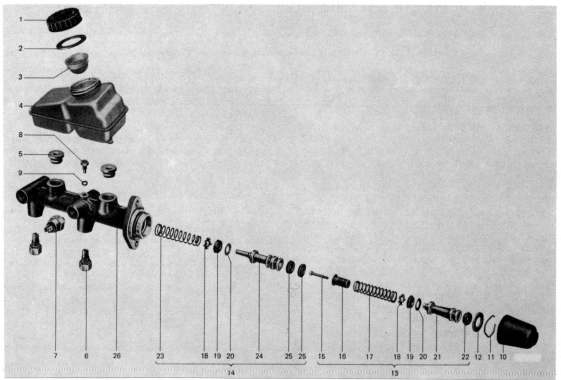

FIG 11:10   Components of the master cylinder (without servo unit)

Key to Fig 11:10   1 Cap   2 Washer   3 Strainer   4 Reservoirs   5 Plug   6 Residual pressure valve   7 Brake warning light switch (2-pin type)   8 Stop screw   9 Washer   10 Boot   11 Circlip   12 Stop washer   13 Primary piston assembly   14 Secondary piston assembly   15 Stroke limiting screw   16 Stop sleeve   17 Cylindrical spring   18 Combined support ring   19 Primary cup   20 Cup washer   21 Pushrod piston   22 Secondary cup   23 Conical spring   24 Secondary piston   25 Piston seal   26 Master cylinder housing

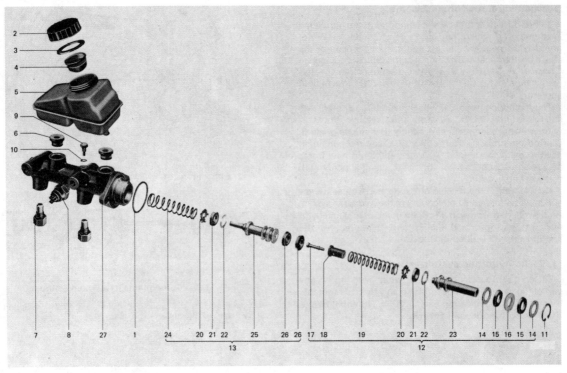

FIG 11:11   Components of the master cylinder (with servo unit)

Key to Fig 11:11   1 'O' ring   2 Cap   3 Washer   4 Strainer   5 Reservoirs   6 Plug   7 Residual pressure valve
8 Brake warning light (2-pin type)   9 Stop screw   10 Washer   11 Circlip   12 Primary piston assembly   13 Secondary
piston assembly   14 Washer   15 Secondary cup   16 Plastic washer   17 Stroke limiting screw   18 Stop sleeve
19 Cylindrical spring   20 Combined support ring   21 Primary cup   22 Cup washer   23 Primary piston   24 Conical spring
25 Secondary piston

The components of the master cylinder which is not fitted with a servo assistance unit are shown in **FIG 11:10**. The components of the master cylinder which is fitted with a servo assistance unit are shown in **FIG 11:11**. Both types have tandem pistons. Each piston serves a separate hydraulic section. Each section operates one front wheel brake and the diagonally opposite rear brake. In the event of a pipe or a seal failure in one section, the other will continue to operate normally. Certain models are provided with a servo unit which augments the braking effort applied by the foot brake pedal. The servo effort arises from atmospheric pressure and intake manifold partial vacuum acting across a diaphragm. Should the servo unit become inoperative, unassisted braking effort is available. Later models are fitted with a pressure regulator in each dual line. Their purpose is explained in **Section 11:1**.

Brake pedal adjustment:

Access for pedal adjustment on all models requires removal of the pedal which is retained by three Phillips screws.

On models without servo units, loosen the clevis locknut, turn the pushrod until there is .16 to .27 inch (4 to 7 mm) free play at the brake pedal pad and retighten the locknut.

On models with servo units, remove the spring retained clevis pin, refer to **FIG 11:12**, loosen the clevis locknut 11,

turn the pushrod 10 until the hole in the clevis 12 aligns exactly with the hole in the brake pedal lever when it is in the normal, at rest, position (that is, zero free play), refit the spring retained clevis pin and retighten the locknut.

Servo unit:

A defective servo unit should be removed and replaced by a new unit. Before condemning a suspect unit, ensure that the in-line non-return valve is serviceable, that there are no leaks in the vacuum pipeline, that the filter 8 in **FIG 11:12** and the seals 4 and 5 are serviceable and that the slots in washer 7 and filter are not in line with each other. With the engine stationary, depress the brake pedal a number of times to evacuate the partial vacuum. Depress the pedal under medium pressure and hold this position while starting the engine. If the servo is operating correctly, the pedal will be felt to give slightly as servo assistance becomes effective.

To remove a servo, uncouple the pushrod from the brake pedal arm, remove the nuts which retain the master cylinder to it, remove the nuts which retain the unit to the bulkhead, dismount the regulators (if fitted) and dismount the servo unit. Fitment is the reverse of this sequence and must be followed by adjustment of the brake pedal as described earlier.

Pressure-sensitive regulators:

If fitted, these are located immediately below the master cylinder on a bracket which is attached to the servo unit. The righthand regulator controls the hydraulic pressure to the righthand rear wheel and vice versa. If the brake pedal is firmly depressed once and then released, a slight 'knock' should be felt as the regulator pistons return to a neutral position.

If the operation of the regulators is suspect, a pressure test should be carried out. As the equipment required will not be readily available to an owner, professional assistance will be needed. **FIG 11:13** shows a zero to 1400 lb/sq in (0 to 1000 kg/sq cm) range pressure gauge and pipe (with bleed connection) fitted to a caliper bleed position. A second pipe and pressure gauge must, at the same time, be similarly connected to the **diagonally opposite** rear wheel bleed position. Bleed both lines via the incorporated bleed connections. Operate the brake pedal firmly several times then apply the brakes hard until the gauge on the front wheel shows a pressure of 500 lb/sq in (35 kg/sq cm). The gauge at the rear wheel should read 380 lb/sq in (27 kg/sq cm). Depress the pedal harder until the front gauge reads 1400 lb/sq in (100 kg/sq cm). The rear gauge should now read 810 lb/sq in (57 kg/sq cm). If the rear pressure reading is not within 5% of that specified, the regulator should be changed for a new unit.

Load-sensitive regulator:

This is attached to the body above the rear axle and is operated from the axle by means of a spring. Rear brake hydraulic pressure is regulated according to the attitude of the car when weight is transferred to the front under heavy braking and thus prevents rear wheel locking. As special tools are required for checking and adjusting the regulator, the car should be taken to a service station in the event of malfunction.

Master cylinder:

The master cylinder should be overhauled every 30,000 miles (50,000 km).

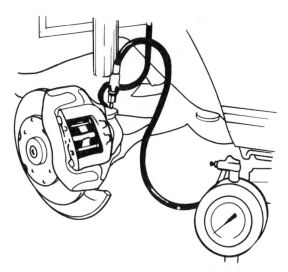

FIG 11:13   Checking a regulator

FIG 11:14   Using a conical tool

Removal and fitment:

Uncouple the hydraulic pipes and blank off the open ends to prevent loss of fluid and entry of dirt. Remove the retaining nuts and washers and dismount the unit.

Fitment is the reverse of this sequence and must be followed by bleeding the complete system as described in **Section 11:6.**

Dismantling:

Discard the fluid from the reservoirs. Refer to **FIG 11:11** or to **FIG 11:12** and dismantle the parts in the sequence in which they are numbered in the illustration. Keep the parts carefully identified and, in particular, ensure that the circular primary spring 17 and 19 is not interchanged with the conical secondary spring 23 or 24. Discard all cups and seals. Discard circlip 11. Clean the internal parts in methylated spirits.

Assembly:

Follow the reverse of the dismantling sequence. Where relevant, use a conical sleeve as shown in **FIG 11:14** to fit new cups or seals. Lubricate the shaft of the primary piston and the secondary cup (23 and 15 in **FIG 11:11**) with the silicone grease included in the overhaul kit. Coat all other cups and pistons in both types of master cylinder with brake cylinder paste before installing them. Keep the cylinder housing vertical to prevent parts from sliding out. Ensure that the new circlip 11 is fully seated in its groove.

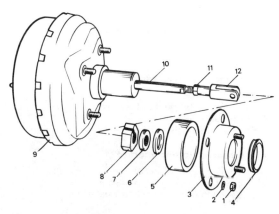

FIG 11:12   The servo unit

Key to Fig 11:12   1 Nut   2 Washer   3 Bracket   4 Seal   5 Seal   6 Cap   7 Damping washer   8 Filter   9 Servo unit   10 Pushrod   11 Locknut   12 Clevis

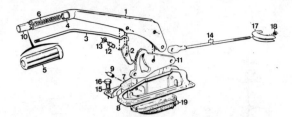

FIG 11 :15 Components of the handbrake control

Key to Fig 11 :15   1 Lever   2 Ratchet   3 Ratchet release rod   4 Spring seat   5 Hand grip   6 Spring   7 Bracket   8 Bracket   9 Pin   10 Ratchet release button   11 Ratchet quadrant   12 Ratchet pivot pin   13 Circlip   14 Rod   15 Washer   16 Bolt   17 Equalizer yoke   18 Nut (adjuster)   19 Boot

11 :6 Bleeding the hydraulic system

This procedure, for which two operators are required, is only necessary if air has entered the system. This may result from the level of the fluid in the reservoirs having fallen too low; because the system has been drained of old fluid or because part of the system has been dismantled. It is important to keep the reservoirs topped up during the bleeding procedure to avoid further air from entering the system. **Do not re-use fluid which has been bled from the system as it will have become aerated.** Use fresh fluid straight from the supply tin. The bleed screws are shown in **FIGS 11 :1** and **11 :9**.

Sequence:

If only one caliper or wheel cylinder has been disconnected, bleed at that point. If the master cylinder has been disconnected or if the system has been drained, bleed in the following sequence: righthand rear, lefthand rear, righthand front, lefthand front.

Procedure:

1 Remove the cap from the bleed nipple and attach a length of rubber or plastic tubing. Submerge the free end of the tubing in a container which is partially filled with brake fluid. Loosen the bleed screw by approximately half a turn.
2 Depress the brake pedal through its full travel, close the bleed screw and release the brake pedal. Repeat this sequence until the fluid from the drain tube is free from air bubbles.
3 Close the bleed screw, remove the drain tube and refit the cap. Repeat the procedure on the other wheels in the sequence specified earlier.

11 :7 The handbrake

The components of the handbrake control are shown in **FIG 11 :15**. The handbrake operates only on the rear wheels. When applied, the control pulls on the equalizer 17 via rod 14 and tensions the cable which is looped round the equalizer. The cable, pulling with equal force on each, applies the brakes to both rear wheels.

An adjuster is provided, item 18 in **FIG 11 :15**, for shortening the effective length of the operating cable when handbrake travel becomes excessive due to cable stretch after long usage. The procedure is as follows:

Adjustment:

1 Adjust the rear brake shoes (on manual adjustment models) as described in **Section 11 :4**. Leave the front wheels chocked and the rear wheels lifted.
2 In the case of models with manual adjustment, apply the handbrake control lever by two notches of the ratchet quadrant. In the case of models with automatic adjustment, apply the handbrake control lever by four notches.
3 Refer to **Chapter 9, FIG 9 :5** and tighten the adjuster nut (arrowed 1) until the rear wheels cannot be turned by hand in either direction.
4 Release the handbrake control lever and confirm that both wheels can now be rotated freely. Repeat the adjustment if necessary. Apply the handbrake and lower the vehicle.

11 :8 Fault diagnosis

(a) 'Spongy' pedal

1 Leak in hydraulic system
2 Worn master cylinder
3 Defective master cylinder seals
4 Defective caliper or wheel cylinder seals
5 Air in hydraulic system

(b) Excessive pedal movement

1 Check 1 and 5 in (a)
2 Rear brake shoes require adjustment
3 New pads and/or shoe linings required
4 Very low fluid level in reservoirs

(c) Brakes inefficient

1 Distorted drum or disc
2 Contaminated pad or shoe lining
3 Loose caliper assembly
4 Seized piston in caliper or wheel cylinder
5 Blocked hydraulic pipe
6 Seized handbrake cable or linkage pivot
7 Broken pull-off spring
8 Defective regulator(s)

(d) Absence of servo assistance

1 Air filter blocked
2 Vacuum pipe blocked or fractured
3 Check valve defective
4 Servo unit defective

(e) All brakes do not operate

1 Check 2, 4, 5 and 8 in (c)
2 One section of reservoir empty
3 One section of master cylinder defective

(f) Rear brake(s) lock before front brakes

1 Check 8 in (c)
2 Pipeline to front brake(s) blocked or fractured
3 Regulator incorrectly adjusted

CHAPTER 12

THE ELECTRICAL SYSTEM

12:1 Description

All models covered by this manual have 12-volt electrical systems in which the negative battery terminal is earthed. Wiring diagrams are included in the **Toohnical Data** section of the **Appendix**.

The battery is housed in the engine compartment as also is the combined fuse and relay box. The starter motor incorporates positive engagement of the drive pinion. The starter motor switch is combined with the ignition switch and operates a solenoid which is integral with the starter motor assembly. The starter motor is mounted on the righthand side of the engine and is carried by the intermediate plate immediately between the engine rear face and the transmission bellhousing.

The generator is belt driven from the crankshaft by the same belt that drives the cooling system water pump. It is a 3-phase AC machine and incorporates a transistorized rectifier. The electronic regulator is included in the alternator assembly. A 'no charge' warning light is provided in the instrument panel.

Although instructions for servicing of electrical equipment are given in this Chapter, it must be accepted that it is not sensible to attempt repairs to units which are seriously defective, electrically or mechanically. Such defective equipment should be replaced by new units. The testing of certain equipment requires specialist services and facilities.

12:2 The battery

The negative terminal is earthed. **Do not, under any circumstances, reverse the terminal connections.** The connections must be tight on the battery posts and a light coating of petroleum jelly should be applied to the terminal clamps and posts to retard corrosion and oxidation. If the connections are corroded, remove the clamps and wash them in bicarbonate of soda. Dry them thoroughly, apply non-metallic grease or Vaseline and refit the terminal clamps tightly.

Keep the fluid in each cell topped up to .2 inch (5 mm) above the plates and separators by adding distilled water.

Never add undiluted acid. If it is necessary to prepare a new solution of oloctrolyte due to spillage or loss, add the acid to the distilled water. It is highly dangerous to add water to acid.

If the charge state of the battery is suspect, test the electrolyte with a hydrometer. The indications from the specific gravity readings given by the hydrometer are approximately as follows.

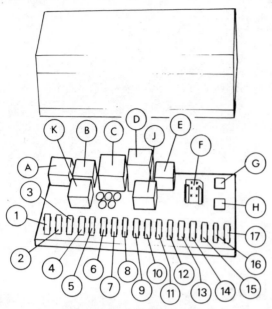

FIG 12:1 The fuses and relays

Key to Fig 12:1   See text tabulation

number of changes in fuse box layout and it is not possible to list the variations for every model. A quick check of the electrical equipment with a fuse removed will indicate which circuit it protects. Optional equipment is asterisked.

Fuse No.	Capacity	Circuit
1	8 amp	Lefthand headlamp
2	8 amp	Righthand headlamp
3	8 amp	Lefthand headlamp
4	8 amp	Righthand headlamp
5	8 amp	Heater fan; warning lights
6	8 amp	Horn
7	8 amp	Direction indicators
8	16 amp	Heated rear window
9	16 amp	Cigar lighter; radio
10	8 amp	Stoplights; interior lights; clock
11	16 amp	Windscreen wiper
12	16 amp	Windscreen wiper and washer
13	8 amp	Righthand rear light
14	8 amp	Lefthand rear light
15	8 amp	Instrument panel and glovebox illumination
16	25 amp	Air conditioning equipment*
17	16 amp	Fog lights*

Cells fully charged—Specific gravity 1.240 to 1.260.
Cells half charged—Specific gravity 1.170 to 1.190.
Cells discharged—Specific gravity 1.100 to 1.120.

The above readings will apply when the battery temperature is about 20°C (68°F). For the same cell condition, specific gravity will increase when the electrolyte temperature is more than 20°C and vice versa. Add .002 for every 3°C (5°F) above 20°C and subtract .002 for every 3°C below 20°C.

If the state of the battery is low take the car for a long daylight run or put the battery on charge at 4 to 5 amps. If this does not correct the battery charge state, have the individual cells voltage tested to ascertain whether the battery should be replaced by a new one. If the battery is to be put on charge without dismounting it from the vehicle, disconnect both leads from the battery.

If the battery is to stand for a long period, give it a freshening-up charge every month. If it is left discharged, it will deteriorate and be ruined.

12:3 Fuses and relays

The combined fuse and relay box is located on the lefthand side of the engine compartment. In addition to standard electrical equipment, the box caters for optional extra equipment and, depending upon the actual equipment fitted to a particular vehicle, all the relays identified in FIG 12:1 may not be fitted nor all the fuses be in use.

Never fit a replacement fuse of greater capacity than that specified for the position in the fuse box since, by doing so, the protection of the relevant circuit may be jeopardized. If a fuse blows repeatedly, trace the reason for it doing so without delay.

Fuses:

The following typical tabulation identifies the fuses and quotes their current capacities. There have been a

Relays:

The following tabulation identifies the relays as lettered in FIG 12:1 and, where relevant, quotes their J numbers in the Wiring Diagrams in the Appendix. Optional equipment is marked *.

A (J126)	Radiator cooling fan
B (J)	Headlamp circuits
C (J25)	Lighting circuits
D (J2)	Direction indicators
E (J24)	Windscreen wiper
F (J31)	Automatic windscreen washer*
G (J32)	Air conditioning equipment*
H (J5)	Fog lights*
J (J9)	Heated rear window
K (J33)	Iodine headlamps*

12:4 The starter motor

The components of the starter motor assembly are shown in FIG 12:2. When the ignition switch is turned to the start position, the starter solenoid is energized. The solenoid armature operates the forked lever 36 and this brings the pinion 37 into engagement with the ring gear of the flywheel or, in the case of automatic transmission models, the torque converter driving plate. At the same time the starter motor switch within the solenoid is closed, the starter rotates and turns the engine.

Tests for a starter which does not operate:

Check the condition of the battery and its connections. If these are in order, switch on the lights and operate the starter switch. Current is reaching the starter if the lights go dim. If the lights do not go dim, check with a voltmeter or test light if there is voltage at the solenoid when the switch is operated. If there is, suspect a defective solenoid. If there

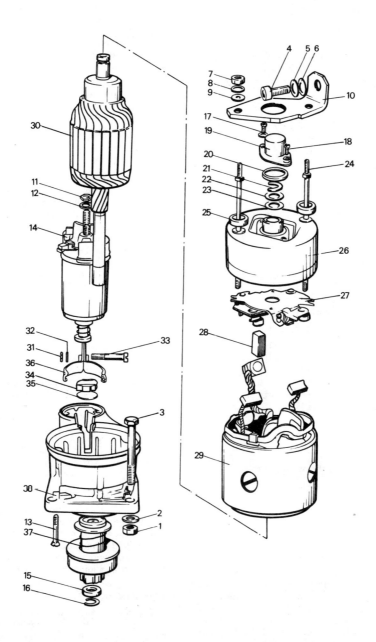

FIG 12:2   Components of the starter motor

Key to Fig 12:2   1 Nut   2 Washer   3 Bolt   4 Socket headed bolt   5 Washer   6 Washer   7 Nut   8 Washer
9 Washer   10 Support plate   11 Nut   12 Washer   13 Bolt   14 Solenoid   15 Stop ring   16 Circlip   17 Screw
18 Washer   19 Cap   20 Seal   21 Lockwasher   22 Spacer   23 Spacer   24 Bolt   25 Distance sleeve   26 End cover
27 Brush holder   28 Rubber sleeve   29 Housing   30 Armature   31 Nut   32 Washer   33 Bolt   34 Seal   35 Washer
36 Forked lever   37 Pinion   38 Mounting housing

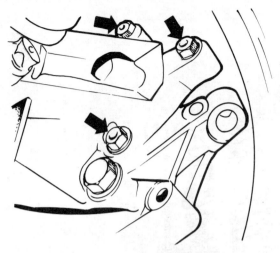

FIG 12:3 The starter motor retaining bolts are arrowed

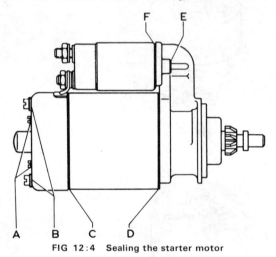

FIG 12:4 Sealing the starter motor

Key to Fig 12:4 Use D3 sealing compound at the positions lettered

is not suspect the ignition switch or the wiring continuity. If these are in order, remove the starter motor for further investigation and to check the brush gear.

Starter removal and fitment:

Disconnect the battery earth connection. Identify and disconnect the wiring from the solenoid. Remove the three nuts, bolts and washers 1, 2, and 3 in **FIG 12:2** and arrowed in **FIG 12:3** which attach the starter motor to the intermediate plate. Remove the socket headed bolt 4 from the support plate 10 and withdraw the motor forwards.

Fitment is the reverse of this sequence. Tighten the attachment bolt nuts and the socket headed bolt to a torque of 14 lb ft (2 kg m).

Fitting a new solenoid:

A new solenoid can be fitted without removing the starter motor from the vehicle. Loosen the nut which

retains the starter motor positive to the solenoid and remove the shoe. Remove the two bolts 13 in **FIG 12:2** which retain the solenoid. Withdraw the solenoid. When fitting the new solenoid, ensure that the armature engages correctly with the forked lever. Seal the solenoid/mounting bracket (**F** in **FIG 12:4**) with compound. The remaining operations are the reverse of the removal sequence. Check the operation of the starter assembly.

Dismantling the starter motor:

The components in **FIG 12:2** are numbered in the sequence in which they should be removed when completely dismantling a starter motor.

Inspection:

Use a brush to clean dust from the field coils, armature, casings and brush gear. Check the insulation of the brush holders. Check the brushes and their springs. Check the armature and field coils for open circuit and for insulation. Polish the commutatator with very fine (00 or 000 grade) sandpaper. Skim a badly worn commutator in a lathe. Use a high speed and take light cuts with a sharp tool. Remove the minimum amount to clean up (a refinished diameter of 1.357 inch (34.5 mm) is a minimum) and undercut the mica insulation by .02 to .03 inch (.5 to .8 mm). Armature axial play should be within .004 to .012 inch (.1 to .3 mm). The bush in the end cover 26 may, if necessary, be removed and new replacement pressed in.

Check the brushes for wear. The wear limit length is $\frac{1}{2}$ inch (13 mm). New brushes have to be soldered to their connecting wires. Remove old brushes by crushing them. Clean the end of the wire, insert it into the tinned drilling of the new brush and splay it out. Use silver solder and an iron of not more than 250 watt capacity to solder the connection. Ensure that the solder is confined by holding the wire with pliers close up behind the brush. File off any surplus solder. Confirm that the brushes move easily in their holders. Relieve any sluggishness by polishing the sides of the brushes with a smooth file.

Assembly:

Assembly is the reverse of the dismantling sequence. Lubricate the starter pinion splines, the forked lever pivot and the end cover bush sparingly with multi-purpose grease. Use a new circlip 16 and note that the stop ring is fitted with the ring groove outwards and that it must move freely on the armature shaft. Use D3 sealing compound at the points and joints indicated in **FIG 12:4**.

12:5 The alternator

This may be either of Bosch or Motorola type. There are slight differences in design, but servicing procedures are substantially the same. The components of a Bosch alternator are shown in **FIG 12:5**. It is an AC machine and is belt driven together with the water pump from a pulley on the crankshaft. The stationary 3-phase output coils are connected to the integral diode rectifier. The field coils are wound on the rotor and are connected to two slip rings on which the brushes run. A cooling fan 7 is incorporated immediately behind the drive pulley. Brushes should be renewed when

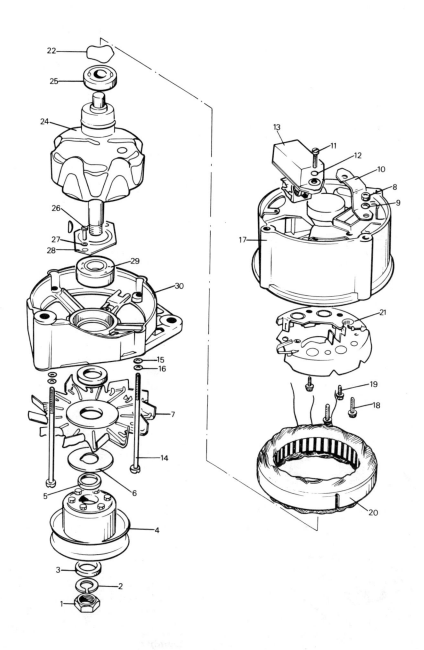

FIG 12:5 Components of the alternator

Key to Fig 12:5   1 Nut   2 Washer   3 Washer   4 Pulley   5 Spacer ring   6 Washer   7 Fan   8 Nut   9 Washer
10 Bracket   11 Screw   12 Washer   13 Regulator and brush assembly   14 Bolts   15 Washer   16 Washer   17 Housing
18 Screw and washer   19 Screw and washer   20 Stator   21 Diode carrier   22 Washer   23 Spacer ring   24 Rotor
25 Bearing   26 Screw   27 Washer   28 Bearing plate   29 Bearing   30 End plate

they have worn down to .2 inch (5 mm). The procedure is described in **Section 12:6.**

Observe the following precautions:

1 Never disconnect the regulator or the battery while the alternator is being driven.
2 Never disconnect or dismount the alternator without first disconnecting the battery.

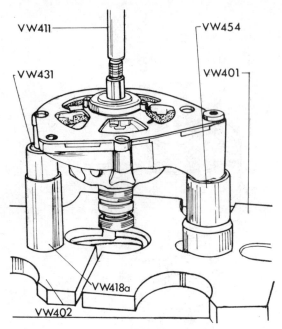

FIG 12:6   Removing the rotor from the end plate

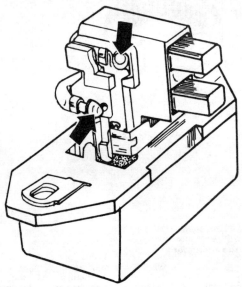

FIG 12:7   The regulator and brush assembly

3 Never operate the regulator independently from the alternator.
4 Never test the alternator either in the vehicle or on a test bench unless the battery is in circuit. Ensure that the battery is in good condition and fully charged and that the negative is earthed. **Never reverse the polarity.**

Tests on an alternator which is not charging:

During normal driving, if the ignition warning light (no charge) does not go out, investigate the reason why the alternator is not charging. Check that the connections to the battery and to the alternator are intact and firm. Check that the belt drive is intact and that it is correctly tensioned as described in **Chapter 4, Section 4:5.** Check that the brushes are of serviceable length and that they are not sticking in their holders. If these are in order, remove the alternator for further investigation as described in **Section 12:6.**

Alternator removal and fitment:

Disconnect the battery earth connection. Withdraw the multi-point socket from the alternator and disconnect the earth strap if fitted. Remove the drive belt as described in **Chapter 4, Section 4:5.** Remove the attachment bolts and dismount the alternator.

Fitment is the reverse of this sequence. Fit and tension the drive belt as described in **Chapter 4, Section 4:5.**

When refitting the alternator on early 1297 cc engines a new type bolt—N44714.1—should be used for the bracket mounting position and tightened to a torque of 2 kg m (14 lb ft). This will prevent wear in the end plate due to the play previously existing between the alternator and mounting bracket.

Dismantling the alternator:

The components in **FIG 12:5** are numbered in the order in which they should be removed when an alternator is to be completely dismantled.

Mark the relative position of the housing 17 and the end plate 30 before separating them. To separate the stator 20 from the diode carrier 21, it is necessary to unsolder the connections and care must be taken and 'heat sink' pliers used. If necessary the rotor can be separated from the end plate under a press as shown in **FIG 12:6.** Bearings 25 and 29 should be renewed. Note, if a new stator 20 is required, that one of the same width must be obtained. The stator for the 55 amp capacity alternator is .256 inch (6.5 mm) wider than that for the 35 amp capacity alternator. Note that screws 18 and 19 are of different lengths.

Renewal of the brushes which have a wear limit length of .2 inch (5 mm) is described in **Section 12:6.**

Assembly:

Assembly is the reverse of the dismantling sequence. Ensure that the fan 7 is fitted the correct way round.

12:6 The alternator regulator

The regulator (13 in **FIG 12:5**) is an electronic type and is combined with the alternator brush holder. It is mounted

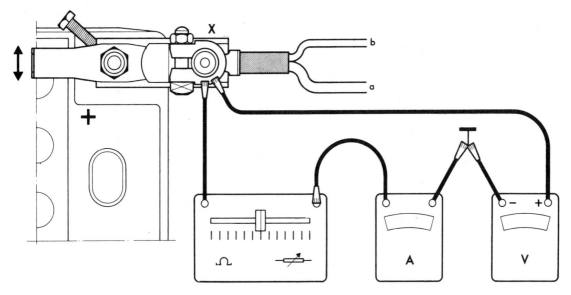

FIG 12:8 The alternator/regulator test set-up

Key to Fig 12:8   a To starter   b To fuse box terminal 30   X Battery cut-out switch mounted on battery + terminal

at the rear of the alternator and can be removed for replacement or for inspection of the brushes without dismounting the alternator from the vehicle.

Regulator removal and fitment:

Disconnect the battery earth connection. Remove the two screws and washers 11 and 12 in **FIG 12:5** and withdraw the regulator and brush assembly 13. Examine the brushes and, if necessary, renew them as described later.

Refitment is the reverse of the removal sequence.

Brush renewal:

Remove the regulator and brush assembly as described earlier. Wear limit length of brushes is .2 inch (5 mm). New brushes are .4 inch (10 mm) long. The points at which the brush connections are soldered are arrowed in **FIG 12:7**. Unsolder and remove the old brushes. Solder the connections of the new brushes and check that the brushes move easily in their holders. Relieve any sluggishness by polishing the sides of the brushes with a smooth file.

Alternator/regulator testing:

The following procedure is for testing with the unit installed in the vehicle and driven by the engine in the normal way. A zero to 18 range voltmeter, a —10, zero, +50 range ammeter, a variable resistance of 100 amp load capacity and a heavy duty battery cut-out switch are required. The test set-up is shown in **FIG 12:8**. The test sequence is as follows.

1 Disconnect the battery (negative) earth connection. Disconnect the battery positive connection. Connect the battery cut-out switch to the battery positive post. Connect the positive cable to the cut-out switch.

2 Close the battery cut-out switch. Connect the load resistance and ammeter in series between the cut-out switch and a well made earth. Connect the voltmeter between the cut-out switch and earth. The connections will now be as shown in **FIG 12:8**.

3 Connect the battery (negative) earth connection. Start the engine and run at 2500 to 3000 rev/min.

4 Adjust the load resistance until the ammeter reads 20 to 30 amps. Open the battery cut-out switch. This disconnects the battery from the switch. The load current is now controlled solely by the load resistance.

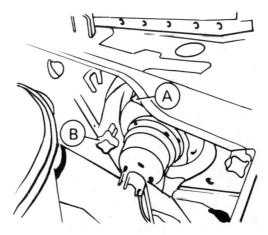

FIG 12:9   Headlamp beam adjustment points

Key to Fig 12:9   A Vertical adjustment   B Horizontal adjustment

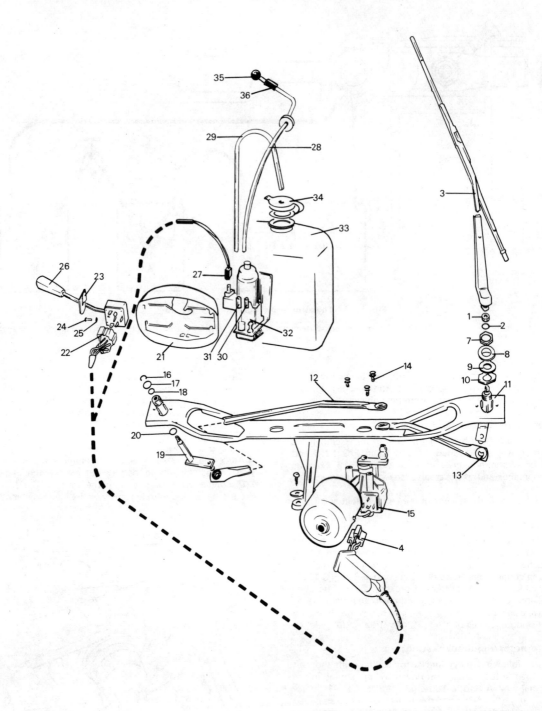

FIG 12:10 The windscreen wiper and washer

Key to Fig 12:10   1 Nut   2 Washer   3 Arm and blade   4 Multi-point connector   5 Bolt   6 Washer   7 Nut
8 Distance sleeve   9 Sealing washer   10 Washer   11 Frame   12 Drive link (righthand)   13 Drive link (lefthand)   14 Bolt
and washer   15 Motor (with crank set for lefthand drive vehicle, see **FIG 12:11**)   16 Circlip   17 Washer   18 Rubber
ring   19 Shaft   20 Washer   21 Switch cover   22 Multi-point connector   23 Cover   24 Phillips screw   25 Washer
26 Switch   27 Pump connector (2-point)   28 Hose for jet   29 Hose to container   30 Rubber grommet   31 Rubber
grommet   32 Pump   33 Fluid container   34 Cover   35 Jets   36 Rubber grommet

5 Adjust the load resistance until the ammeter reads 25 amps. The voltmeter should now read 12.5 to 14.5 volts.

6 If the voltage reading is not within the prescribed range, fit a new regulator as described earlier and repeat the test sequence from operation 3.

If, on the repeat test, a reading within the 12.5 to 14.5 volts range is obtained, the first regulator was defective. If, on the other hand, a reading within the prescribed range is again not obtained, the alternator is defective. A defective alternator should be passed to a specialist for repair or replaced by a new machine.

12:7 Headlamps

Professional facilities are required for a complete and accurate alignment of the main and dipped beams but acceptable adjustments may be made as follows.

Alignment:

Position the vehicle on level ground and 33 ft (10 m) from a vertical wall. With the tyres correctly inflated, one person or a weight of about 160 lb (70 kg) in a front seat

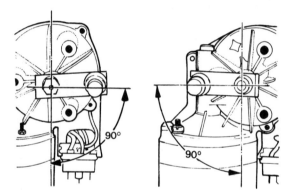

FIG 12:11 Lefthand drive and righthand drive parking positions

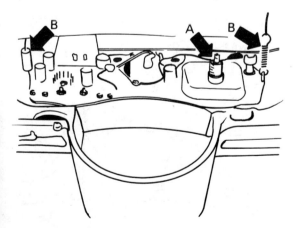

FIG 12:12 Removing the instrument cluster

Key to Fig 12:12   A Speedometer drive connection B Springs

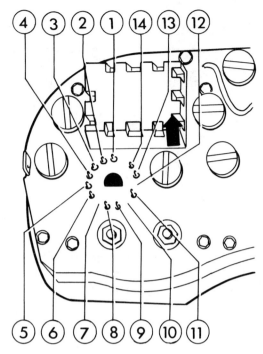

FIG 12:13 Multi-point connections and voltage stabiliser (arrowed)

Key to Fig 12:13   1 Direction indicator warning light (terminal 49a)   2 Earth connection (terminal 31)   3 Fuel gauge transmitter   4 Alternator warning light (terminal 15) 5 Alternator warning light (terminal D+)   6 Oil pressure warning light from oil pressure switch 7 Vacant   8 Positive wire (terminal 15)   9 Temperature gauge transmitter 10 Vacant   11 Clock + (terminal 30a)   12 Brake circuit warning light   13 Instrument lighting + (terminal 57) 14 Main beam warning light + (terminal 56a)

and the fuel tank full, adjust the headlights so that the main beams are parallel and 4 inch (100 mm) below the level of the headlamp centres.

The vertical (A) and the horizontal (B) adjustment screws are shown in FIG 12:9.

12:8 Lighting circuits

Lighting circuits are included in the Wiring Diagrams in the **Appendix** and their fuses and relays are identified in **FIG 12:1** and tabulated in **Section 12:3**.

Bulbs burn out frequently:

If the bulbs burn out frequently, suspect that the alternator regulator is defective. Check the regulator as described in **Section 12:6**.

Brilliance of lights varies with engine speed:

Check the condition of the battery connections, clean the battery terminal posts and ensure that the connections to the battery are making good contact. Renew the battery earth cable if it is not in first class condition.

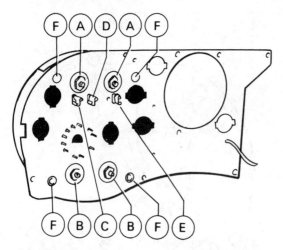

FIG 12:14   Removing temperature and fuel gauges

Key to Fig 12:14   A Fuel gauge retaining nuts   B Temperature gauge retaining nuts   C Earth (terminal 31)   D Terminal J   E + (terminal 15)   F Trim plate retaining bolts

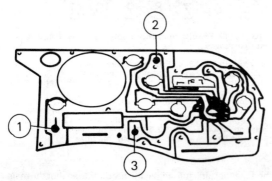

FIG 12:15   Cluster printed circuit board

Key to Fig 12:15   1 Connection for speedometer lighting   2 Connection for tachometer (terminal 15)   3 Connection for clock (terminal 30)

Confirm that the alternator drive belt is in good condition and that it is correctly tensioned as described in **Chapter 4, Section 4:5**.

12:9 Horn

If the horn does not operate, check that its fuse (6 in **FIG 12:1**) is intact, that the steering wheel horn button is making contact and that the wiring continuity (see Wiring Diagrams in the **Appendix**) is in order. If the horn itself is suspect, dismount it and, using jump wires, connect it directly across the battery terminals. A defective horn should be replaced by a new unit.

Pitch adjustment is made at the adjusting screw but, unless the vehicle is out of warranty, no adjustment should be attempted by an owner.

12:10 Windscreen wiper and washer

The components of the windscreen wiper and washer are shown in **FIG 12:10**. Parts are numbered in the sequence in which they should be removed when completely dismantling the equipment. They should be removed starting with 1 for the wiper mechanism and motor and with 27 for the washer pump and tank. Do not reverse the connector 27 or the washer pump will not supply fluid.

Ensure that the fluid in the washer tank is absolutely free of grit and foreign matter. Blockage of washer nozzles by dirt is the main reason for defective operation. Use a needle to adjust the aim of the nozzles. If either the wiper motor or the washer motor fails to operate, check, by using jump wires, that the relevant switch is not at fault. If the switch is serviceable but there is no voltage at the motor, check the fuses, the relay and the wiring continuity. If there is voltage at the motor but it fails to operate, fit a replacement. No servicing or overhaul procedures are prescribed for wiper or washer motors.

When correctly parked, the wiper blades should be parallel with the lower edge of the windscreen and $1\frac{3}{8}$ inch (35 mm) up from it. **FIG 12:11** shows the different wiper crank installation positions for LH and RH drive vehicles when in the parked position.

12:11 Instruments

Cluster removal:

Disconnect the battery earth connection. Refer to **FIG 12:12** and uncouple the speedometer drive cable from the back of the speedometer (arrowed **A**). Using long-nosed pliers, detach the left and right springs (arrowed **B**). Swing the cluster forwards and disconnect the multi-point connector. **FIG 12:13** shows the back of the cluster and identifies the multi-point pins.

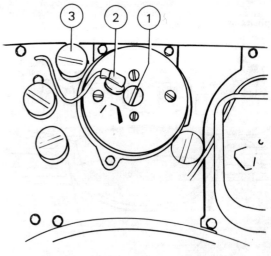

FIG 12:16   Tachometer installation

Key to Fig 12:16   1 Terminal 1 (to coil)   2 + (terminal 15)   3 Tachometer lighting

Speedometer:

The speedometer is driven by flexible cable from the transmission final drive. The cable is supported by rubber grommets at the bulkhead and at the instrument panel carrier. Do not lubricate the drive cable. Access to the speedometer requires the removal of the cluster as described earlier. An unserviceable speedometer should be passed to a specialist for repair. To remove, withdraw the bulb and holder and remove three bolts.

Oil pressure:

If, with a stationary engine but with the ignition switched on, the oil pressure warning light does not come on, check the bulb. If the bulb is intact, suspect that there is a discontinuity in the wiring or that the pressure switch contacts have remained open. The transmitter is located at the rear of the cylinder head and, if defective, must be replaced by a new unit.

Coolant temperature and fuel gauges:

The coolant temperature transmitter is located in the elbow at the rear of the cylinder head. The fuel gauge transmitter is located in the top of the fuel tank.

Both these gauges are fed electrically via the voltage stabilizer arrowed in **FIG 12:13** (this is J6 in the Wiring Diagrams in the **Appendix**). If both the coolant temperature gauge and the fuel gauge give no or erroneous readings, suspect that the stabilizer is defective. Withdraw it and fit a new unit.

To remove the coolant temperature and the fuel gauges, refer to **FIG 12:14** and remove nuts **A** and **B** and remove bolts **F** holding the gauge trim plate. Withdraw the gauges.

A defective coolant temperature transmitter should be replaced by a new unit as also should a defective fuel gauge transmitter. It is permissible, however, to correct the fuel gauge readings by judicious bending of the float arm. To withdraw the fuel gauge transmitter, remove the cover plate which is retained by three screws. Identify and disconnect the two wires. Uncouple the fuel feed pipe. Unclip and withdraw the transmitter and its seal. Note, that a plastic union nut is used to secure the transmitter when a plastic fuel tank is fitted. A special tool—2012—is required for the removal and refitting of this nut.

Clock or tachometer:

Either a clock or a tachometer may be fitted. A printed circuit board with circuit track for speedometer lighting is available as a spare part for vehicles not so fitted in the factory. Refer to **FIG 12:15.** If a clock or a tachometer is to be connected, an additional track must be soldered in. **FIG 12:16** shows a tachometer installation.

12:12 Fault diagnosis

(a) Battery discharged

1 Lights left on
2 Shortcircuit in electrical system
3 Alternator not charging
4 Regulator defective
5 Battery internally defective

(b) Insufficient charging rate

1 Check 4 in (a)
2 Loose or dirty terminal connections
3 Drive belt slipping

(c) Battery overcharged

1 Check 4 in (a)

(e) Alternator output low or nil

1 Check 4 in (a); 3 in (b)
2 Drive belt broken
3 Stator and/or rotor windings defective
4 Slip rings worn, burned or shorted
5 Brushes worn or sticking

(f) Starter motor lacks power or will not operate

1 Battery discharged; cable connection loose
2 Starter switch or solenoid defective
3 Brushes worn or sticking
4 Commutator worn, burned or shorted
5 Pinion engagement mechanism defective
6 Armature and/or field coils defective

(g) Starter motor rough or noisy

1 Retaining bolts loose
2 Damaged teeth on pinion or flywheel ring gear

(h) Lights inoperative or erratic

1 Battery discharged; bulb(s) burned out
2 Faulty earth connection; discontinuity in wiring
3 Defective switch or relay; fuse blown

(j) Wiper motor sluggish

1 Defective motor
2 Seized linkage pivot

(k) Washer inoperative

1 Blocked jet
2 Empty tank
3 Pump or motor defective

(l) Temperature or fuel gauge inoperative

1 Voltage stabilizer defective
2 Transmitter disconnected or defective
3 Gauge defective
4 Fuse blown; loose or broken wiring

(m) Oil pressure warning light inoperative

1 Check 2 and 4 in (l)
2 Bulb blown

(n) Warning light(s) inoperative

1 Check 4 in (l) and 2 in (m)

NOTES

CHAPTER 13

THE BODYWORK

13:1 Bodywork finish

Large-scale repairs to body panels are best left to expert panel beaters. Even small dents can be tricky, as too much hammering will stretch the metal and make things worse instead of better. Filling minor dents and scratches is probably the best method of restoring the surface. Use a modern filling compound and work to the manufacturer's instructions. The touching-up of paintwork is well within the ability of most owners, particularly as self-spraying cans of the correct colours are now readily available. Paint may change colour with age and it is better to spray a whole wing or panel rather than to touch-up a small area.

Before spraying, remove all traces of wax polish with white spirit. More drastic treatment will be required if silicone polish has been applied. Use a primer surfacer or a paste stopper or a filler according to the amount of filling required, and when it is dry, rub it down with 400 grade 'Wet or Dry' paper until the surface is smooth and flush with the surrounding area. Spend time on getting a good finish as this will control the final effect. Apply the retouching paint keeping it wet in the centre and light and dry round the edges. After a few hours drying, use a cutting compound to remove the dry spray and finish off with a liquid polish.

Take great care when working with hydraulic brake fluid not to spill any on the paintwork.

13:2 Bonnet removal and fitment

Two operators are required to dismount and refit the bonnet.

Removal:

1 Open the bonnet. Mark across both hinges and the underside of the bonnet panel so that refitment may be made with the minimum of adjustment.
2 While the bonnet is being held firmly, remove the two bolts which retain the bonnet to each hinge. Lift off the bonnet.

Fitment:

Fitment of the bonnet is the reverse of the removal sequence. Before finally tightening the bolts which secure the bonnet to the hinges, position the panel to the marks made before removal. When fitted, the gap round the bonnet should be equal and even. The elongated holes in the hinges allow fore and aft adjustment. Vertical adjustment, when necessary, is made at the elongated holes in the attachment points of the forward catches and at the hinge pivots.

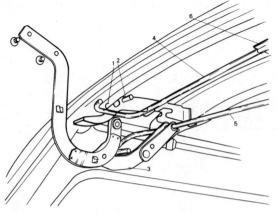

FIG 13:1 A tail door hinge

Key to Fig 13:1   1 Circlip   2 Hinge pin   3 Hinge
4 Torsion bar   5 Torsion bar   6 Anti-rattle pad

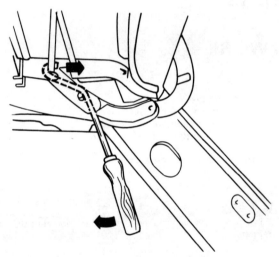

FIG 13:2   Removing a torsion bar

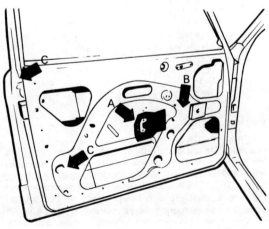

FIG 13:3   A front door with trim removed

Bonnet catch cable:

The cable operates directly on the lefthand catch. A link rod from the lefthand catch operates the righthand catch.

Removal:

Access requires removal of the radiator grille. This is retained by four clips to the upper crossmember, two lower supports, two side springs and eight Phillips type screws on the forward skirt.

Remove the two bolts which retain the lefthand catch and unhook the cable. Remove the two Phillips type screws which retain the hand lever and dismount the lever assembly. Remove the clip which retains the lever itself, remove the lever and unhook the cable. Remove the cable by pulling out forwards.

Fitment:

The fitment procedure is the reverse of the removal sequence. Ensure that the rubber grommet in the water trap is correctly fitted. Adjust the catches as necessary vertically to level the forward line of the bonnet panel. Refit the radiator grille.

13:3 Luggage compartment lid and tail door

The first part of this section covers the boot lid and is only relevant to saloon models. The second part is only relevant to estate vehicles.

Luggage compartment lid removal:

Two operators are required to dismount and refit the boot lid.
1 Open the lid. Mark the position of each hinge in relation to the lid so that refitment may be carried out with the minimum of adjustment.
2 With the weight of the lid being taken securely, remove the two bolts which retain the lid to each hinge and lift off the lid.

Fitment of the lid:

Fitment is the reverse of the removal sequence. Any necessary adjustment of the lid to equalize the surrounding gap is made before finally tightening the retaining bolts fully.

The lid catch is adjustable as also is the catch striker.

The lid is balanced in the open position by a tension spring at each hinge and, if a spring breaks, the balance will be impaired. Unhook the broken spring and hook in a new replacement.

Tail door removal:

The tail door is carried by two hinges and its weight is counterbalanced by two torsion bar springs. A lefthand hinge is shown in **FIG 13:1**. Two operators are required to dismount and refit the tail door.
1 Open the tail door. Mark each hinge position in relation to the door. This will minimize adjustment on refitment.
2 With the door being firmly supported, remove the two bolts which retain the door to each hinge. Dismount the door.

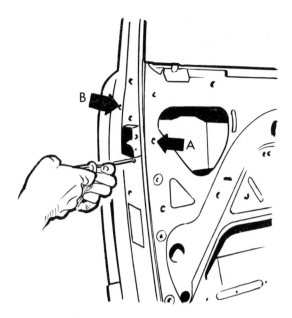

FIG 13:4 Removing a lock

Fitment:

Fitment of the tail door is the reverse of this sequence. Before finally tightening the hinge bolts fully, check that the gap between the door and the body aperture is equal and even. The tail door catch and the catch striker are both adjustable.

Hinge pin removal and fitment:

With the tail door dismounted, press down the hinge partially, block the hinge in this position with the head of a hammer, remove the circlip from the hinge pin and extract the pin. Fitment is the reverse of this sequence.

Torsion bar removal and fitment:

Remove the hinge pin as described earlier. Remove the blocking hammer. Refer to **FIG 13:2** and, using special tool VW 709 as shown in the illustration or an equivalent lever, prise the bar out of engagement. **FIG 13:2** shows a righthand hinge. The procedure for a lefthand hinge is the same.

Fitment of a new torsion bar is substantially the reverse of this procedure. Refit the hinge pin and rehang the tail door.

13:4 Doors, locks and fittings

Each door is carried on a pair of hinges. The fixed half of each hinge is welded to and consequently integral with body. Doors are bolted to the swinging half of each hinge by three bolts in the case of front doors and, in the case of four door models, by two bolts to each rear door.

Door trim panel removal:

Remove the central screw and pull off the window winding mechanism handle. Remove the elbow rest which is retained by three screws. Commencing at a bottom corner, disengage the twelve spring clips. Swing the bottom edge of the trim panel away from the door and disengage the top edge from the retaining angle. Collect the foam packing pieces and sheet plastic insulation.

Door trim fitment:

This is the reverse of the removal procedure. Ensure that the insulation material is evenly repositioned before refitting the trim panel.

Door latch remote control:

The latch remote control is retained to the door inner panel by two Phillips type screws and may be removed after dismounting the trim panel as described earlier and withdrawing these screws and unhooking the actuating rod. The location of the screws is indicated by arrow **A** in **FIG 13:3**.

On refitment, the rod must be reconnected with the lock before attaching the remote control unit to the door inner panel.

Door lock:

Refer to **FIG 13:4**. The door lock is attached to the flange of the door by two Phillips type screws and by a third screw (arrowed **A**) to the door inner panel. Removal of these screws allows the lock to be dismounted and the remote control actuating rod to be unhooked if it has not been removed as described earlier.

Fitment is this sequence reversed.

Exterior door handle:

The exterior handle is retained by a single Phillips type screw (arrowed **B** in **FIG 13:4**) in the flange of the door and by two stop plates on the inside.

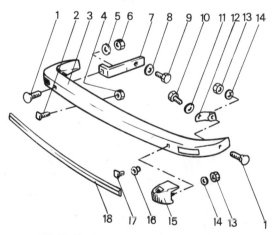

FIG 13:5 Components of a front bumper

Key to Fig 13:5   1 Bolt   2 Bolt   3 Bumper   4 Nut
5 Washer 6 Nut 7 Bracket 8 Washer 9 Bolt 10 Bolt
11 Washer 12 Bracket 13 Nut 14 Washer 15 Trim
16 Ferrule 17 Clip 18 Trim strip

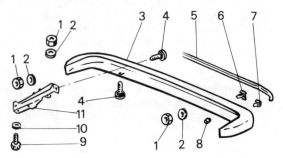

FIG 13:6   Components of a rear bumper

Key to Fig 13:6   1 Nut   2 Washer   3 Bumper   4 Bolt
5 Trim strip   6 Bolt   7 Clip   8 Ferrule

Door removal and fitment:

Two operators are essential when removing a door. Uncouple the check strap by removing the pivot pin. Withdraw the hinge pivot pins while the door is being firmly supported. Dismount the door. It is recommended that a door be removed by withdrawing the pivot pins and not by removing the hinge bolts. If necessary, the half hinges may be detached from the door after it has been dismounted.

Fitment is effected by refitting the pivot pins while the door is supported and accurately registered with the body half of the hinges. Recouple the check strap.

Door and lock adjustment:

If the original door is being refitted and the hinges and lock have not been disturbed, adjustment should not be necessary. If a new door, lock or striker has been fitted, adjustment will almost certainly be required. Proceed as follows:

1 Loosen the lock striker so that under fairly heavy load it can take up a new position. Loosen the hinge retaining

FIG 13:7   Front wing

Key to Fig 13:7   1 Hexagon-headed screws   2 Phillips type screws   3 Wing

bolts to a similar extent. Remove the trim panel as described earlier.

2 Centre the door and adjust the alignment and the level of the outside panel in relation to the body.

3 From inside the door through the relevant apertures, tighten the hinge retaining bolts. Hold the outside handle with the latch in the open position. Push the door fully closed and release the latch. This will move the striker into the required position.

4 Again hold the exterior handle and press the latch to the open position. Gently open the door without disturbing the striker.

5 Tighten the striker fully. Close the door and tighten the hinge retaining bolts fully. Check the adjustment. Repeat the procedure as necessary until a satisfactory fit is achieved. Refit the trim panel.

13:5   Door window winder and glass

Window glass winder mechanism:

When removing the window winding mechanism the window glass must be in the fully raised position. Remove the four retaining screws (indicated by arrow **B** in **FIG 13:3**) from the door inner panel, push the winder spindle into the door cavity and draw the unit downwards to disengage the two plastic sliders from the arm. Withdraw the mechanism through the bottom forward aperture in the door inner panel.

Fitment of the winder mechanism is the reverse of this sequence.

Window glass:

Remove the window winding mechanism as described earlier leaving the window glass in the fully raised position. Unscrew the lock button so that the interior jointing can be removed. Disengage the exterior chrome moulding and, by giving each a quarter turn with a screwdriver, unlatch the five clips which retain the outer jointing. Take careful note of the run taken by the tension cable assembly before unhooking and removing the cable and its spring. Dismount the rear guide channel which is retained by an upper and lower screw (these are indicated by arrows **C** in **FIG 13:3**). Lower the glass to the bottom of the door cavity. Remove the three screws which retain the forward guide channel. Remove the glass front steady and withdraw the guide channel upwards. Withdraw the window glass upwards.

Fitment is the reverse of this sequence and procedure.

13:6   Windscreen and backlight glass

The procedure for replacing a windscreen, backlight or tail door glass is similar. If the windscreen is being dealt with, remove the windscreen wiper arms and place a protective covering over the bonnet and instrument panel.

Removing the original glass:

1 Run a thin-bladed tool round the aperture to break the seal between the moulding and the body aperture.

2 Press the glass by hand from inside the vehicle and dismount it complete with the moulding. If the glass was shattered, remove sections until the moulding can be pulled away from the aperture.

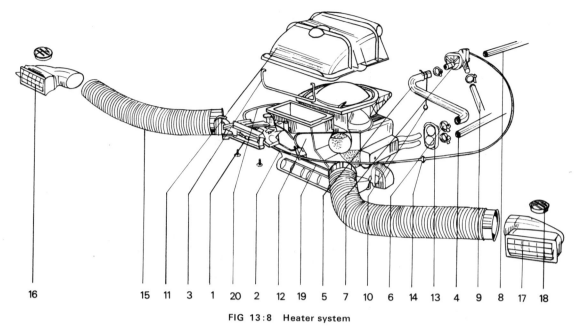

FIG 13:8 Heater system

Key to Fig 13:8   1 Controls   2 Heater valve cable   3 Clip   4 Hose   5 Hose   6 Hose clip   7 Heater valve   8 Hose
9 Hose   10 Hose support   11 Heater cover   12 Housing   13 Double grommet   14 Grommet   15 Air hose   16 Vent
17 Vent   18 Vent   19 Control cable   20 Control cable

3 Ensure that the moulding channel is cleaned thoroughly of old sealer and that all particles of shattered glass have been removed from it. Small particles of old glass left in the moulding channel may induce breakage of the new glass.

4 Clean the body aperture which was in contact with the moulding and remove all traces of old sealer from its surfaces. Check that the aperture is undamaged. File away any bumps. These could induce breakage of the new glass.

Fitting new glass:

1 Fit the cleaned moulding to the glass with the moulding joint at the centre top. Fit the trim mouldings and angle pieces. Fit a strong cord of about $\frac{1}{8}$ inch (3 mm) in diameter into the moulding channel which will engage the aperture flange.

2 Arrange the ends of the cord to emerge at the bottom centre point of the moulding and on the inside. With the aid of an assistant, locate the glass against the outside of the aperture and ensure that it registers evenly and accurately with the aperture.

3 From outside the vehicle, apply hand pressure to the edge of the moulding over the aperture flange. Pull alternate ends of the cord while the assistant maintains a steady hand pressure. Pull the cord first across the bottom and then up the sides and finally across the top.

4 Check that the lips of the moulding fit correctly inside and outside all the way round. Use a pressure gun fitted with a copper nozzle (which will not scratch the glass) and inject sealing compound between both the glass and the moulding and between the moulding and the

body flange. Remove excess sealer with a rag and white spirit. Do not use thinners as this will damage the paintwork.

3:7 Consoles

Centre console:

The centre console (if fitted to the particular model) may be removed after withdrawing three screws: one at the rear edge; one on the left and one on the right forward side and inclined upwards. Disconnect the radio and additional instruments if fitted and withdraw the console.

Fitment is the reverse of this sequence.

Selector lever console:

This unit is applicable only to automatic transmission models and access to the starter inhibitor switch, etc. necessitates its removal as described in **Chapter 7, Section 7:10.**

13:8 Dashboard and glove box

Removal:

1 Disconnect the battery earth cable. Dismount the centre console (if fitted to the particular model) as described in **Section 13:7**. Dismount the instrument cluster as described in **Chapter 12, Section 12:11.**

2 Dismount the centre cover which is retained by four Phillips type screws and disconnect the cigar lighter. Remove the two nuts from inside the glove box and dismount the glove box lid. Remove one Phillips type screw from below the glove box.

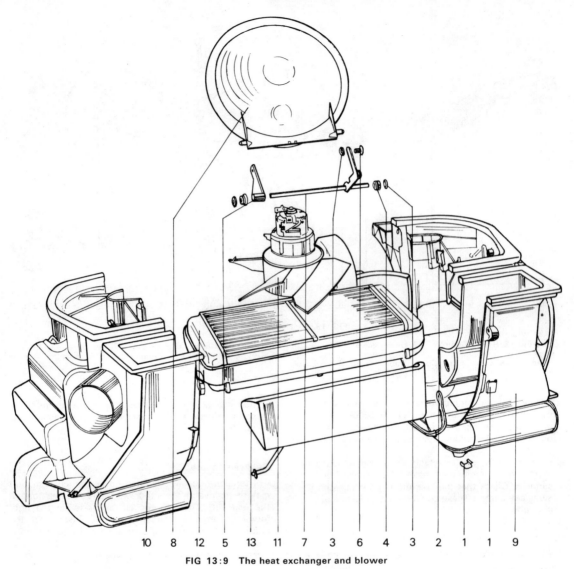

FIG 13:9 The heat exchanger and blower

Key to Fig 13:9   1 Clip   2 Clip   3 Circlip   4 Bush   5 Levers   6 Pin   7 Rod   8 Cut-off flap   9 Half housing
10 Half housing   11 Blower   12 Heat exchanger   13 Control flap

3 Remove one Phillips type screw from the front upper edge of the shelf at the side of the steering column. Remove a further screw from the opposite side of the column and a third screw from the lower panel adjacent to the control pedals.

4 Remove the Phillips type screw from each extremity of the dashboard. Remove two dashboard attachment nuts from below the cowl panel water trap in the engine compartment.

5 Remove the air hose from the lefthand and the righthand vents. Pull off the heater control knobs and remove the coverplate which is attached to the dashboard by two screws.

6 Remove the steering wheel as described in **Chapter**

10, Section 10:3. Remove the switch assembly from the steering column. Check that all relevant wiring has been disconnected and that nothing is caught up in the assembly. Dismount the dashboard.

Fitment:

Installation of the dashboard is the removal sequence in reverse.

13:9 Bumper removal and fitment

Front bumper:

The components of a front bumper and its attachment brackets are shown in **FIG 13:5**.

Removal:

1 Open the bonnet, disconnect the battery earth cable and disconnect the wiring from the front direction indicator lights.
2 Remove the bolts which attach the side ends of the bumper to the front wings. Remove the nuts and washers which retain the bumper to the main support brackets. The bumper can now be dismounted.
3 If necessary the brackets may be removed from the chassis and the trim parts may be separated from the bumper channel.

Fitment:

Follow the reverse of the removal sequence.

Rear bumper:

The components of a rear bumper and its attachment brackets are shown in **FIG 13:6**.

Removal:

Open the boot lid and dismount the rear number plate illumination wiring. Remove the nuts, bolts and washers which attach the bumper channel to the wings and to the main support brackets. Dismount the bumper. If necessary, the brackets may be removed from the chassis and the trim may be separated from the bumper channel.

Fitment:

This is the reverse of the dismounting sequence.

13:10 Front wing removal and fitment

The panel which comprises a front wing and is removable is shown in **FIG 13:7**. Each wing is attached to the body by 14 screws.

Removal:

Remove the front bumper as described in **Section 13:9**. Remove the trim strips. Remove seven hexagon-headed screws from along the top of the wheel arch. The bonnet must be opened to give access to these screws. Remove three hexagon-headed screws from inside at the front, one Phillips type screw at the junction with the windscreen, one Phillips type screw from the lower body and two hexagon-headed screws from the forward skirt. Dismount the wing.

Fitment is the reverse of this sequence. Two operators will be required as the wing needs to be accurately positioned when engaging the screws. Apply undercoating to all bare metal areas and to the heads of the attachment screws and bolts.

13:11 Heater system

The layout of the standard heater system is shown in **FIG 13:8**. Hot coolant from the engine cooling system, when the heater system control valve is open, is circulated through the heat exchanger. Ambient air is drawn across the heat exchanger by the blower and distributed into the interior of the vehicle as selected by the controls. If the heat selection valve is closed, ambient air may be distributed.

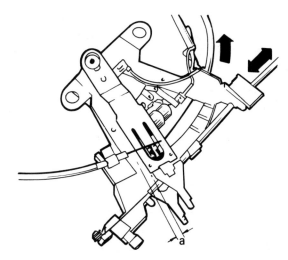

FIG 13:10   Control adjustment

Key to Fig 13:10   a Gap of .08 inch (2 mm)

Maintenance:

The hose connections will require renewal in due course and, as described later, the controls may require to be adjusted to compensate for cable stretch, etc. The blower electrical circuit is controlled by fuse 5 (see **Chapter 12, Section 12:3**). If the blower does not operate, check this fuse. If the fuse is intact, check the switch or the wiring circuit for discontinuity.

Removal:

In the event of the heat exchanger developing a leak or the blower motor becoming unserviceable, it will be necessary to partially or fully remove the heater system. Refer to **FIG 13:8** and proceed substantially in the same order as the parts are numbered as far as may be necessary to deal with a fault.

1 From inside the vehicle, pull off the control knobs. Remove two screws and dismount the coverplate. Disconnect the control cables and, if necessary, remove the control block.
2 Partially drain the engine cooling system as described in **Chapter 4, Section 4:2**. Release hose clips 6 and disconnect hoses 4, 5, 8 and 9 from the control valve 7 and hose support 10.
3 Remove two pins and dismount the heater cover 11. Withdraw the double grommet 13. Remove the dashboard as described in **Section 13:8**. Uncouple the hoses 15.
4 Refer to **FIG 13:9**. Dismount the heat exchanger/blower unit, remove the clips and separate the housing into its two halves. Withdraw the component that is at fault.

Reassembly and refitment:

Reverse the full or partial sequence as taken on dismantling the assembly. At the appropriate stage, adjust the controls as described later.

Adjustments:

There are three controls each of which is adjusted separately as follows.

Cut-off cable:

Press the flap in the water drain box to the closed position. Hook the cable to the upper slide. Press this slide to the left until gap **a** in **FIG 13:10** is .08 inch (2 mm). Secure the cable with its clip.

Control flap cable:

Hook the cable to the lower slide. Press the lower slide fully to the left and hold it in this position. Push the outer cable fully to the right until the inner cable cannot be pulled further out of the outer cable (see **FIG 13:10**) and secure the outer cable with its clip.

Heater valve cable:

Push the lever on the valve (7 in **FIG 13:8**) in the direction of the cable until it is against its stop. Attach the inner cable to the lever. Move the outer cable until the finger grip on the control dial is vertically upwards. Secure the outer cable with its clip.

13:12 Air conditioning system

The optional air conditioning system incorporates a refrigeration circuit, the compressor of which is belt driven from a pulley forward of the water pump and alternator drive pulley. An electro-magnetic clutch between the compressor and its pulley is brought into action by the air conditioning controls.

All work involving air conditioning system components must be entrusted to a service station having the necessary special equipment and trained personnel. If the pressurised system is opened, liquid refrigerant will escape, immediately freezing anything it contacts. Uncontrolled release of the refrigerant will cause severe frostbite or possibly even more serious injury if it contacts any part of the body. Consequently, it is dangerous for an unqualified person to attempt to disconnect any part of the circuit.

Units may be dismounted from their locations without the assistance of a qualified refrigeration engineer **provided that pipe connections are not disturbed.** An owner must enlist specialist assistance if it is necessary to discharge, evacuate or recharge the system.

If the system does not operate, check that the compressor drive belt is intact and correctly tensioned. If this is in order, check that the fuse (see **Chapter 12, Section 12:3**) is intact and that relay J32 is serviceable. If these are in order, check the switch and the relevant circuit for a possible wiring discontinuity.

APPENDIX

TECHNICAL DATA

WIRING DIAGRAMS

HINTS ON MAINTENANCE AND OVERHAUL

GLOSSARY OF TERMS

INDEX

Inches	Decimals	Milli-metres	Inches to Millimetres		Millimetres to Inches	
			Inches	mm	mm	Inches
1/64	.015625	.3969	.001	.0254	.01	.00039
1/32	.03125	.7937	.002	.0508	.02	.00079
3/64	.046875	1.1906	.003	.0762	.03	.00118
1/16	.0625	1.5875	.004	.1016	.04	.00157
5/64	.078125	1.9844	.005	.1270	.05	.00197
3/32	.09375	2.3812	.006	.1524	.06	.00236
7/64	.109375	2.7781	.007	.1778	.07	.00276
1/8	.125	3.1750	.008	.2032	.08	.00315
9/64	.140625	3.5719	.009	.2286	.09	.00354
5/32	.15625	3.9687	.01	.254	.1	.00394
11/64	.171875	4.3656	.02	.508	.2	.00787
3/16	.1875	4.7625	.03	.762	.3	.01181
13/64	.203125	5.1594	.04	1.016	.4	.01575
7/32	.21875	5.5562	.05	1.270	.5	.01969
15/64	.234375	5.9531	.06	1.524	.6	.02362
1/4	.25	6.3500	.07	1.778	.7	.02756
17/64	.265625	6.7469	.08	2.032	.8	.03150
9/32	.28125	7.1437	.09	2.286	.9	.03543
19/64	.296875	7.5406	.1	2.54	1	.03937
5/16	.3125	7.9375	.2	5.08	2	.07874
21/64	.328125	8.3344	.3	7.62	3	.11811
11/32	.34375	8.7312	.4	10.16	4	.15748
23/64	.359375	9.1281	.5	12.70	5	.19685
3/8	.375	9.5250	.6	15.24	6	.23622
25/64	.390625	9.9219	.7	17.78	7	.27559
13/32	.40625	10.3187	.8	20.32	8	.31496
27/64	.421875	10.7156	.9	22.86	9	.35433
7/16	.4375	11.1125	1	25.4	10	.39370
29/64	.453125	11.5094	2	50.8	11	.43307
15/32	.46875	11.9062	3	76.2	12	.47244
31/64	.484375	12.3031	4	101.6	13	.51181
1/2	.5	12.7000	5	127.0	14	.55118
33/64	.515625	13.0969	6	152.4	15	.59055
17/32	.53125	13.4937	7	177.8	16	.62992
35/64	.546875	13.8906	8	203.2	17	.66929
9/16	.5625	14.2875	9	228.6	18	.70866
37/64	.578125	14.6844	10	254.0	19	.74803
19/32	.59375	15.0812	11	279.4	20	.78740
39/64	.609375	15.4781	12	304.8	21	.82677
5/8	.625	15.8750	13	330.2	22	.86614
41/64	.640625	16.2719	14	355.6	23	.90551
21/32	.65625	16.6687	15	381.0	24	.94488
43/64	.671875	17.0656	16	406.4	25	.98425
11/16	.6875	17.4625	17	431.8	26	1.02362
45/64	.703125	17.8594	18	457.2	27	1.06299
23/32	.71875	18.2562	19	482.6	28	1.10236
47/64	.734375	18.6531	20	508.0	29	1.14173
3/4	.75	19.0500	21	533.4	30	1.18110
49/64	.765625	19.4469	22	558.8	31	1.22047
25/32	.78125	19.8437	23	584.2	32	1.25984
51/64	.796875	20.2406	24	609.6	33	1.29921
13/16	.8125	20.6375	25	635.0	34	1.33858
53/64	.828125	21.0344	26	660.4	35	1.37795
27/32	.84375	21.4312	27	685.8	36	1.41732
55/64	.859375	21.8281	28	711.2	37	1.4567
7/8	.875	22.2250	29	736.6	38	1.4961
57/64	.890625	22.6219	30	762.0	39	1.5354
29/32	.90625	23.0187	31	787.4	40	1.5748
59/64	.921875	23.4156	32	812.8	41	1.6142
15/16	.9375	23.8125	33	838.2	42	1.6535
61/64	.953125	24.2094	34	863.6	43	1.6929
31/32	.96875	24.6062	35	889.0	44	1.7323
63/64	.984375	25.0031	36	914.4	45	1.7717

UNITS	Pints to Litres	Gallons to Litres	Litres to Pints	Litres to Gallons	Miles to Kilometres	Kilometres to Miles	Lbs. per sq. In. to Kg. per sq. Cm.	Kg. per sq. Cm. to Lbs. per sq. In.
1	.57	4.55	1.76	.22	1.61	.62	.07	14.22
2	1.14	9.09	3.52	.44	3.22	1.24	.14	28.50
3	1.70	13.64	5.28	.66	4.83	1.86	.21	42.67
4	2.27	18.18	7.04	.88	6.44	2.49	.28	56.89
5	2.84	22.73	8.80	1.10	8.05	3.11	.35	71.12
6	3.41	27.28	10.56	1.32	9.66	3.73	.42	85.34
7	3.98	31.82	12.32	1.54	11.27	4.35	.49	99.56
8	4.55	36.37	14.08	1.76	12.88	4.97	.56	113.79
9		40.91	15.84	1.98	14.48	5.59	.63	128.00
10		45.46	17.60	2.20	16.09	6.21	.70	142.23
20				4.40	32.19	12.43	1.41	284.47
30				6.60	48.28	18.64	2.11	426.70
40				8.80	64.37	24.85		
50					80.47	31.07		
60					96.56	37.28		
70					112.65	43.50		
80					128.75	49.71		
90					144.84	55.92		
100					160.93	62.14		

UNITS	Lb ft to kgm	Kgm to lb ft	UNITS	Lb ft to kgm	Kgm to lb ft
1	.138	7.233	7	.967	50.631
2	.276	14.466	8	1.106	57.864
3	.414	21.699	9	1.244	65.097
4	.553	28.932	10	1.382	72.330
5	.691	36.165	20	2.765	144.660
6	.829	43.398	30	4.147	216.990

TECHNICAL DATA
Dimensions are in inches unless otherwise stated

Manufacturer's spares are in mm sizes and consequently, where relevant, dimensions in the following tabulation are given in mm

ENGINE

Bore and stroke:

1297 cc	75 × 73.4 mm
1471 cc	76.5 × 80 mm
1588 cc	79.5 × 80 mm

Compression ratios:

Passat models	8.2, 8.5 or 9.7 to 1
Dasher models	8.0 or 8.5 to 1

Crankshaft:

Main bearings	5	
Desired dia. clearance	.0012 to .0032	
Wear limit	.0067	
Desired axial clearance	.003 to .007	
Wear limit	.010	
Journal diameters	*Main*	*Crankpin*
New	53.96 − .02 mm	45.96 − .02 mm
1st regrind size	53.71 − .02 mm	45.71 − .02 mm
2nd regrind size	53.46 − .02 mm	45.46 − .02 mm
3rd regrind size	53.21 − .02 mm	45.21 − .02 mm
Maximum ovality	.03 mm	
Bearing shells	Available to suit these diameters	

Connecting rods:

Big end:

Desired diametrical clearance	.0012 to .0032
Wear limit	.0047
Axial wear limit	.010

Pistons:

Standard diameter:

1297 cc	74.98 to 75.00 mm		
1471 cc	76.48 to 76.50 mm		
1588 cc	79.48 to 79.50 mm		
Oversizes	.25, .50, 1.00 mm		
Clearance in bore	.0012		
Wear limit	.0028		
2nd oversize	76.98	77.01	701
	76.99	77.02	702
	77.00	77.03	703
3rd oversize	77.48	77.51	751
	77.49	77.52	752
	77.50	77.53	753

Piston rings:

Gap wear limit	.040
Groove clearance wear limit	.060

Cylinder block:

Head face flatness	Within .004

Cylinder head:

Block face flatness	Within .004
Camshaft bearing bores	1.0236 + .0008

Camshaft:

Axial clearance	.006
Journal diameters	1.0220 – .0008
Camshaft bend at centre	.004 maximum
Cam 'heel to toe' dimension	1.902

Valves:

Dimensions	See **Chapter 1, FIG 1 : 6**
Stem to guide clearance:	
Inlet	.016
Exhaust	.032

Valve clearances:

	Cold	*Hot*
Inlet	.006 to .010	.008 to .012
Exhaust	.014 to .018	.016 to .020

Valve springs:

Spring test load:	
Outer	96 to 106 lb at .916
Inner	46 to 51 lb at .719

Valve timing:

Inlet opens	9 deg. BTDC
Inlet closes	41 deg. ABDC
Exhaust opens	49 deg. BBDC
Exhaust closes	1 deg. ATDC

Oil pump

Gear type

Pressure:	
Minimum	14 lb/sq inch
Maximum	94 lb/sq inch
Warning light	4 to 8 lb/sq inch (pre 1976)
	2 to 6 lb/sq inch (from 1976)

FUEL SYSTEM

Fuel octane ratings:

Passat models:	
1297 cc engines	91
1470 cc engines	98
Dasher models	91

Filters:

Air cleaner	Dry, paper
Fuel	Incorporated in fuel pump

Fuel pump

Mechanical diaphragm

Pressure	2.8 to 3.5 lb/sq inch

Single barrel carburetters

Solex 30/35 PDSIT

Passat 1300 ZA and ZF engines	056 129 015A
Venturi dia.	27 mm
Main jet	X 137.5
Air correction jet	110
Pilot jet	50
Pilot air jet	180
Passat 1500 LC engines FF	075 129 015F
Venturi dia.	27 mm
Main jet	X 135
Air correction jet	90
Pilot jet	55
Pilot air jet	180
Passat 1500 (Manual) ZB engine	056 129 015C
Venturi dia.	27 mm
Main jet	X 140
Air correction jet	100

Pilot jet	..	.. ..	50
Pilot air jet	..	.. .. ..	180
Passat 1500 (Automatic) ZB engine		.. ..	056 129 015D
Venturi dia.	..	.. ..	27 mm
Main jet	..	.. ..	X 135
Air correction jet	..	.. .. ..	100
Pilot jet	..	.. ..	50
Pilot air jet	..	.. .. ..	180

Single barrel carburetters   .. .. .. Solex 35 PDSIT

Passat 1300 (1975)		.. .. ..	056 129 015AD
Venturi dia.	..	.. .. ..	27
Main jet	..	.. .. ..	X 140
Air correction jet	..	.. ..	100
Pilot jet	..	.. ..	52.5
Pilot air jet	..	.. .. ..	150
Passat 1500 (1975) YJ engines (Manual)		..	062 129 015B
Main jet	..	.. .. ..	X142.5
Air correction jet	..	.. ..	110
Pilot jet	..	.. .. ..	52.5
Pilot air jet	..	.. ..	150
Passat 1500 (1975) (Automatic)		.. ..	062 129 015A
As Manual except:			
Main jet	..	.. ..	137.5
Passat 1600 (1976)	..	.. ..	049 129 015 B and C
Main jet	..	.. .. ..	140
Air correction jet	..	.. ..	110
Idle jet	..	.. .. ..	55
Idle air jet	..	.. .. ..	150
Auxiliary fuel jet	..	.. ..	50/100

Double barrel carburetters   .. .. .. Solex 32/35 TDID

Passat TS (Manual) ZC engine	..	.. ..	056 129 015
Venturi dia.	..	.. .. ..	24/27 mm
Main jet	..	.. .. ..	X117.5/X140
Air correction jet	..	.. ..	140/140
Pilot jet	..	.. .. ..	45
Pilot air jet	..	.. .. ..	180
Auxiliary fuel jet	..	.. ..	60
Auxiliary air jet	..	.. ..	130
Enrichment	..	.. ..	57.5/75
Passat TS (Automatic) ZC engine	..	..	056 129 015E
As Manual except:			
Main jet	..	.. .. ..	X115/X140
Enrichment	..	.. ..	57.5/80
Passat TS 1975 (Manual) ZC engine	..	..	056 129 015AE
As pre-1975			

Double barrel carburetters   .. .. .. Solex 32/35 DIDTA

Passat TS (Manual)	..	.. ..	056 129 015P
As TS (Automatic)			
Passat TS 1975 (Automatic)	..	..	056 129 015 AH
As pre-1975 except:			
Enrichment	..	.. ..	57.5/100
Passat 1600 (1976)	..	.. ..	049 129 015
Main jet	..	.. ..	X 117.5/X150
Air correction jet	..	.. ..	140/120
Idle jet	..	.. .. ..	47.5
Idle air jet	..	.. .. ..	175

Dasher 1973:
    Type .. ..   Solex 32/35 DIDTA
    Series No. ZD engines 056 129 015M
      Main jet X120/X140
      Air correction jet 140/140
      Pilot jet   45
      Pilot air jet   180
      Auxiliary fuel jet   60
      Auxiliary air jet   100

Dasher 1974, except California:
    Series No. (Manual) XW engines ..   055 129 015B
      (Automatic) XV engines ..   055 129 015C
      Main jet .. ..   X135/X140 (X130/X140 Auto)
      Air correction jet .. ..   150/140 (140/140 Auto)
      Idle jet 52.5/50
      Idle air jet 180/100
      Auxiliary fuel jet 42.5
      Auxiliary air jet   110

Dasher 1974, California only:
    Series No. (Manual) XZ engines 056 129 015G
      (Automatic) XY engines ..   056 129 015L
      Main jet .. ..   X122.5/X142.5 (X120/X145 Auto)
      Air correction jet .. ..   130/140 (140/140 Auto)
      Idle jet 45/50
      Idle air jet 180/100
      Auxiliary fuel jet   60
      Auxiliary air jet   130

Passat 1600 (late 1975) .. ..   Zenith 2B2
    Series No. (Manual) 049 129 015D
      (Automatic) 049 129 015E
      Main jet X117.5/X125
      Air correction jet 135/92.5
      Idle jet 52.5/40
      Idle air jet 135/125
      Bypass jet 42.5
      Bypass air jet   130

Dasher 1975, USA.. .. .. ..   Zenith 2B3
    Series No. (Manual) 055 129 017F
      (Automatic) 055 129 017G
      Main jet 117.5/137.5
      Air correction jet 140/92.5
      Idle jet 52.5/65
      Idle air jet 130/110
      Bypass fuel jet .. .. ..   —/42.5
      Bypass air jet .. .. ..   —127.5

Fuel injection system:
    Make and type .. .. ..   Bosch Continuous Injection (CIS)
    Fuel pump delivery rate .. ..   1500 cc/min
    Fuel pressure .. .. ..   4.6 to 5.2 bar
    Idle speed .. ..   850 to 1000 rev/min
    CO content .. ..   See **Chapter 2**

IGNITION SYSTEM

Firing order 1, 3, 4, 2
Sparking plugs:
    Diameter and reach .. .. ..   14 mm × 19 mm
    Points gap 028

Recommended types:

	Passat and L	Passat S and LS	Passat TS
Model			
Bosch	175 T30	200 T30	225 T30
Beru	175-14-3A	200-14-3A1	225-14-3A
Champion	N8Y	N8Y	N7Y

Distributor .. .. Bosch JFU 4
  Dwell angle:
    Passat .. .. 50 ± 3 deg.
    Dasher (California) .. .. .. 50 ± 3 deg.
    Dasher (other States) .. .. .. 47 ± 3 deg.
  Points gap .. .. .016
Coil .. .. Bosch KW12V

COOLING SYSTEM

Filler cap pressure rating .. .. .. 13 to 15 lb/sq inch
Thermostat:
  Starts opening at .. .. 80°C
  Fully open at .. .. 90°C
  Stroke .. .. .27 approx.
Cooling fan thermo switch:
  Contacts close .. .. Between 90°C and 95°C
  Contacts open .. .. Between 85°C and 90°C

CLUTCH

Type .. .. Single dry plate
Driven plate:
  1297 cc engines .. .. 180 mm dia.
  1471 cc engines .. .. 190 mm dia.
  Maximum runout .. .. .016 at 3.45 radius
Pressure plate:
  Maximum 'dishing' .. .. .. .012 inwards
Pedal free play 6

TRANSMISSION

Manual .. .. Synchro on all forward gears
  Gear ratios:
    1st 3.454
    2nd .. .. 2.055 (later 1.94)
    3rd 1.370
    4th .. .. .968
    Reverse 3.168
  Final drive ratio:
    1297 cc models 4.555
    1471 and 1588 cc models 4.111
Automatic .. .. With torque converter
  Gear ratios:
    1st 2.65
    2nd 1.59
    3rd 1.00
    Reverse 1.80
  Final drive ratio:
    Passat (not TS) 4.09
    Dasher 4.09
    Passat TS 3.818

SUSPENSION

Front:

Springing	Coil, independent McPherson type struts, transverse arms, anti-roll bar
Dampers	Telescopic, hydraulic, integral with strut

Rear:

Springing	Coil on trailing beam axle
Dampers	Telescopic, hydraulic
Stabiliser	Panhard type rod
Anti-roll bar	Integral with beam axle

Tyre pressures:

Saloon models, front and rear	26 lb/sq inch
Estate models, front	26 lb/sq inch
rear	26 to 30 lb/sq inch

STEERING

Type	Rack and pinion
Turning circle	33 ft 10 inch diameter
Ratio	18.52:1
Turns, lock to lock	4

BRAKES

Operation:

Foot	Hydraulic, dual (diagonal) line
Hand	Mechanical on rear drums
Rear brakes	Drum
Saloon models	180 mm dia.
Estate	200 mm dia.
Drum wear limit	1 mm oversize
Shoe lining thickness (new)	6 mm
Shoe lining wear limit	2.5 mm
Front brakes	Disc
Disc diameter	239 mm
Disc thickness:	
Manual trans.	10 mm
Automatic trans.	12 mm
Disc wear limit	8.5 mm
Friction pad thickness:	
Manual trans. (new)	10 mm
Automatic trans. (new)	14 mm
Wear limit	6 mm
Pedal free play:	
With servo unit	Zero
Without servo unit	.16 to .27

ELECTRICAL EQUIPMENT

Battery:

Voltage	12-volt
Earthing system	Negative earth
Starter motor	Bosch
Type	EF 12V
Reference No.	0 001 211 209
Pinion engagement	Positive

						13 mm
Brush wear limit length	..	..	..	..	..	13 mm
Commutator min. dia.	..	..	..	..	..	34.5 mm (remachined)

Alternator ..   ..   Bosch
    Type K1 14V 35A 20
    Rectifier   ..   ..   Integral diodes
    Brush wear limit length   ..   ..   5 mm
Regulator ..   ..   Bosch
    Type   ..   ..   EE 14V 20 (integral with alternator brush carrier)
    Reference No. 0192 052 004
Fuses   ..   ..   See page 120

CAPACITIES

Engine:				_Imperial_	_USA_	_Litres_
Passat, with oil filter change	..	..	..	5.25 pts	6.3 pts	3.0
Dasher, with oil filter change	..	..	..	6.2 pts	7.4 pts	3.5
Filter only	..	..	..	.9 pt	1.0 pt	.5
Cooling system (total)	..	..	..	11.4 pts	13.7 pts	6.5
G10 antifreeze in total:						
for −25°C protection	..	..	..	4.6 pts	5.5 pts	2.6
for −35°C protection	..	..	..	5.75 pts	6.8 pts	3.25
Fuel tank:						
Saloon models	..	..	..	10 galls	12 galls	46
Estate	..	..	..	11 galls	13 galls	50
Transmission:						
Manual, single system:						
Gearbox and final drive	..	..	..	3.5 pts	4.2 pts	2
Automatic, dual system:						
Final drive	..	..	..	1.75 pts	2.1 pts	1
Gearbox and torque converter from 'dry'		..	..	10.6 pts	12.6 pts	6
Gearbox and torque converter refill	..	..	..	5.3 pts	6.3 pts	3

DIMENSIONS

Overall length   ..   ..   13 ft 9 inch (4190 mm)
Overall width   ..   ..   5 ft 3 inch (1600 mm)
Overall height   ..   ..   4 ft 5.5 inch (1360 mm)
Track:
  Front   ..   ..   4 ft 4.8 inch (1340 mm)
  Rear   ..   ..   4 ft 4.6 inch (1335 mm)
Wheelbase ..   ..   8 ft 1.2 inch (2470 mm)
Ground clearance at partial load ..   ..   ..   4.7 inch (120 mm)
Weight:
  Manual transmission models:
    Saloon ..   ..   1951 lb
    Estate ..   ..   2006 lb
  Automatic transmission models:
    Saloon ..   ..   2006 lb
    Estate ..   ..   2061 lb

TORQUE WRENCH SETTINGS

Torques are in lb ft unless otherwise stated

Engine:

Oil filter canister	Tighten by hand
Oil pump retaining bolts	14
Sump:	
Drain plug	22
Attachment bolts	7
Camshaft drive tensioner locknut	32
Camshaft drive wheels:	
Camshaft bolt	58
Intermediate shaft bolt	58
Crankshaft bolt	58
Connecting rod cap nuts	33
Main bearing cap bolts	47
Cylinder head bolts	See **Chapter 1, Section 1:4**
Camshaft bearing cap nuts	14

Ignition system:

Sparking plugs	21
Clamp bracket bolt	14

Clutch to flywheel bolts 18

Fuel system:

Pump attachment bolts	14

Transmission:

Drain and filler plugs	18
Final drive casing to engine	40
Drive shafts:	
Socket-headed bolts	25
Hub nut	180 to 216
Manual:	
Pinion shaft nut	72
Gearbox to drive casing nuts	14
Gearbox to gearchange housing nuts	14
Automatic	
Torque converter to drive plate bolts	21
Gearbox sump bolts (repeat as gasket settles)	7

Front suspension:

Ball joint flange nuts	47
Strut assembly to body nuts	18
Strut assembly top nut	43

Rear suspension:

Stub axle attachment bolts	47
Damper attachment bolts	43
Diagonal arm attachment bolts	61
Axle arm pivot bolts	32

Steering:

Steering wheel retaining nut	36
Tie rod to steering unit bolts	40
Steering unit mounting nuts	14
Linkage ball joint nuts	29

Brakes:

Caliper attachment bolts	43

Road wheel bolts 65

WIRING DIAGRAMS

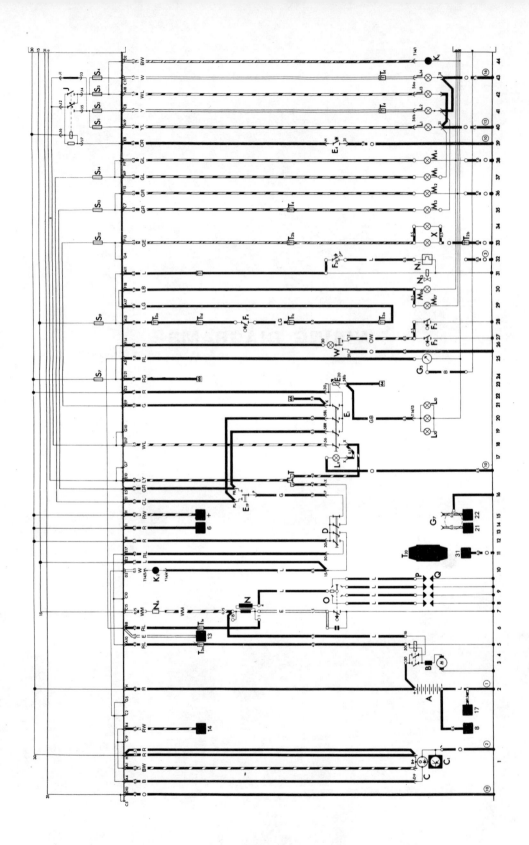

158

FIG 14:1 Current flow diagram, Passat—part 1

Key to Fig 14:1 *Numbers on right relate to those on diagram base line to locate items*

A	Battery	2
B	Starter	3, 4, 5
C	Generator	1
C1	Voltage regulator	1
D	Ignition/starter switch	10–16
E1	Lighting switch	17–23
E4	Headlight dip and flasher switch	39
E19	Parking light switch	16
E20	Instrument panel lighting control/ switch	
F2	Door contact switch, front, left	23
F3	Door contact switch, front, right	27
F4	Reversing light switch	28
F26	Thermoswitch for cold start device	28
G5	Rev counter	32
G7	TDC sender unit connection	25
J	Headlight dip and flasher relay	14–16
K1	High beam warning lamp	39–43
K2	Generator warning lamp	44
L1	Low beam headlight, left	10
L2	Low beam headlight, right	40, 41

L9	Bulb for lighting switch illumination	17
L10	Instrument panel light	19–21
L13	High beam headlight, left	42
L14	High beam headlight, right	43
M1	Side light, left	37
M2	Tail light, right	36
M3	Side light, right	35
M4	Tail light, left	38
M16	Reversing light, left	30
M17	Reversing light, right	29
N	Ignition coil	7, 8
N1	Automatic choke	32
N3	Electro-magnetic cut-off valve	31
N6	Series resistance wire for coil	7
O	Distributor	9
P	Spark plug connector	9
Q	Spark plugs	9
S1, S2, etc.	Fuses in fuse box	

T	Adaptor behind instrument panel	
T1c	Connector single, near front partition	
T1d	Connector single, near front partition	
T1e	Connector single, near fuse box	
T2b	Connector 2 point, in luggage compartment	
T3a	Connector 3 point, near fuse box	
T4	Connector 4 point, near fuse box	
T20	Central socket	11
W	Interior lights	26
X	Number plate light	33, 34

Circled numbers:

1	Earthing strap from battery to body	
2	Earthing strap from generator to cylinder block	
10	Earthing point on body	

Black squares are numbered terminals in diagnostic test socket T20

Wiring colour code: B Blue   E Green   G Grey   L Black   M Mauve   O Brown   R Red   W White   Y Yellow
When wires have two colour code letters the first denotes the main colour, the second the stripe. Numbers in wires (eg 2.5, 0.5) indicate cross-sectional area of wire in sq mm

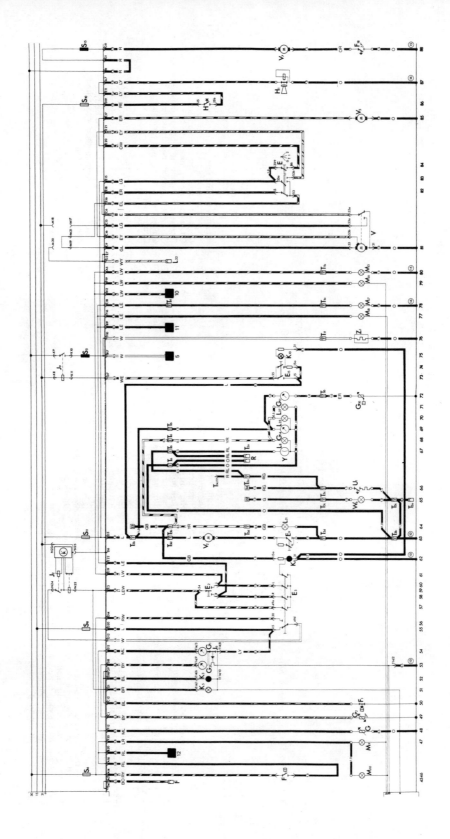

160

FIG 14:2 Current flow diagram, Passat—part 2

Key to Fig 14:2 *Numbers on right relate to those on diagram base line to locate items*

Code	Item	No.
E	Windscreen wiper switch	82–84
E2	Turn signal switch	58–60
E3	Emergency light switch	56–62
E9	Fresh air blower motor switch	63
E15	Heated rear window switch	73–75
F	Brake light switch	46
F1	Oil pressure switch	50
F18	Thermoswitch for radiator fan motor	88
G	Fuel gauge sender unit	48
G1	Fuel gauge	54
G2	Temperature gauge sender unit	49
G3	Temperature gauge	53
G10	Oil pressure sender unit	72
G11	Oil pressure gauge	72
H	Voltmeter	68
H1	Horn plate	86
	Horn	87
J2	Emergency warning light relay	59
J6	Voltage stabiliser	53, 54
J9	Heated rear window relay	73, 75
K3	Oil pressure warning lamp	52

Code	Item	No.
K5	Turn signal warning lamp	51
K6	Emergency light warning lamp	62
K10	Heated rear window warning lamp	75
L8	Clock light	68
L21	Heater control levers light	64
L22	To lefthand and righthand foglights	
L25	Voltmeter light	70
L27	Oil pressure gauge light	71
M5	Turn signal, front, left	80
M6	Turn signal, rear, left	79
M7	Turn signal, front, right	78
M8	Turn signal, rear, right	77
M9	Brake light, left	47
M10	Brake light, right	46
R	Radio connection	
S5, S6, etc.	Fuses in fuse box	
T1a	Connector single, in engine compartment, front right	
T1b	Connector single, in engine compartment, front left	

Code	Item	No.
T1f	Connector single, in luggage compartment, left	
T2a	Connector 2 point, behind instrument panel	
T3b	Connector 3 point, behind instrument panel	
T3c	Connector 3 point, behind instrument panel	
T4	Connector 4 point, near fuse box	
T6	Connector 6 point, behind console	
U1	Cigarette lighter	66
V	Windscreen wiper motor	81
V2	Blower motor	63
V5	Washer pump motor	85
V7	Radiator fan motor	88
W6	Glove box light	65
Y	Clock	67
Z1	Heated rear window	76

Circled numbers:

18	Earthing point on body
15	Earthing point in engine compartment, front, left
10	Earthing point in engine compartment, front, right

Black squares are numbered terminals in diagnostic test socket T20

Wiring colour code: **B** Blue **E** Green **G** Grey **L** Black **M** Mauve **O** Brown **R** Red **W** White **Y** Yellow
When wires have two colour code letters the first denotes the main colour, the second the stripe. Numbers in wires (eg 2.5, 0.5) indicate cross-sectional area of wire in sq mm

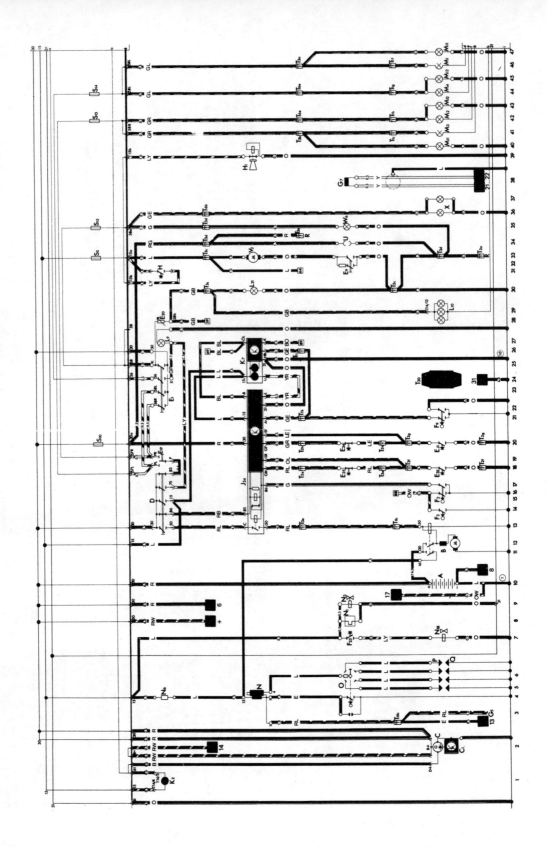

162

FIG 14:3 Current flow diagram. Dasher—part 1

Key to Fig 14:3 *Numbers on right relate to those on diagram base line to locate items*

A	Battery	10
B	Starter	11, 12
C	Alternator	2
C1	Regulator	2
D	Ignition/starter switch	13, 14, 15, 17, 18
E1	Light switch	22, 23, 24, 25, 32, 33
E9	Fresh air fan	
E20	Instrument panel lighting control switch	28
E24	Safety belt lock, left	20
E25	Safety belt lock, right	18
E31	Contact strip in driver seat	20
E32	Contact strip in passenger seat	18
F2	Door contact and buzzer alarm switch, left	16, 17
F3	Door contact switch, right	14
F9	Parking brake control light switch	21, 22
F25	Throttle valve switch	7
G5	To tachometer terminal 1	3
G7	TDC sensor	38
H	Horn button	31
H1	Horn	39
J34	Safety belt warning system relay	13, 14, 17, 18, 19, 20, 21, 22, 23
K2	Alternator charging warning light	1
K7	Dual circuit brake warning and safety belt warning system control light	24, 25, 26, 27
L9	Light switch illumination	27
L10	Instrument panel light	28, 29
L21	Heater lever illumination	30
M1	Parking light, left	46
M2	Tail light, right	42
M3	Parking light, right	41
M4	Tail light, left	44
M11	Sidemarker lights, front	40, 47
M12	Sidemarker lights, rear	43, 45
N	Ignition coil	4
N1	Automatic choke	8
N3	Electromagnetic cut-off valve	9
N6	Series resistance	4
N18	EGR valve	7
O	Ignition distributor	4, 6
P	Spark plug connectors	5, 6
Q	Spark plugs	5, 6
R	Radio	33, 34
S	Fuses	
T1a	Connector, behind dashboard	
T1b	Connector, in engine compartment	
T1c	Connector, in engine compartment, right	
T1d	Connector, in engine compartment, right	
T1e	Connector, in engine compartment, left	
T1f	Connector, in engine compartment, left	
T1g	Connector, in luggage compartment, left	
T1h	Connector, in luggage compartment, right	
T1i	Connector, behind dashboard	
T1k	Connector, behind dashboard	
T2a	Connector, behind dashboard	
T2b	Connector, in engine compartment	
T2c	Connector, next to radiator	
T2d	Connector, in luggage compartment	
T2e	Connector, in body bottom	
T2f	Connector, below passenger seat	
T2g	Connector, below driver seat	
T2h	Connector, on body bottom	
T3a	Connector, in engine compartment, left, front	
T3b	Connector, in engine compartment, right, front	
T3c	Connector, behind dashboard	
T3d	Connector, behind dashboard	
T3e	Connector, behind dashboard	
T3f	Connector, behind dashboard	
T6a	Connector, behind dashboard	
T6c	Connector, behind dashboard	
T6d	Connector, behind dashboard	
T6e	Connector, behind dashboard	
T14	Connector, on dashboard cluster	
T20	Test network/test socket	24
U	Cigarette lighter	34
V2	Fresh air fan	33
W6	Glove compartment light	35
X	Licence plate light	36

Circled numbers:

1	Ground strap, battery-body-engine	
10	Ground connector, instrument cluster	

Black squares are numbered terminals in diagnostic test socket T20

Wiring colour code: B Blue   E Green   G Grey   L Black   M Mauve   O Brown   R Red   W White   Y Yellow

When wires have two colour code letters the first denotes the main colour, the second the stripe. Numbers in wires (eg 2.5, 0.5) indicate cross-sectional area of wire in sq mm

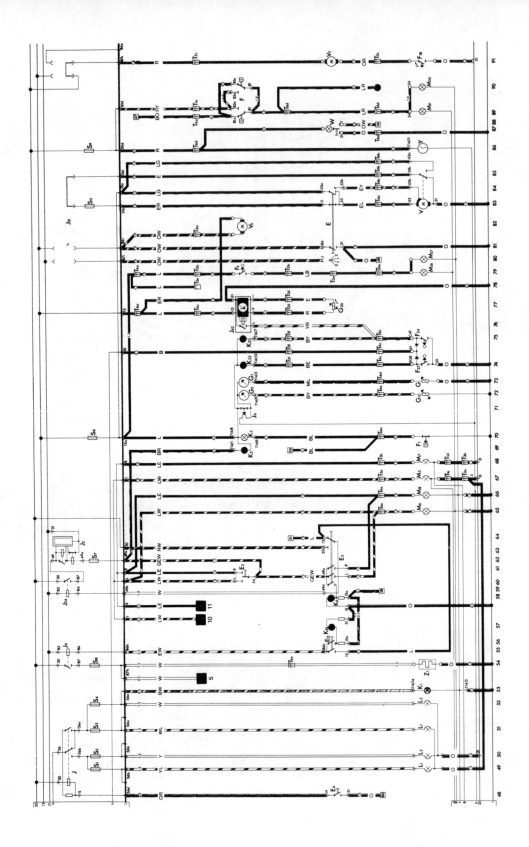

FIG 14:4   Current flow diagram, Dasher—part 2

Key to Fig 14:4   *Numbers on right relate to those on diagram base line to locate items*

E	Windshield wiper switch	81, 83, 84,
E2	Turn signal switch	60, 61
E3	Emergency flasher switch	59, 60, 61, 62, 63, 64
E4	Headlight dimmer switch	48
E15	Rear window defogger switch	55, 56
F	Brake light switch	88, 89, 90
F1	Engine oil pressure switch	70
F4	Backup light switch	79
F18	Radiator cooling fan thermo switch	91
F24	Elapsed CAT mileage odometer	75
F27	Elapsed EGR mileage odometer	74
G	Fuel gauge sending unit	73
G1	Fuel gauge	73
G2	Coolant temperature sending unit	72
G3	Coolant temperature gauge	72
G20	Catalytic converter temperature sensor	77
J	Headlight dimmer relay	48, 49, 50, 51, 52
J2	Emergency flasher relay	63, 64
J6	Voltage stabiliser	71
J9	Rear window defogger relay	54, 55
J24	Relay activating emergency flasher relay	59, 6C
J31	Windshield washer/wiper intermittent relay (optional)	80, 81, 83, 85
J42	Catalytic converter relay	76, 77
K1	Headlight high beam warning light	53
K3	Engine oil pressure light	70
K5	Turn signal warning light	69
K6	Emergency flasher warning light	58
K10	Rear window defogger warning light	57
K21	Catalytic converter warning light	75
K22	EGR warning light	74
L1	Sealed beam unit, left	49, 51
L2	Sealed beam unit, right	50, 52
M5	Turn signal, front left	67
M6	Turn signal, rear left	65
M7	Turn signal, front right	68
M8	Turn signal, rear right	66
M9	Brake light, left	89
M10	Brake light, right	90
M16	Backup light, left	79
M17	Backup light, right	80
S	Fuses	
T1a	Connector, behind dashboard	
T1b	Connector, in engine compartment	
T1c	Connector, in engine compartment, right	
T1d	Connector, in engine compartment, right	
T1e	Connector, in engine compartment, left	
T1f	Connector, in engine compartment, left	
T1g	Connector, single, in luggage compartment, left	
T1h	Connector, single, in luggage compartment, right	
T1i	Connector, single, behind dashboard	
T1k	Connector, single, behind dashboard	
T2a	Connector, double, behind dashboard	
T2b	Connector, double, in engine compartment	
T2c	Connector, double, next to radiator	
T2d	Connector, double, in luggage compartment	
T2e	Connector, double, on body bottom	
T2f	Connector, double, below passenger seat	
T2g	Connector, double, below driver seat	
T2h	Connector, double, on body bottom	
T3a	Connector, 3 point, in engine compartment, left, front	
T3b	Connector, 3 point, in engine compartment, right, front	
T3c	Connector, 3 point, behind dashboard	
T3d	Connector, 3 point, behind dashboard	
T3e	Connector, 3 point, behind dashboard	
T3f	Connector, 3 point, behind dashboard	
T6a	Connector, 6 point, behind dashboard	
T6b	Connector, 6 point, behind dashboard	
T6c	Connector, 6 point, behind dashboard	
T6d	Connector, 6 point, behind dashboard	
T6e	Connector, 6 point, behind dashboard	
T14	Connector, 14 point, on dashboard cluster	
V	Windshield wiper motor	83, 84, 85
V5	Windshield washer pump	82
V7	Radiator cooling fan	91
W	Interior light	87, 88
Y	Clock	86
Z1	Rear window defogger heating element	54

Black squares are numbered terminals in diagnostic test socket T20

Wiring colour code: **B** Blue   **E** Green   **G** Grey   **L** Black   **M** Mauve   **O** Brown   **R** Red   **W** White   **Y** Yellow

When wires have two colour code letters the first denotes the main colour, the second the stripe. Numbers in wires (eg 2.5, 0.5) indicate cross-sectional area of wire in sq mm

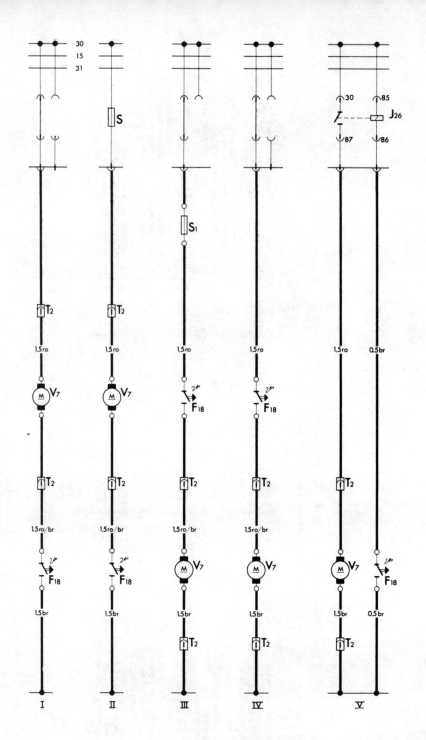

FIG 14:5 Alternative circuits for radiator fan

Key to Fig 14:5   **I** Negative control   **II** Negative control with fuse in fuse box   **III** Positive control with separate fuse
IV Positive control   **V** Relay control   F18 Thermoswitch for radiator fan   J26 Radiator fan relay   S Fuse in fuse box
S1 Separate fuse   V7 Radiator fan motor

Wiring colour code: **br** brown   **ro** red

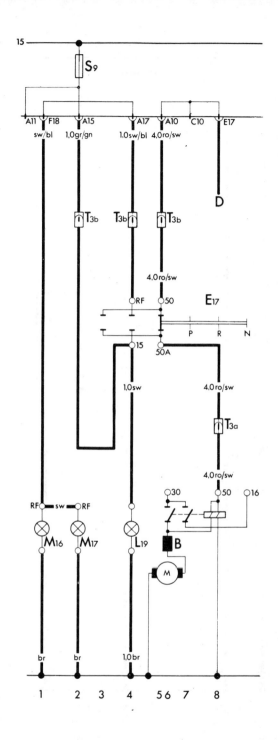

FIG 14:6   Additional current flow diagram for automatic transmission

Key to Fig 14:6   B Starter   D To ignition/starter switch terminal 50   E17 Starter inhibitor and reversing light switch
L19 Selector lever light   M16 Reversing light, left   M17 Reversing light, right   T3a Connector in engine compartment
T3b Connector under dash

Wiring colour code: **bl** blue   **br** brown   **gn** green   **gr** grey   **ro** red   **sw** black

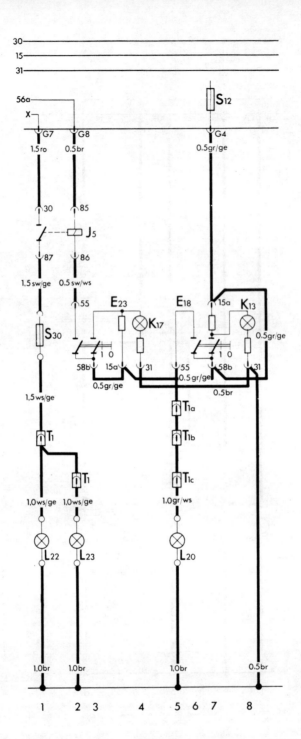

FIG 14:7 Additional current flow diagram for fog lamps and rear fog lamps

Key to Fig 14:7   E18 Rear fog lamp switch   E23 Fog lamp switch   J5 Fog lamp relay   K13 Rear fog lamp warning light
K17 Fog lamp warning light   L20 Rear fog lamp   L22 Fog lamp, left   L23 Fog lamp, right   S12 Fuse in fuse box
S30 Separate fuse   T1 Flat connector   T1a Connector behind dash   T1b, T1c Connectors in luggage compartment

Wiring colour code: **br** brown   **ws** white   **ge** yellow   **sw** black   **ro** red   **gr** grey   **gn** green

HINTS ON MAINTENANCE AND OVERHAUL

There are few things more rewarding than the restoration of a vehicle's original peak of efficiency and smooth performance.

The following notes are intended to help the owner to reach that state of perfection. Providing that he possesses the basic manual skills he should have no difficulty in performing most of the operations detailed in this manual. It must be stressed, however, that where recommended in the manual, highly-skilled operations ought to be entrusted to experts, who have the necessary equipment, to carry out the work satisfactorily.

Quality of workmanship:

The hazardous driving conditions on the roads to-day demand that vehicles should be as nearly perfect, mechanically, as possible. It is therefore most important that amateur work be carried out with care, bearing in mind the often inadequate working conditions, and also the inferior tools which may have to be used. It is easy to counsel perfection in all things, and we recognise that it may be setting an impossibly high standard. We do, however, suggest that every care should be taken to ensure that a vehicle is as safe to take on the road as it is humanly possible to make it.

Safe working conditions:

Even though a vehicle may be stationary, it is still potentially dangerous if certain sensible precautions are not taken when working on it while it is supported on jacks or blocks. It is indeed preferable not to use jacks alone, but to supplement them with carefully placed blocks, so that there will be plenty of support if the car rolls off the jacks during a strenuous manoeuvre. Axle stands are an excellent way of providing a rigid base which is not readily disturbed. Piles of bricks are a dangerous substitute. Be careful not to get under heavy loads on lifting tackle, the load could fall. It is preferable not to work alone when lifting an engine, or when working underneath a vehicle which is supported well off the ground. To be trapped, particularly under the vehicle, may have unpleasant results if help is not quickly forthcoming. Make some provision, however humble, to deal with fires. Always disconnect a battery if there is a likelihood of electrical shorts. These may start a fire if there is leaking fuel about. This applies particularly to leads which can carry a heavy current, like those in the starter circuit. While on the subject of electricity, we must also stress the danger of using equipment which is run off the mains and which has no earth or has faulty wiring or connections. So many workshops have damp floors, and electrical shocks are of such a nature that it is sometimes impossible to let go of a live lead or piece of equipment due to the muscular spasms which take place.

Work demanding special care:

This involves the servicing of braking, steering and suspension systems. On the road, failure of the braking system may be disastrous. Make quite sure that there can be no possibility of failure through the bursting of rusty brake pipes or rotten hoses, nor to a sudden loss of pressure due to defective seals or valves.

Problems:

The chief problems which may face an operator are:
1 External dirt.
2 Difficulty in undoing tight fixings.
3 Dismantling unfamiliar mechanisms.
4 Deciding in what respect parts are defective.
5 Confusion about the correct order for reassembly.
6 Adjusting running clearance.
7 Road testing.
8 Final tuning.

Practical suggestions to solve the problems:

1 Preliminary cleaning of large parts—engines, transmissions, steering, suspensions, etc,—should be carried out before removal from the car. Where road dirt and mud alone are present, wash clean with a high-pressure water jet, brushing to remove stubborn adhesions, and allow to drain and dry. Where oil or grease is also present, wash down with a proprietary compound (Gunk, Teepol etc,) applying with a stiff brush—an old paint brush is suitable—into all crevices. Cover the distributor and ignition coils with a polythene bag and then apply a strong water jet to clear the loosened deposits. Allow to drain and dry. The assemblies will then be sufficiently clean to remove and transfer to the bench for the next stage.

On the bench, further cleaning can be carried out, first wiping the parts as free as possible from grease with old newspaper. Avoid using rag or cotton waste which can leave clogging fibres behind. Any remaining grease can be removed with a brush dipped in paraffin. If necessary, traces of paraffin can be removed by carbon tetrachloride. Avoid using paraffin or petrol in large quantities for cleaning in enclosed areas, such as garages, on account of the high fire risk.

When all exteriors have been cleaned, and not before, dismantling can be commenced. This ensures that dirt will not enter into interiors and orifices revealed by dismantling. In the next phases, where components have to be cleaned, use carbon tetrachloride in preference to petrol and keep the containers covered except when in use. After the components have been cleaned, plug small holes with tapered hard wood plugs cut to size and blank off larger orifices with greaseproof paper and masking tape. Do not use soft wood plugs or matchsticks as they may break.

2 It is not advisable to hammer on the end of a screw thread, but if it must be done, first screw on a nut to protect the thread, and use a lead hammer. This applies particularly to the removal of tapered cotters. Nuts and bolts seem to 'grow' together, especially in exhaust systems. If penetrating oil does not work, try the judicious application of heat, but be careful of starting a fire. Asbestos sheet or cloth is useful to isolate heat.

Tight bushes or pieces of tail-pipe rusted into a silencer can be removed by splitting them with an open-ended hacksaw. Tight screws can sometimes be started by a tap from a hammer on the end of a suitable screwdriver. Many tight fittings will yield to the judicious use of a hammer, but it must be a soft-faced hammer if damage is to be avoided, use a heavy block on the opposite side to absorb shock. Any parts of the steering system which have been damaged should be renewed, as attempts to repair them may lead to cracking and subsequent failure, and steering ball joints should be disconnected using a recommended tool to prevent damage.

3 It often happens that an owner is baffled when trying to dismantle an unfamiliar piece of equipment. So many modern devices are pressed together or assembled by spinning-over flanges, that they must be sawn apart. The intention is that the whole assembly must be renewed. However, parts which appear to be in one piece to the naked eye, may reveal close-fitting joint lines when inspected with a magnifying glass, and, this may provide the necessary clue to dismantling. Lefthanded screw threads are used where rotational forces would tend to unscrew a righthanded screw thread.

Be very careful when dismantling mechanisms which may come apart suddenly. Work in an enclosed space where the parts will be contained, and drape a piece of cloth over the device if springs are likely to fly in all directions. Mark everything which might be reassembled in the wrong position, scratched symbols may be used on unstressed parts, or a sequence of tiny dots from a centre punch can be useful. Stressed parts should never be scratched or centre-popped as this may lead to cracking under working conditions. Store parts which look alike in the correct order for reassembly. Never rely upon memory to assist in the assembly of complicated mechanisms, especially when they will be dismantled for a long time, but make notes, and drawings to supplement the diagrams in the manual, and put labels on detached wires. Rust stains may indicate unlubricated wear. This can sometimes be seen round the outside edge of a bearing cup in a universal joint. Look for bright rubbing marks on parts which normally should not make heavy contact. These might prove that something is bent or running out of truth. For example, there might be bright marks on one side of a piston, at the top near the ring grooves, and others at the bottom of the skirt on the other side. This could well be the clue to a bent connecting rod. Suspected cracks can be proved by heating the component in a light oil to approximately 100°C, removing, drying off, and dusting with french chalk, if a crack is present the oil retained in the crack will stain the french chalk.

4 In determining wear, and the degree, against the permissible limits set in the manual, accurate measurement can only be achieved by the use of a micrometer. In many cases, the wear is given to the fourth place of decimals; that is in ten-thousandths of an inch. This can be read by the vernier scale on the barrel of a good micrometer. Bore diameters are more difficult to determine. If, however, the matching shaft is accurately measured, the degree of play in the bore can be felt as a guide to its suitability. In other cases, the shank of a twist drill of known diameter is a handy check.

Many methods have been devised for determining the clearance between bearing surfaces. To-day the best and simplest is by the use of Plastigage, obtainable from most garages. A thin plastic thread is laid between the two surfaces and the bearing is tightened, flattening the thread. On removal, the width of the thread is compared with a scale supplied with the thread and the clearance is read off directly. Sometimes joint faces leak persistently, even after gasket renewal. The fault will then be traceable to distortion, dirt or burrs. Studs which are screwed into soft metal frequently raise burrs at the point of entry. A quick cure for this is to chamfer the edge of the hole in the part which fits over the stud.

5 **Always check a replacement part with the original one before it is fitted.**

If parts are not marked, and the order for reassembly is not known, a little detective work will help. Look for marks which are due to wear to see if they can be mated. Joint faces may not be identical due to manufacturing errors, and parts which overlap may be stained, giving a clue to the correct position. Most fixings leave identifying marks especially if they were painted over on assembly. It is then easier to decide whether a nut, for instance, has a plain, a spring, or a shakeproof washer under it. All running surfaces become 'bedded' together after long spells of work and tiny imperfections on one part will be found to have left corresponding marks on the other. This is particularly true of shafts and bearings and even a score on a cylinder wall will show on the piston.

6 Checking end float or rocker clearances by feeler gauge may not always give accurate results because of wear. For instance, the rocker tip which bears on a valve stem may be deeply pitted, in which case the feeler will simply be bridging a depression. Thrust washers may also wear depressions in opposing faces to make accurate measurement difficult. End float is then easier to check by using a dial gauge. It is common practice to adjust end play in bearing assemblies, like front hubs with taper rollers, by doing up the axle nut until the hub becomes stiff to turn and then backing it off a little. Do not use this method with ballbearing hubs as the assembly is often preloaded by tightening the axle nut to its fullest extent. If the splitpin hole will not line up, file the base of the nut a little.

Steering assemblies often wear in the straight-ahead position. If any part is adjusted, make sure that it remains free when moved from lock to lock. Do not be surprised if an assembly like a steering gearbox, which is known to be carefully adjusted outside the car, becomes stiff when it is bolted in place. This will be due to distortion of the case by the pull of the mounting bolts, particularly if the mounting points are not all touching together. This problem may be met in other equipment and is cured by careful attention to the alignment of mounting points.

When a spanner is stamped with a size and A/F it means that the dimension is the width between the jaws and has no connection with ANF, which is the designation for the American National Fine thread. Coarse threads like Whitworth are rarely used on cars to-day except for studs which screw into soft aluminium or cast iron. For this reason it might be found that the top end of a cylinder head stud has a fine thread and the lower end a coarse thread to screw into the cylinder block. If the car has mainly UNF threads then it is likely that any coarse threads will be UNC, which are not the same as Whitworth. Small sizes have the same number of threads in Whitworth and UNC, but in the $\frac{1}{2}$ inch size for example, there are twelve threads to the inch in the former and thirteen in the latter.

7 After a major overhaul, particularly if a great deal of work has been done on the braking, steering and suspension systems, it is advisable to approach the problem of testing with care. If the braking system has been overhauled, apply heavy pressure to the brake pedal and get a second operator to check every possible source of leakage. The brakes may work extremely well, but a leak could cause complete failure after a few miles.

Do not fit the hub caps until every wheel nut has been checked for tightness, and make sure the tyre pressures are correct. Check the levels of coolant, lubricants and hydraulic fluids. Being satisfied that all is well, take the car on the road and test the brakes at once. Check the steering and the action of the handbrake. Do all this at moderate speeds on quiet roads, and make sure there is no other vehicle behind you when you try a rapid stop.

Finally, remember that many parts settle down after a time, so check for tightness of all fixings after the car has been on the road for a hundred miles or so.

8 It is useless to tune an engine which has not reached its normal running temperature. In the same way, the tune of an engine which is stiff after a rebore will be different when the engine is again running free. Remember too, that rocker clearances on pushrod operated valve gear will change when the cylinder head nuts are tightened after an initial period of running with a new head gasket.

Trouble may not always be due to what seems the obvious cause. Ignition, carburation and mechanical condition are interdependent and spitting back through the carburetter, which might be attributed to a weak mixture, can be caused by a sticking inlet valve.

For one final hint on tuning, never adjust more than one thing at a time or it will be impossible to tell which adjustment produced the desired result.

NOTES

GLOSSARY OF TERMS

Allen key Cranked wrench of hexagonal section for use with socket head screws.

Alternator Electrical generator producing alternating current. Rectified to direct current for battery charging.

Ambient temperature Surrounding atmospheric temperature.

Annulus Used in engineering to indicate the outer ring gear of an epicyclic gear train.

Armature The shaft carrying the windings, which rotates in the magnetic field of a generator or starter motor. That part of a solenoid or relay which is activated by the magnetic field.

Axial In line with, or pertaining to, an axis.

Backlash Play in meshing gears.

Balance lever A bar where force applied at the centre is equally divided between connections at the ends.

Banjo axle Axle casing with large diameter housing for the crownwheel and differential.

Bendix pinion A self-engaging and self-disengaging drive on a starter motor shaft.

Bevel pinion A conical shaped gearwheel, designed to mesh with a similar gear with an axis usually at 90 deg. to its own.

bhp Brake horse power, measured on a dynamometer.

bmep Brake mean effective pressure. Average pressure on a piston during the working stroke.

Brake cylinder Cylinder with hydraulically operated piston(s) acting on brake shoes or pad(s).

Brake regulator Control valve fitted in hydraulic braking system which limits brake pressure to rear brakes during heavy braking to prevent rear wheel locking.

Camber Angle at which a wheel is tilted from the vertical.

Capacitor Modern term for an electrical condenser. Part of distributor assembly, connected across contact breaker points, acts as an interference suppressor.

Castellated Top face of a nut, slotted across the flats, to take a locking splitpin.

Castor Angle at which the kingpin or swivel pin is tilted when viewed from the side.

cc Cubic centimetres. Engine capacity is arrived at by multiplying the area of the bore in sq cm by the stroke in cm by the number of cylinders.

Clevis U-shaped forked connector used with a clevis pin, usually at handbrake connections.

Collet A type of collar, usually split and located in a groove in a shaft, and held in place by a retainer. The arrangement used to retain the spring(s) on a valve stem in most cases.

Commutator Rotating segmented current distributor between armature windings and brushes in generator or motor.

Compression ratio The ratio, or quantitative relation, of the total volume (piston at bottom of stroke) to the unswept volume (piston at top of stroke) in an engine cylinder.

Condenser See capacitor.

Core plug Plug for blanking off a manufacturing hole in a casting.

Crownwheel Large bevel gear in rear axle, driven by a bevel pinion attached to the propeller shaft. Sometimes called a 'ring gear'.

'C'-spanner Like a 'C' with a handle. For use on screwed collars without flats, but with slots or holes.

Damper Modern term for shock-absorber, used in vehicle suspension systems to damp out spring oscillations.

Depression The lowering of atmospheric pressure as in the inlet manifold and carburetter.

Dowel Close tolerance pin, peg, tube, or bolt, which accurately locates mating parts.

Drag link Rod connecting steering box drop arm (pitman arm) to nearest front wheel steering arm in certain types of steering systems.

Dry liner Thinwall tube pressed into cylinder bore

Dry sump Lubrication system where all oil is scavenged from the sump, and returned to a separate tank.

Dynamo See Generator.

Electrode Terminal, part of an electrical component, such as the points or 'Electrodes' of a sparking plug.

Electrolyte In lead-acid car batteries a solution of sulphuric acid and distilled water.

End float The axial movement between associated parts, end play.

EP Extreme pressure. In lubricants, special grades for heavily loaded bearing surfaces, such as gear teeth in a gearbox, or crownwheel and pinion in a rear axle.

Fade	Of brakes. Reduced efficiency due to overheating.	**Journals**	Those parts of a shaft that are in contact with the bearings.
Field coils	Windings on the polepieces of motors and generators.	**Kingpin**	The main vertical pin which carries the front wheel spindle, and permits steering movement. May be called 'steering pin' or 'swivel pin'.
Fillets	Narrow finishing strips usually applied to interior bodywork.		
First motion shaft	Input shaft from clutch to gearbox.	**Layshaft**	The shaft which carries the laygear in the gearbox. The laygear is driven by the first motion shaft and drives the third motion shaft according to the gear selected. Sometimes called the 'countershaft' or 'second motion shaft.'
Fullflow filter	Filters in which all the oil is pumped to the engine. If the element becomes clogged, a bypass valve operates to pass unfiltered oil to the engine.		
FWD	Front wheel drive.	**lb ft**	A measure of twist or torque. A pull of 10 lb at a radius of 1 ft is a torque of 10 lb ft.
Gear pump	Two meshing gears in a close fitting casing. Oil is carried from the inlet round the outside of both gears in the spaces between the gear teeth and casing to the outlet, the meshing gear teeth prevent oil passing back to the inlet, and the oil is forced through the outlet port.		
		lb/sq in	Pounds per square inch.
		Little-end	The small, or piston end of a connecting rod. Sometimes called the 'small-end'.
		LT	Low Tension. The current output from the battery.
		Mandrel	Accurately manufactured bar or rod used for test or centring purposes.
Generator	Modern term for 'Dynamo'. When rotated produces electrical current.	**Manifold**	A pipe, duct, or chamber, with several branches.
Grommet	A ring of protective or sealing material. Can be used to protect pipes or leads passing through bulkheads.	**Needle rollers**	Bearing rollers with a length many times their diameter.
Grubscrew	Fully threaded headless screw with screwdriver slot. Used for locking, or alignment purposes.	**Oil bath**	Reservoir which lubricates parts by immersion. In air filters, a separate oil supply for wetting a wire mesh element to hold the dust.
Gudgeon pin	Shaft which connects a piston to its connecting rod. Sometimes called 'wrist pin', or 'piston pin'.		
Halfshaft	One of a pair transmitting drive from the differential.	**Oil wetted**	In air filters, a wire mesh element lightly oiled to trap and hold airborne dust.
Helical	In spiral form. The teeth of helical gears are cut at a spiral angle to the side faces of the gearwheel.	**Overlap**	Period during which inlet and exhaust valves are open together.
Hot spot	Hot area that assists vapourisation of fuel on its way to cylinders. Often provided by close contact between inlet and exhaust manifolds.	**Panhard rod**	Bar connected between fixed point on chassis and another on axle to control sideways movement.
		Pawl	Pivoted catch which engages in the teeth of a ratchet to permit movement in one direction only.
HT	High Tension. Applied to electrical current produced by the ignition coil for the sparking plugs.	**Peg spanner**	Tool with pegs, or pins, to engage in holes or slots in the part to be turned.
Hydrometer	A device for checking specific gravity of liquids. Used to check specific gravity of electrolyte.	**Pendant pedals**	Pedals with levers that are pivoted at the top end.
Hypoid bevel gears	A form of bevel gear used in the rear axle drive gears. The bevel pinion meshes below the centre line of the crownwheel, giving a lower propeller shaft line.	**Phillips screwdriver**	A cross-point screwdriver for use with the cross-slotted heads of Phillips screws.
		Pinion	A small gear, usually in relation to another gear.
		Piston-type damper	Shock absorber in which damping is controlled by a piston working in a closed oil-filled cylinder.
Idler	A device for passing on movement. A free running gear between driving and driven gears. A lever transmitting track rod movement to a side rod in steering gear.	**Preloading**	Preset static pressure on ball or roller bearings not due to working loads.
		Radial	Radiating from a centre, like the spokes of a wheel.
Impeller	A centrifugal pumping element. Used in water pumps to stimulate flow.		

Radius rod	Pivoted arm confining movement of a part to an arc of fixed radius.
Ratchet	Toothed wheel or rack which can move in one direction only, movement in the other being prevented by a pawl.
Ring gear	A gear tooth ring attached to outer periphery of flywheel. Starter pinion engages with it during starting.
Runout	Amount by which rotating part is out of true.
Semi-floating axle	Outer end of rear axle halfshaft is carried on bearing inside axle casing. Wheel hub is secured to end of shaft.
Servo	A hydraulic or pneumatic system for assisting, or, augmenting a physical effort. See 'Vacuum Servo'.
Setscrew	One which is threaded for the full length of the shank.
Shackle	A coupling link, used in the form of two parallel pins connected by side plates to secure the end of the master suspension spring and absorb the effects of deflection.
Shell bearing	Thinwalled steel shell lined with anti-friction metal. Usually semi-circular and used in pairs for main and big-end bearings.
Shock absorber	See 'Damper'.
Silentbloc	Rubber bush bonded to inner and outer metal sleeves.
Socket-head screw	Screw with hexagonal socket for an Allen key.
Solenoid	A coil of wire creating a magnetic field when electric current passes through it. Used with a soft iron core to operate contacts or a mechanical device.
Spur gear	A gear with teeth cut axially across the periphery.
Stub axle	Short axle fixed at one end only.
Tachometer	An instrument for accurate measurement of rotating speed. Usually indicates in revolutions per minute.

TDC	Top Dead Centre. The highest point reached by a piston in a cylinder, with the crank and connecting rod in line.
Thermostat	Automatic device for regulating temperature. Used in vehicle coolant systems to open a valve which restricts circulation at low temperature.
Third motion shaft	Output shaft of gearbox.
Threequarter floating axle	Outer end of rear axle halfshaft flanged and bolted to wheel hub, which runs on bearing mounted on outside of axle casing. Vehicle weight is not carried by the axle shaft.
Thrust bearing or washer	Used to reduce friction in rotating parts subject to axial loads.
Torque	Turning or twisting effort. See 'lb ft'.
Track rod	The bar(s) across the vehicle which connect the steering arms and maintain the front wheels in their correct alignment.
UJ	Universal joint. A coupling between shafts which permits angular movement.
UNF	Unified National Fine screw thread.
Vacuum servo	Device used in brake system, using difference between atmospheric pressure and inlet manifold depression to operate a piston which acts to augment brake pressure as required. See 'Servo'.
Venturi	A restriction or 'choke' in a tube, as in a carburetter, used to increase velocity to obtain a reduction in pressure.
Vernier	A sliding scale for obtaining fractional readings of the graduations of an adjacent scale.
Welch plug	A domed thin metal disc which is partially flattened to lock in a recess. Used to plug core holes in castings.
Wet liner	Removable cylinder barrel, sealed against coolant leakage, where the coolant is in direct contact with the outer surface.
Wet sump	A reservoir attached to the crankcase to hold the lubricating oil.

NOTES

INDEX

NOTES

NOTES

NOTES

NOTES

NOTES